THE TURKISH ECONOMY IN CRISIS

THE TURKISH ECONOMY IN CRISIS

Editors

ZİYA ÖNİŞ

BARRY RUBIN

Routledge
Taylor & Francis Group

LONDON AND NEW YORK

First published in 2003 in Great Britain by
Routledge
2 Park Square, Milton Park, Abingdon, Oxon, OX14 4RN
270 Madison Ave, New York NY 10016

Transferred to Digital Printing 2006

British Library Cataloguing in Publication Data

The Turkish economy in crisis
   1. Financial crises – Turkey 2. Turkey – Economic policy
   3. Turkey – Economic conditions – 1960–
   I. Onis, Ziya II. Rubin, Barry
   338.5'42'09561

ISBN 0 7146 5497 3 (cloth)
ISBN 0 7146 8397 3 (paper)

Library of Congress Cataloging-in-Publication Data

The Turkish economy in crisis / editors Ziya Öniş, Barry Rubin.
   p.cm.
Includes bibliographical references and index.
   ISBN 0-7146-5497-3 (cloth) – ISBN 0-7146-8397-3 (pbk.)
   1. Turkey–Economic conditions–1960– 2. Turkey–Economic policy. 3.
   Finance–Turkey–History–20th century. I. Öniş, Ziya. II. Rubin,
   Barry M. III. Title.
   HC492.T877 2003
   330.9561–dc21

                              2003007111

This group of studies first appeared in a Special Issue of *Turkish Studies*
(ISSN 1468-3849), Vol.4, No.2 (Summer 2003) [The Turkish Economy in Crisis].
Turkish Studies is a project of the Turkish Studies Institute (TSI) of the
Global Research in International Affairs (GLORIA) Center,
Interdisciplinary Center (IDC).

Publisher's Note
The publisher has gone to great lengths to ensure the quality of this reprint
but points out that some imperfections in the original may be apparent

Printed and bound by CPI Antony Rowe, Eastbourne

Contents

Preface

This book originated as a special issue of the *Turkish Studies* journal, produced with the great skill, knowledge, and coordinating efforts of Ziya Öniş. One of Turkey's most impressive accomplishments has been its dramatic economic development, but during 2001 and 2002 the economic crises facing Turkey were clearly the worst in at least half a century.

While the foundation of Turkey's economy remains strong, the problems can be traced back to a mixture of domestic shortcomings and international conditions. It is of the greatest importance to analyze the roots and solutions of these crisis, which have had the greatest impact on the Turkish people. Although the worst aspects of the crises were already over by 2003, these experiences require serious thought and reform in order to avoid a recurrence.

In particular, we wish to thank the support given this project by Attila Aşkar and Mete Soner, President and Dean of the College of Administrative Sciences and Economics, Koç University, and also the financial assistance provided by the College of Administrative Sciences and Economics for the workshop at which most of the papers were presented. Since 2003 marks the university's tenth anniversary, it seems appropriate to dedicate this book to that event.

We wish to thank especially Elisheva Rosman, Özgül Erdemli and Ehud Waldoks for their hard work on this book. We also wish to acknowledge the able assistance of Evren Tok and Gamze Sezer and to thank Vicky Johnson of Frank Cass for her assistance in publishing this project.

B.R.
Summer 2003

Domestic Politics versus Global Dynamics: Towards a Political Economy of the 2000 and 2001 Financial Crises in Turkey

ZİYA ÖNİŞ

Development in Turkey during the postwar period has occurred in the context of democratic institutions and representative government. Breakdowns of democracy have typically accompanied periods of economic crisis, notably in the late 1950s and the late 1970s. Nonetheless, military interludes have been relatively short-lived and the democratic order has been restored after a brief period of transition. This pattern makes an interesting contrast with Brazil, for example, where a military government had been institutionalized for a period of 20 years following the simultaneous collapse of the import-substitution model and democracy in the mid-1960s. Hence, compared to the dominance of bureaucratic authoritarian politics during crucial periods of strategy shift in both East Asia and Latin America, Turkey has managed to combine moderate growth and significant industrial transformation within a broad framework of democratic institutions.[1]

Yet, a closer and a more critical investigation raises serious questions concerning the quality of economic development and the performance of the democratic regime in the postwar Turkish context. Turkey managed to sustain moderately high rates of economic growth over a period of five decades. While this performance could not be described as inadequate by the standards of middle-income economies in general, it was certainly not the kind of growth that would lead to a steady convergence with the per capita income levels prevailing in the developed world, particularly in the presence of high population growth.[2] Turkey, unlike the East Asian "NICs" (newly industrialized countries) such as South Korea and Taiwan, failed to establish its credentials as a major catch-up story. What is also striking is that the pattern of growth has been associated with high-income inequality, rather reminiscent of Latin American styles of development.[3]

Moving to the political realm, Turkey's nascent democratic order has also displayed some serious deficiencies. A neo-patrimonial political

culture together with clientelistic patterns of interaction involving the state
and key segments of society have been identified as enduring features of
the Turkish political system. Thus, Turkey's performance in the economic
and political realms is heavily interrelated. The performance of the
democratic regime has clearly been inadequate in terms of generating high
rates of economic growth on a sustained basis. What seemed to underlie
this inadequate performance was the failure to effectively manage the
severe distributional conflicts—with different groups in society aiming to
obtain a greater share of the "rents" associated with easy access to
state resources.[4]

Indeed, "populist cycles" and periodic fiscal crises of the state have
emerged as persistent features of the Turkish economy ever since the
Menderes era of the 1950s. "Populism" in the present context is defined as
using state resources and "manipulating economic outcomes in ways that
disproportionately benefit select groups and classes, whose strength and
support the elite relies on to maintain its rule."[5] Democratically elected
governments, then, have typically initiated populist cycles in order to
establish broad electoral support. The resultant fiscal disequilibrium and
high inflation have, in turn, been followed by a balance of payments crisis
and an inevitable encounter with the International Monetary Fund (IMF).
The difficulties inherent in applying a severe monetary contraction and
deep cuts in government expenditure in the midst of a major economic
crisis resulted in the collapse of the democratic regime and its replacement
by military rule. In the absence of distributional constraints, military rule
has been effective in terms of restoring macroeconomic stability. However,
restoration of democracy has eventually brought to the surface the
accumulated distributional claims, thus marking the upward trend in the
populist cycle. One should note, though, that military interludes have
created temporary stability at the expense of further instability in the
future. Such episodes have helped to undermine trust on the part of key
social actors and have also prevented the institutionalization of the party
system, leading to discontinuity and fragmentation—which contribute
towards instability.[6]

The endemic nature of populist cycles clearly highlights the weakness
of Turkish democracy in providing effective governance of the economy.
Populist cycles and the ensuing crises have been costly in the sense that
they have reduced the rate of growth below what would otherwise have
been the case. Moreover, in a rather ironic and yet typical Latin American
fashion, populist cycles have been associated with high, rather than low,
inequality. A central problem in this context concerns the question of
whether the system can release itself from the exigencies of short-term

politics and clientelistic patterns of interaction and devote resources to areas desperately needed for building competitiveness and long-term improvements in the distribution of income.

It is also interesting that major policy changes in Turkey have not been initiated on the basis of a broad social consensus. Rather, such changes have taken place in a top-down fashion, often in response to influences originating from the international economy. The adoption of the neo-liberal model in 1980 is a striking example of this pattern of top-down and externally induced restructuring. In retrospect, the role of the Turkish state in the economic domain has been reactive as opposed to the proactive role that the state has performed in the historically more successful cases of South Korea and Taiwan.[7]

Given this broad background, some interesting structural shifts become evident in the trajectory of Turkey's political economy in the era of financial globalization following the complete liberalization of the capital account in August 1989. The duration of populist cycles has been reduced and crises have become more frequent (with successive crises taking place in 1994, 2000, and 2001) in an environment characterized by unrestricted exposure to highly volatile short-term capital flows (see Table 1).

Consequently, towards the end of the 1990s, Turkey found itself confronted with a serious low growth-high inequality syndrome. Although crises have become frequent, they have not been accompanied with an explicit breakdown of the democratic order (see Table 1).[8] The changing international order of the post-cold war era, the cultural context of neo-liberal globalization—with its increasing emphasis on the extension of civil and human rights—and, most important of all, the political conditionality associated with European Union (EU) membership, have all been instrumental in excluding the possibility of an authoritarian exit as an easy way out of the economic impasse. The party system experienced serious fragmentation for a variety of reasons, and—within a fragmented democratic order—weak and unstable coalition governments failed to provide effective governance in an environment where the option of authoritarian exit was excluded by definition and the economy was exposed to the instability of global capital markets.

From a comparative perspective, the recent Turkish experience clearly highlights the difficulties that countries located in the middle—in-between the two extremes of authoritarianism and established democracy—face in terms of adapting themselves effectively to the intrinsically unstable environment of open capital account regimes. Clearly, this is not a problem unique to Turkey but is confronted by many other "emerging markets"—Argentina being the most typical recent example.[9]

TABLE 1

CHARACTERISTICS OF ECONOMIC CRISES IN TURKEY

	1958/59	1978/79	1994	2000/1
Nature of the crises	Balance of payments crisis originating from the current account, primarily caused by domestic imbalances.	Balance of payments crisis, originating from the current account, caused mainly by domestic imbalances.	Balance of payments crises, originating mainly from the capital account, caused partly by domestic imbalances.	Balance of payments crisis caused by successive speculative attacks and massive outflows of capital leading to the collapse of growth and heavy unemployment in 2001. Both internal and external imbalances are important.
Origins	Fiscal imbalances; steady appreciation of the real exchange rate; export stagnation and rising trade deficit.	Fiscal imbalances; steady appreciation of the real exchange rate; export stagnation and rising trade deficit; distorted production and trade structure caused by ISI.	Fiscal imbalances; steady appreciation of the real exchange rate; export stagnation, import boom, outflow of short-term capital.	Primarily originated from disequilibrium in the banking sector (private banks in 2000 and public banks in 2001); a strong link may be formulated between disequilibria in the banking sector and fiscal imbalances.
External dimension	Peripheral; falling world demand for agricultural products in the latter half of the decade.	Successive oil shocks have contributed to the crises; oil shocks largely aggravated the problem created primarily by domestic imbalances.	Significant over-dependence on fragile short-term capital inflows following premature capital account liberalization in August 1989.	Highly volatile external environment characterized by recurrent crisis in emerging markets and reversible capital flows, especially after the Asian crisis of 1997. Export performance negatively affected by the Russian crisis and weak global demand. Rendered the economy highly vulnerable to a crisis.

TABLE 1 (Cont.)

	1958/59	1978/79	1994	2000/1
International actors in the post-crisis context	IMF is the dominant actor in the post-crisis period. A typical short-term stabilization program.	Both IMF and the World Bank are heavily involved; official assistance through the OECD is also important.	IMF is the primary actor; EU is also involved through the Customs Union.	IMF is the critical actor both in the pre- and post-crisis era; the role of the EU is decisive for the first time. IMF and EU anchors are increasingly interrelated. World Bank is also involved as a secondary actor.
Political consequences	Collapse of the democratic regime. Restoration of democracy occurs over a relatively short period of time.	Collapse of the democratic regime; longer military rule; restoration of full or unrestricted party competition occurs over a longer period.	Democratic regime remained intact; an implicit link could be formulated between the negative effect of 1994 crisis, the rise of political Islam and indirect or "postmodern" military intervention in February 1997.	A decisive turning point, the democratic regime proved to be highly resilient in the face of the crisis; the impact of the changed international environment and the presence of a powerful EU anchor are significant.

PREMATURE CAPITAL ACCOUNT LIBERALIZATION AND THE DEBT TRAP:
THE ECONOMIC AND POLITICAL BACKGROUND TO THE TWIN CRISES

Turkey began implementing neo-liberal reforms in 1980. The program
initiated in 1980 was one of the first of its kind and was devoted to both
short-term stabilization and long-term structural adjustment. Based on
close collaboration between the IMF and the World Bank and involving
the application of "cross-conditionality," it was radical and far-reaching.
At the same time, it was a gradualist program that envisaged, if not in a
totally systematic manner, a stage-by-stage liberalization and integration
into the world markets. In the early 1980s, Turkey obtained a record five
consecutive structural adjustment loans from the World Bank. It may
appear rather paradoxical today, but during the mid-1980s key
international organizations highlighted the Turkish experiment as a model
case of successful adjustment. Perhaps the most striking achievement of
Turkish neo-liberalism concerned the dramatic increase in exports and a
structural shift in favor of manufactured exports in a comparatively short
space of time. Turkey has also been able to sustain reasonably rapid
economic growth—in the order of four to five percent per annum during
its first decade of neo-liberalism.[10]

After a decade of rapid economic growth, the momentum of the reform
process was in decline towards the end of the 1980s. Two critical turning
points, which are important in terms of understanding the origins of
subsequent imbalances and the increasingly unimpressive economic
performance during the 1990s, are September 1987 and August 1989.
September 1987 marked the return of unrestricted party competition and
the distributional pressures naturally associated with this process. The
inability of democratically elected governments to contain severe
distributional pressures that had been largely repressed in the early years
of the 1980s manifested itself in the form of larger fiscal deficits and
higher rates of inflation. In worsening economic conditions, the Turkish
government conceived large inflows of capital as a key mechanism to
restore growth and did not focus on basic structural deficiencies in the
economy, namely large fiscal imbalances. The August 1989 measures
completed the last stage in the liberalization of the capital account and the
establishment of the full convertibility of the Turkish lira, which resulted
in a dramatic increase in inflows of short-term international capital.
Arguably, Turkey was able to evade a crisis at the end of the 1980s, but at
the expense of a highly fragile pattern of debt-led economic growth—
which resulted in successive financial crises in the post-1990 era.[11]

Central to the economics of recurrent financial crises in Turkey is an
extraordinarily high ratio of public sector borrowing requirement (PSBR)

to gross national product (GNP). This is not a novel issue in Turkey as the problem also existed in the 1970s. However, financial liberalization largely altered the process whereby public deficits have traditionally been financed. The establishment of domestic capital markets presented the government with the opportunity to borrow domestically. As a result, domestic debt started to increase. While Turkey had a domestic debt stock close to zero in 1987, this grew continuously and reached 25–30 percent of GDP by 2000.

High real rates of interest emerged as a striking feature of the Turkish economy during the 1990s. The size of the government's financial requirement compared to the size of the domestic financial system was at the heart of these high real interest rates. The growth in the government's financial requirements outstripped the increase in the size of the financial system. This naturally increased the burden on the financial markets, and —in turn—the domestic financial system responded by adjusting prices. Therefore, Turkey's high and downwardly rigid interest rates are a direct outcome of the government's demand for funds.

Not surprisingly, the increase in real interest rates has caused an increase in interest payments and hence an increase in budget deficits. The change in the deficit financing policies of governments after 1987 has had a clear impact on deficit dynamics. Indeed, one can detect an important change in the nature of PSBR after the crisis of 1994. In striking contrast to the pre-1994 era, the movements in budget deficits in the post-1994 period are almost completely dominated by interest payments on domestic debt. The impact of financial liberalization in the presence of a large budget deficit was a systematic increase in the domestic debt and short-term domestic borrowing requirements, which caused a move towards higher interest rates. As a result, Turkey has been caught in a vicious circle of increasing deficits and rising interest rates.[12]

When the government increased its financing requirements via new issues of debt instruments, the commercial sector became the major customer for such securities. The financing policy of the government being based on short-term borrowing led the commercial banks to change their asset management policies. They shifted from direct loan extensions to purchasing government securities. In this way, domestic agents who increasingly borrowed from abroad started to finance public deficits. This indirect form of borrowing by domestic agents replaced direct borrowing by the public sector from international capital markets.

In addition, the deficit-financing policies led the commercial banks to open short positions in foreign currencies. In order to finance their massive investment in government bonds, many Turkish banks made short-term borrowings from international markets against which the government bonds were pledged as collateral. Essentially, banks were borrowing short-term money to hold long-term Turkish government bonds. The high rates of return on government bonds made the privately-owned banks reluctant to manage the market risks, but as the banks started to operate in short positions in foreign currency-denominated assets, financing policy based on short-term borrowing made the banking sector progressively more vulnerable to foreign exchange and interest rate risks. The fact that the banks involved were typically small and medium-sized banks rendered the situation even more risky. High rates of return coupled with the existing policies, which provided a unique set of tax and regulatory incentives, allowed highly favorable profit margins for the Turkish banks and many of them turned to arbitrage activities to generate a substantial proportion of their profits. An important consequence of these profitable short-term positions has been the increasing trend of dollarization in the banking system. The share of foreign currency-denominated assets and liabilities started to increase, especially after 1987. Prior to the recent crises, the share of foreign currency-denominated assets in total assets rose from 26 percent in 1998 to 38 percent in 1999. Similarly, the share of foreign currency-denominated liabilities rose from 25 percent in 1998 to 48 percent in 1999.[13]

Looking back, a central lesson to be learned is that Turkey paid the price for premature exposure to financial globalization. Although the capital account was opened fully nearly a decade after the program's inception, the necessary domestic infrastructure for such a policy had not been created. In the context of a highly fragmented party system, successive coalition governments in the 1990s lacked the capacity and the incentives necessary for undertaking fiscal stabilization and regulation of the banking sector—measures which are critical to the success of both financial and capital account liberalization. Consequently, a lopsided pattern of development occurred whereby economic growth in Turkey has been increasingly dependent on inflows of highly volatile short-term capital. Yet another negative ramification of this concerns the inability of Turkey to attract significant amounts of direct foreign investment, which constitutes an important source of economic development in the current international context. Clearly, it was not democracy *per se* but the specific populist nature of the Turkish party system that failed to provide an appropriate environment for capitalizing on the benefits and minimizing the losses associated with financial globalization.[14]

THE CRISES OF NOVEMBER 2000 AND FEBRUARY 2001:
INTERNAL DYNAMICS AND SYSTEMIC INFLUENCES

Ever since Turkey implemented one of the very first IMF programs in 1958, frequent encounters with the Fund have been inevitable occurrences due to periodic macroeconomic crises. More recently, Turkey made a serious attempt to deal with the structural causes of the budget deficits and the chronic inflation process, a context in which the IMF once again was involved as a central actor. In July 1998, the Staff Monitoring Program was agreed with the IMF. This, in turn, initiated a number of targets and precautions related to the budget, monetary policies, and various structural reforms, and also led to a stand-by agreement with the IMF in December 1999.[15]

The stand-by agreement was certainly ambitious: aiming to bring consumer price inflation down to 25 percent by the end of 2000, 12 percent by the end of 2001, and to seven percent by the end of 2002. It was hoped that the program—through its single-minded emphasis on the disinflation component—would contribute towards the reduction of real interest rates to acceptable levels and the increase of the growth potential of the economy, leading to a more efficient and equitable distribution of resources. A tight fiscal policy, an incomes policy in line with targeted inflation, and monetary and exchange rate policies formulated in line with decreasing inflation were the basis of the disinflation program. A pre-announced exchange rate strategy constituted the only novel element in an otherwise rather orthodox program of inflation stabilization.

The program also tried to tackle fundamental structural problems in the key areas of taxation, privatization, banking regulation, and the reform of agricultural price support schemes. Reduction of agricultural support prices and their replacement by direct income support schemes were crucial components of the program since the support prices involved were substantially above the EU norms and, consequently, the agricultural sector continued to be a major source of disequilibrium in the Turkish economy.

During the early months of 2000, there appeared to be considerable optimism concerning the prospects for stabilization and reform in Turkey. To a significant extent this optimism was the outcome of the EU's Helsinki summit, which took place during the same month as the signing of the IMF stand-by agreement. The endorsement of Turkey's candidacy for full membership at the Helsinki summit of the European Council provided a powerful incentive for undertaking both political and economic reforms. Furthermore, by the end of the 1990s, governments had discovered that progressively smaller amounts of resources were available for populist redistribution once the principal sum and interest on domestic debt had been paid out. Stated somewhat differently, the fiscal crisis of the state appeared to have reached its limits, forcing the politicians and the public at large to seriously reconsider the feasibility of continuing on a populist trajectory.[16]

A superficial glance at Turkish politics also seemed to point towards a certain change in the underlying political culture and behavior. Coalition governments in Turkey, both in the late 1970s and the early to mid-1990s, have been associated with instability and lacked the credibility and commitment to undertake serious fiscal adjustment. The new coalition government formed after the general elections of April 1999, incorporating the left nationalist Democratic Left Party (*Demokratik Sol Parti*—DSP) under the leadership of Bülent Ecevit, the radical-nationalist Nationalist Action Party (*Milliyetçi Hareket Partisi*—MHP) under Devlet Bahçeli, and the right-of-center Motherland Party (*Anavatan Partisi*—ANAP) under Mesut Yılmaz, gave the impression of having significant commitment towards implementing a far-reaching program of disinflation and reform. This appeared to be a rather paradoxical development given the wide ideological spectrum that characterized the coalition government. It was also a puzzling development in the sense that the two dominant partners of the coalition, DSP and MHP, drew their support primarily from low-income segments of society or, in other words, from the losers of neo-liberal globalization. Finally, the fact that an IMF program was concluded for the first time in Turkish history without the presence or influence of a major crisis seemed to provide additional support for these optimistic assessments.

The performance of the coalition government in office, however, failed to match the optimistic mood that prevailed in the early months of 2000. In time, it became apparent that the coalition government lacked cohesion and that its commitment to the economic program was half-hearted. Serious conflicts emerged during the year between the second dominant member of the coalition, the ultra-nationalist MHP, and the two other partners over key aspects of economic policy. In particular, the MHP opposed central elements of the economic program that involved the reduction of agricultural subsidies and the sale of state assets in telecommunications. Reduction of agricultural subsidies generated resistance on income distributional grounds, while the sale of the majority of the shares in the state telecommunications enterprise to foreign investors was considered unacceptable on the grounds of the alleged strategic importance of the enterprise and the loss of national sovereignty entailed by this decision. Perhaps the attempts on the part of the MHP to block the implementation of key aspects of the program were not surprising given that the party drew its support primarily from the rural poor; implementing the program would seriously jeopardize its future electoral prospects.

The coalition government agreed to implement the economic program in the face of major external pressure—originating from both the international financial community and the EU—in an environment where the fiscal situation was diagnosed as unsustainable. This, however, did not mean a deep commitment to reform on the part of all coalition partners, and the half-hearted nature of the commitment became increasingly apparent by the summer of 2000. This, in turn, progressively undermined investor confidence and constituted one of the underlying sources of the speculative attack and the massive exodus of short-term capital in November 2000.

A key point to emphasize in this context is that a coalition government itself is not necessarily a source of instability. Many examples exist, notably in Western Europe, of coalition governments being able to achieve the cohesion and cooperation needed for effective governance of the economy. By 2000, though, Turkey had not reached that stage of political development. One should bear in mind that the ideological distance between the principal coalition partners was considerably wider than most of their Western European counterparts. Furthermore, it was also clear from the experience of the post-1999 era that the basic orientation of political parties in Turkey had not fundamentally changed over time. The parties continued to act as patronage networks serving narrowly based sectional interests as opposed to serving the interests of broad segments of the society as a whole. This narrow focus also prevented them from playing a more constructive role in terms of policy implementation.[17]

Leading into the November 2000 crisis, other elements were also involved. In retrospect, it is clear that the program had failed to generate enough credibility on the part of market participants. This was, in part, due to the insufficient cohesion of—and commitment by—the coalition government. Yet, the rise of the current account deficit during the course of 2000 was also a factor that progressively undermined investor confidence and raised deep questions concerning the sustainability of the program. The steady increase in the size of the current account deficit originated from the fact that the interest rates dropped too rapidly in the initial stages of the program. This, in turn, helped to sustain a consumption boom and made it difficult for the authorities to control the overall demand, resulting in a major surge in imports with negative repercussions on the current account.[18]

Domestic politics, then, was at the heart of the crisis. Yet, an account of the crisis would be seriously incomplete if it failed to take into account the crucial role of external dynamics. Like Turkey, other middle-income countries also experienced full account liberalization and faced a rather unstable and demanding environment in the context of the 1990s. Certainly, the international financial environment had become much more volatile and the investors far more risk-averse following the Asian crisis of 1997. In this kind of environment, even minor policy disturbances could have dramatic ramifications in terms of undermining investor confidence—leading to sudden and large-scale withdrawal of capital from individual economies.

The inherent instability of the international financial environment was aggravated further by specific developments in the context of the year 2000. Turkey suffered from higher energy prices, higher euro as well as higher interest rates on external borrowings in 2000, which rendered the task of policymakers increasingly more complex. Adverse developments in Argentina were also important in terms of influencing investor confidence.

More specifically, the IMF itself—the key institution involved in the Turkish stabilization and reform program—should share a significant part of the blame for the outbreak of the two successive crises. The fact that the crises occurred in the midst of an IMF program is in itself rather surprising, but clearly demonstrates that even in the presence of IMF support the program failed to inspire sufficient confidence on the part of market participants. Furthermore, IMF action is open to criticism on the following grounds. First, the IMF failed to provide an adequate mix of conditions and incentives for program implementation. Given the demanding conditions imposed, the scale of assistance provided was rather inadequate. The measure of assistance was also inadequate, given the scope of adjustment required.[19] The problem was, in part, due to the IMF lacking significant information. For instance, the IMF did not have full information concerning the range of the disequilibrium in the public banking sector and, hence, the true depth of fiscal disequilibrium in Turkey. Indeed, the information became available just prior to the February 2001 crisis. This may be identified as a serious deficiency considering that the disequilibrium in public banks emerged as a central contributor to the 2001 crisis. This problem reflected the absence of accountability and transparency as key deficiencies of Turkey's domestic political order. Yet, it also reflected insufficient investment on the part of the IMF in terms of acquainting itself with the specific characteristics of individual countries and acquiring the relevant information. The IMF had a standard model and tried to apply it in a number of countries, irrespective of its lack of information concerning the political and institutional environment prevailing in those countries. Hence, the February 2001 crisis constituted a classic case of asymmetric information.[20]

Furthermore, it has been argued—quiet convincingly—that the IMF could have prevented the initial November crisis, which was essentially a liquidity crisis. One of the main tenets of the stabilization program was the "no sterilization rule" as a safeguard against possible monetary indiscipline in order to add credibility to the disinflation program. The conditions engendered by this approach restricted the monetary autonomy of the Central Bank by forcing it to operate like a quasi-currency board, allowing the interest rate to be freely determined by the market while leaving the control of monetary policy in the hands of capital flows. Given the inflexibility of the IMF in this respect, the Central Bank appears to have adhered too rigidly to the program. As a result, Demirbank—the main private bank involved in the 2000 crisis—effectively lost all of its capital in two days. Arguably, through a more flexible approach, the Central Bank could have injected liquidity into the system at the right moment to prevent the collapse of Demirbank and, hence, block the outbreak of the crisis itself. Although the Turkish version was a softer version of such experiments, it clearly highlighted a more general problem associated with the controlled exchange rates and currency board-style experiments typically implemented as part of IMF programs in many other countries. The evidence suggests that, on the whole, such experiments tend to be unsuccessful. Even when they are successful in the short run, they tend to be unsuccessful in the long run—as illustrated vividly by the recent Argentine crisis.[21]

In retrospect, the IMF could have paid explicit attention to the sequencing of reforms. Rather than placing the primary emphasis on the elimination of the budget deficit in the first instance, the restructuring of the banking sector could have received immediate attention. There exists a certain consensus that the 2000 and 2001 crises in Turkey were essentially banking crises, though these were clearly related to underlying fiscal imbalances. The November 2000 crisis was primarily a crisis of the private banking sector whereas the February 2001 crisis stemmed from the disequilibrium in key components of the government-owned banking sector. Thus, a perennial failure to properly regulate the banking sector was at the heart of both crises, a failure which reflected—to a significant extent —the deficiencies of the domestic political system. The IMF, however, was also partly responsible for the under-regulation of the banking system.

Admittedly, the formation of the key regulatory agency—the Bank Regulation and Supervision Authority (BRSA)—constituted a key component of the IMF program in 1999. Indeed, the organization became operative prior to the November crisis. In retrospect, the Fund was rather over-optimistic concerning the ability of such a new institution to play an effective role over a short period of time in a highly problematic banking sector. The ability of such an agency to play a constructive regulatory role was severely hampered by the presence of private banking lobbies that resisted any kind of regulation. Bank regulation also faced resistance from politicians and policymakers who conceived of private banks as a major means of government financing and the public banks as a serious source of rent distribution for building up and sustaining electoral support. Whilst the IMF was justified in its emphasis on the need to create strong regulatory institutions in Turkey, it clearly underestimated the political and institutional problems of constructing autonomous and effective regulatory institutions in the Turkish context. In other words, attempting to engineer reforms in a top-down fashion without paying sufficient attention to problems of political legitimacy tends to reduce the likelihood of effective implementation and the overall viability of the IMF-sponsored reform process.

At a deeper level, one could accuse the IMF of failing to deal with the systemic origins of recurrent financial crises in the "semi-periphery" of inherent imperfections in the global financial markets. Hitherto, the IMF has been impervious to such criticisms and has failed to pay adequate attention to proposals involving internationally coordinated capital controls over short-term capital flows. In spite of the fact that the IMF has been going through a process of transformation in recent years—notably in the aftermath of the Asian crisis, it has clearly not been sympathetic to proposals along the lines of the "Tobin tax" to limit short-term capital flows at either the global, regional or national levels. Turning to the Turkish context and considering the risks of program failure, given the depth of disequilibrium and the magnitude of adjustment required temporary controls over outflows of short-term capital could have been an effective instrument. The fact that the IMF did not pay any attention to such instruments as part of its overall program design in Turkey, or elsewhere for that matter, is clearly an issue that deserves serious criticism.[22]

LOOKING BEYOND FEBRUARY 2001:
THE ECONOMIC AND POLITICAL CONSEQUENCES OF THE CRISES

The economic crisis experienced by Turkey in February 2001 proved to be a far deeper crisis than the one in November 2000. Indeed, it constituted the deepest economic crisis faced by Turkey in modern times. The striking magnitude of the crisis may be illustrated by the fact that GNP in real terms declined by 9.4 percent during the course of the year. The result was a dramatic drop in per capita income from $2,986 to $2,110 per annum and a massive increase in unemployment by 1 million people. The crisis, moreover, had a deep affect on all segments of society. Unlike the 1994 crisis, highly educated and skilled employees also lost their jobs in large numbers. Small- and medium-sized businesses were severely affected, resulting in widespread bankruptcies and layoffs. The crisis also led to a major increase in the number of people living below the $400 per month poverty line and the $200 per month subsistence line.[23]

At a more fundamental level, the two consecutive crises helped highlight the total exhaustion of a model of development based on clientelistic ties and patronage networks. This model was the root cause of the problems involving chronic inflation, massive build-up of domestic and external debt as well as unusual levels of corruption by international standards. Hence, the crises marked a drastic loss of legitimacy on the part of the Turkish state. The lack of trust on the part of the public concerning the politicians and the political parties in general—already a strong sentiment prior to the crises—was amplified considerably in the aftermath.

Considering the intensity of the economic collapse experienced, it was somewhat strange to observe that the crises themselves failed to produce a collapse of the government in power or a major dislocation in society. Occasional protests by civil society associations were observed, but these, though, were certainly not comparable to the massive and violent waves of social protest that accompanied the Argentine crisis of 2001. From a comparative perspective, the Turkish experience deserves attention in the sense that the country's social fabric proved to be quite resilient in the face of a major economic collapse. This was, in part, due to the unusual size and strength of the informal economy, which provided a natural escape route for those who lost their jobs in the formal labor market. The presence of strong informal networks involving the family and other informal mechanisms of social support performed a stabilizing function, helping to prevent massive social and political dislocation. Clearly, the informal sector constitutes an element of social capital and a source of short-term stability in the Turkish context. The very strength of the informal economy, however, prevents an urgency to undertake reforms designed to enlarge the size of the recorded economy and result in more resources for the government and a more efficient economy in the long run.[24]

The fact that the social fabric has proved to be quite resilient so far should not lead one to excessive optimism. In the past, populist cycles also ended with crises. Nonetheless, the economy managed to recover from these crises in a relatively short period and a growth trajectory was soon established. In the current context, given the size of the debt burden that has accumulated over a number of years, restoring growth may not be as smooth as in the previous post-crises episodes. If growth fails to recover over a period of a few years and stagnation becomes the norm, then it would be increasingly more difficult to prevent major social and political instability along the lines recently experienced by Argentina. Restoration of growth, therefore, is a crucial consideration, both for debt repayment and maintaining social harmony.

On a more optimistic note, the outbreak of crises has accelerated the reform process in Turkey. Following the February crisis, the authorities took significant steps towards strengthening the role and augmenting the autonomy of key regulatory institutions such as BRSA. It is certainly too early to judge the performance of institutions like BRSA, given the length of the period under consideration and the absence of sufficient concrete evidence. There is no doubt, however, that BRSA, for example, has been playing an active role in the restructuring and reform of the banking sector, which was clearly not the case in the pre-crisis period. Indeed, some commentators have gone as far as to suggest that the IMF deliberately refrained from preventing both crises in Turkey as a means of breaking down opposition to reform. This line of argument, though, appears to be rather far-fetched. What is significant for our purposes, however, is that the reform process initiated by the 1999 program significantly accelerated during the post-crisis setting.[25]

It is quite striking that the same coalition government which had, in part, been responsible for the outbreak of the two crises played an instrumental role in the passing of a record number of laws through parliament over a period of 18 months. The legislation involved covered not only the economic sphere but also embodied major changes in the political sphere designed to enlarge democratic rights and freedoms in highly critical and sensitive areas. In fact, the sheer number of laws passed during 1999–2002 appears to be remarkable, especially judged by the standards of Turkish coalition governments.[26]

At a superficial level, it may be difficult to reach a firm verdict on the performance of the coalition government given the ambiguities highlighted. A closer investigation, though, suggests quite clearly that the main impetus for reform originated from external actors. In the absence of powerful pressures for change applied by both the international financial community and the EU, major factions of the domestic political elites would continue to resist reform in both the economic and political arena as long as a crisis-free environment prevailed. Successive crises clearly increased the power and influence of key external actors such as the IMF and the EU in pushing through major economic and political reforms.

Turkey was clearly in a more fortunate position than Argentina in the sense that it was supported by two rather powerful external anchors. The IMF was certainly much more generous to Turkey after the February crisis.[27] This was largely due to the geo-strategic importance of Turkey from the point of view of US foreign policy interests. Indeed, the events of September 11 seemed to have accentuated Turkey's geo-strategic importance for the United States. Furthermore, there existed a powerful EU anchor in the Turkish context—especially after the Helsinki decision of 1999—which was absent in the Argentine context. By recognizing Turkey's candidate status, the EU created a powerful and institutionalized framework for dialogue and change in line with the economic and political conditions needed to satisfy the Copenhagen criteria. Argentina's alternative to the EU was LAFTA (Latin American Free Trade Agreement), a much looser form of regional integration and clearly a weak external anchor by the standards of the EU.

Indeed, what is fascinating to observe is that the economic crises accelerated the pace of reforms needed for Turkey's eventual EU membership. The material incentives associated with EU membership seemed all the more attractive in the midst of a deep economic crisis. As a result, it became progressively easier to generate popular support for EU membership, in spite of the rather problematic conditions attached to such membership. This, in turn, provided a favorable environment for passing difficult reforms on sensitive issues—such as the extension of cultural rights for the Kurds and the abolition of the death penalty—with relative ease despite the presence of a powerful "anti-EU coalition."

The military-security establishment and the MHP constitute the leading elements of a highly organized and vocal anti-EU coalition. This coalition is not opposed to EU membership *per se* but is strongly opposed to key conditions associated with full EU membership—both in the economic and political spheres—because the fulfillment of such conditions would undermine national autonomy and threaten the unity of the Turkish state. Given the underlying strength of the anti-EU coalition in Turkey, many of the key reforms would not have passed through parliament, at least not in the near future, were it not for a major economic crisis. In fact, a close inspection of the post-February 2001 developments clearly indicates that the MHP has been extremely active in its attempts to block key elements of the reform agenda. Moreover, the anti-EU coalition is likely to play an important role in the near future in terms of challenging the remaining components of EU-related reforms, notably in the political sphere.

Developments in the post-crisis period are also interesting in the sense that the international financial community itself regards a permanent EU anchor as a crucial element guaranteeing the stability and durability of the reform process in Turkey. The underlying logic here is that the IMF only constitutes a temporary anchor—its intervention being effective only as long as an economic crisis persists. For these reasons, the pressures emanating from the EU and the international financial community have been mutually reinforcing processes that constitute a powerful engine for change in Turkey.[28]

Finally, the crisis itself has helped promote a new kind of political actor in the person of Kemal Derviş. Derviş was recruited from the World Bank and appointed as the minister responsible for the economy with the explicit objective of pulling the economy out of crisis. From a comparative standpoint, the appointment of Derviş signifies the emergence of a new kind of politics in the era of financial globalization. In this context, a key individual can play a critical role in terms of forming a bridge between the domestic political sphere of the country concerned and the interests of the international financial community—or what could be described as "transnational capital."

Considering his particular background, the manner in which Derviş positioned himself in Turkey's domestic politics as a "social democrat" is quite interesting and paradoxical. Clearly, Derviş seems to understand social democracy as a necessary part of building a broad-based, pro-reform coalition that incorporates the winners of the reform process and tries to compensate the losers to a certain extent. This, though, begs a number of questions. First, would it be possible to construct such a broad-based coalition around an advocate of neo-liberal reforms when many conceive of him as an agent of the IMF and the international community? Second, and perhaps more significant, would it be possible to sustain such a broad-based coalition if the material benefits of the reform process fail to accrue to broad segments of society, at least in the short run? These questions highlight the serious dilemmas that seem to confront any attempt to construct a broad, pro-reform coalition in an unequal society. These problems are not likely to disappear in the post-crisis era.

OVERCOMING THE LOW GROWTH-HIGH INEQUALITY SYNDROME: THE CHALLENGES AHEAD AND THE NEED FOR A LONG-TERM STRATEGY

A major dilemma facing the Turkish economy in the post-crisis era is how to restore rapid and sustained economic growth in an environment characterized by heavy debt burden—which has accumulated over the years. Long-term growth, however, depends critically on building up domestic capacity and improvement in the country's competitiveness in international markets—issues which are only tangentially addressed by IMF programs. Overcoming fiscal imbalances and high inflation as well as implementing key regulatory reforms constitute necessary but not sufficient steps in this context. Historically, in Turkey the state has been a dominant entity. The existence of a powerful state tradition, however, does not necessarily produce a "hard state" in the purely economic sense of the term. Indeed, the Turkish state, in spite of its significant contribution to economic development over time, manifested elements of a soft state, as the events leading to the most recent set of crises clearly testified. A key challenge, therefore, is to transform the state from a soft state to an effective, market-augmenting "competition state" in the economic realm whilst softening the "hard state" in the political realm through a process of democratic reform.[29] The need for such a transformation is clearly apparent from an examination of the comparative data on certain key indicators of international competitiveness and economic performance.

A crucial element of success evident from the early stages of the Turkish neo-liberal experiment involved a radical improvement in export performance combined with a structural shift in favor of manufactured exports. Turkey satisfies the criterion of being classified as an NIC, with more than 75 percent of its exports falling into the category of manufactured exports (Figure 1). Yet, a closer examination reveals that Turkey lags behind the first generation Asian NICs and other types of NICs in terms of the technology content of its manufactured exports measured by the ratio of technology-intensive exports as a ratio of total manufactured exports (Figure 1). One may clearly interpret this as a sign of weak competitiveness.

A disproportionate share of Turkish manufactured exports continues to be based on such traditional categories as textiles and clothing, iron and steel, and manufacturing of foodstuffs and beverages. In order to break this pattern of dependence on traditional manufactures and achieve diversification towards exports with high technology content, societies need to direct resources towards human capital and research and development. Comparative data unambiguously illustrates the deficiencies of the Turkish economy with respect to these fundamental categories when judged by the standards of both the Asian NICs and industrialized countries (Figures 2 and 3). Educational expenditure is particularly significant, not only for increasing competitiveness but also in terms of creating a favorable environment for foreign direct investment and improving income distribution over time.

The Turkish Economy in Crisis

FIGURE 1

COMPOSITION OF EXPORTS AND TECHNOLOGY CONTENT OF
MANUFACTURED EXPORTS (1997)

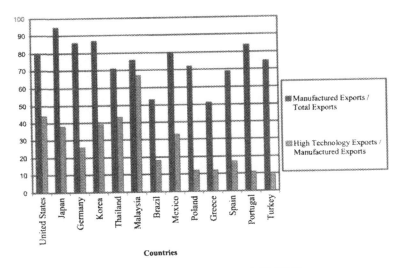

Source: The World Bank, *World Development Report 1999/2000* (2000).

FIGURE 2

RESEARCH AND DEVELOPMENT EXPENDITURE AS % OF GNP
(MOST RECENT BETWEEN 1987–97)

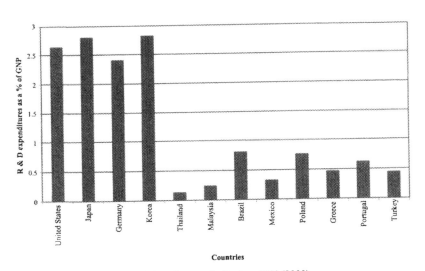

Source: The World Bank, *World Development Indicators 2000* (2000).

FIGURE 3

EDUCATION EXPENDITURE AS % OF GNP (1997)

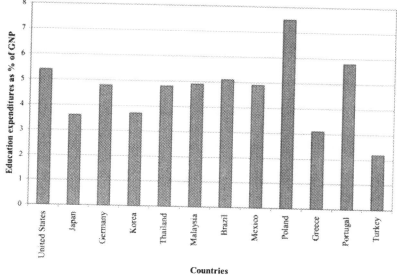

Source: The World Bank, *World Development Indicators 2000* (2000).

This naturally brings us to an area where Turkey has clearly failed to capitalize on one of the positive features of neo-liberal globalization: the availability of a large pool of foreign investment. Foreign direct investment (FDI) would not only generate more capital for economic development but would also help to raise export competitiveness. Data presented in Figure 4 clearly illustrates Turkey's striking inability to attract FDI on an adequate scale compared to other emerging markets in different parts of the world. Research on this issue points towards a multitude of factors that have contributed to the restriction of FDI flows to Turkey. These are—in descending order of importance—political instability, high inflation, uncertainty, deficiencies of the legal system, high tax rates, problems in the financial system, inadequate infrastructure, and pervasive levels of corruption.[30] Undoubtedly, the success of the reform process and rapid progress towards EU membership are likely to play a positive role in this respect. Building domestic capacity in key areas such as education and technological innovation is also likely to create an environment which would be attractive not only for foreign investors but also for the country itself in terms of attracting the right kinds of FDI, involving high technology content and significant linkages with the rest of the economy.

The Turkish Economy in Crisis

FIGURE 4
FDI INFLOWS (1989–94 AND 1995–2000, FIVE-YEAR AVERAGES)

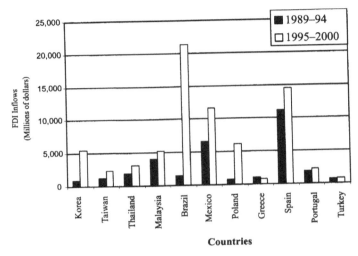

Source: United Nations, *World Investment Report 2001* (2001).

Defense constitutes one area where significant economies are possible. Arguably, the geo-strategic threats facing Turkey in the current regional and international context are somewhat exaggerated and Turkey's defense expenditure is high by international standards (Figure 5). Indeed, lack of transparency and accountability, which applies to all aspects of government expenditure in Turkey, applies with equal force to the case of defense expenditure. Most commentators would argue that published figures on defense expenditure as a proportion of GNP provide a severe underestimate of the true magnitudes involved.[31] Hence, the peace dividend for Turkey is undoubtedly high given the need to generate resources with higher payoffs in such critical areas as civilian technology generation, human capital formation and investment in health. It is obvious, however, that proposals involving sizable cuts in defense expenditure will encounter serious opposition from the powerful military establishment. Nonetheless, we would expect issues relating to defense expenditure to come under increasing scrutiny as Turkey approaches EU membership and deeper issues pertaining to the role of the military in Turkish society gradually come to the forefront of public debate.

Clearly, the issues raised in this section are ultimately political issues in the sense that the ability to tackle these problems effectively hinges on the capacity of the domestic political or party system to alleviate the

FIGURE 5
MILITARY EXPENDITURE AS % OF GNP (1997)

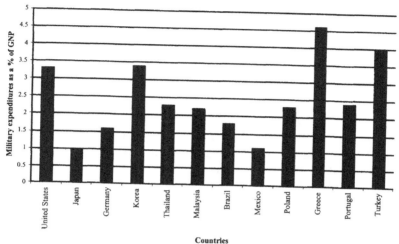

Source: The World Bank, *World Development Indicators 2000* (2000).

pressures of short-term politics and clientelistic patterns of interaction. The Turkish political system is undoubtedly undergoing a process of change in response to powerful domestic and external pressures. Whether this change will be sufficiently rapid in terms of supporting the economic transformation of the Turkish state in the directions outlined within the space of the next few years is rather difficult to predict, especially when writing in a state of flux during the fall of 2002.

THE NEED FOR A PERMANENT EXTERNAL ANCHOR: POLITICAL ECONOMY AND THE SIGNIFICANCE OF EU MEMBERSHIP

It is hard to visualize a decisive break with populist cycles and a transformation of the state in the direction of democratic and accountable competition state in the absence of a powerful EU anchor. Hence, the evolution of Turkey-EU relations and the kinds of signals provided by the EU are likely to have a crucial bearing on Turkey's economic performance over the course of the next decade. Indeed, relations with the European Community (EC) and, more recently, with the European Union have exercised a critical influence over Turkey's political economy throughout the postwar period. The EC/EU has emerged as Turkey's principal trading partner and source of foreign investment over the years. Currently, more than 50 percent of Turkey's foreign trade is with the EU. Turkey, along with Greece, was one of the earliest contenders in the EC/EU enlargement process—both countries acquiring associate membership status in the early 1960s. Whilst the EC/EU has been crucial to Turkey's development experience over the years, the relationship has been a complex and—at times—a mutually disappointing relationship, traditionally dominated by the interplay of economic, political, and security considerations as well as fundamental issues concerning culture and identity.[32]

From a purely economic point of view, Turkey's aspirations to become a full member of the EC/EU have met with resistance. This is due both to Turkey's size and its relative underdevelopment, which pose possible threats—notably in terms of mass migration of labor to high-wage economies of the European core. More recently, political considerations appear to dominate purely economic constraints as the EU has placed a growing emphasis on democratization and human rights. In the context of the 1990s, the crucial development concerns the signing of the Customs Union (CU) Agreement, which became formally operative by the end of 1995. In retrospect, the CU has been instrumental in accelerating the process of trade liberalization in Turkey and exposing Turkish industry to greater external competition. The CU has also created an additional benefit in the sense that it facilitated significant regulatory reforms in the course of the 1990s, notably in the areas of competition policy and intellectual property rights—measures which helped to bring Turkey to global norms of competition. Arguably, weak coalition governments would not have implemented these measures had the EU not demanded them as conditions for activating the CU.[33]

The CU, however, constituted a weak form of integration in the sense that it involved opening Turkey to greater competition but fell considerably short of enabling full membership. Stated somewhat differently, the CU represented a rather unbalanced mix of conditions and incentives. In that respect, the decision of the EU Council to offer the full-membership perspective to Turkey in December 1999 was an important turning point with potentially far-reaching consequences for the Turkish political economy. For countries like Turkey with significant legacies of clientelistic politics, a powerful external anchor is a necessary—albeit not a sufficient—condition for undertaking and consolidating major internal reforms. With full membership in sight, the mix of conditions and incentives became far more favorable. Indeed, the Helsinki decision has facilitated the emergence of a vocal pro-EU coalition in Turkey and has clearly contributed towards the acceleration of the reform process in both the economic and the political spheres—despite considerable opposition. Some of the reforms that passed through parliament in August 2002 would certainly have been unthinkable a few years ago.

Nevertheless, the process is far from complete. Looking to the future, the success of Turkey's economic reforms is likely to be an important consideration in the country's graduation to full membership. Arguably, however, purely political considerations relating to issues such as the Cyprus dispute and the quality of democracy might prove to be formidable obstacles on Turkey's trajectory to this membership. To a certain extent, the ability to create a virtuous cycle depends on the capacity of the political system to satisfy the Copenhagen criteria and achieve step-by-step integration with the EU prior to full membership. This would be made possible by capitalizing on opportunities provided by the EU in such diverse areas as education and technological development. The EU could certainly help in accelerating this process by improving the mix of conditions and incentives further in Turkey's favor, a situation which it could effect through improved financial assistance, a more balanced approach towards the resolution of the Cyprus dispute, and support for civil society organizations that form the backbone of the emerging pro-EU coalition. It is fair to say that the role that the EU played in Turkey has been less constructive compared to the role it played in the earlier wave of southern enlargement and the latest wave of eastern enlargement.[34]

CONCLUDING OBSERVATIONS

Recurrent populist cycles have been a dominant element of the Turkish political economy in the postwar period. Populist cycles, which have inevitably culminated in macroeconomic crises, have been costly to the Turkish economy and have reduced the rate of economic growth below what would otherwise have been the case. The duration of populist cycles has become shorter and crises have become more frequent during the era of open capital account regimes. One may explain this apparent paradox as the combined outcome of the underlying weaknesses of the democratic regime at home and premature exposure to financial globalization. Capital account liberalization in Turkey has been engineered prior to the establishment of a stable macroeconomic environment and a strong regulatory framework for the banking sector. Premature financial and capital account liberalization in the absence of an adequate institutional infrastructure had major negative ramifications. The result was a pattern of a highly fragile debt-led growth which was heavily dependent on domestic borrowing to finance the large fiscal deficit and inflows of short-term capital. This inherently unstable pattern of growth amplified the risks of speculative attacks and, hence, vulnerability to successive crises. The latest of these recurrent crises experienced in February 2001 constituted the deepest crisis experienced by Turkey in the modern era.

There exist certain signs that the underlying continuities in the Turkish political economy are in the process of being dismantled under the impact of powerful pressures for change originating from the international financial community and the EU in recent times. The deep crisis experienced by Turkey in 2001 has clearly helped to accelerate this process. Change, however, is unlikely to proceed in a smooth manner. With the option of the authoritarian exit largely excluded from the political agenda, countries like Turkey face serious dilemmas in establishing the basis for rapid and sustained economic growth in the presence of fragile democratic institutions. The existence of acute distributional pressure and unrestricted exposure to the highly unstable environment of global financial markets make the prospects for rapid and sustained growth in such countries highly problematic. Comparative analysis clearly highlights the difficulties that Turkey faces in developing an effective competition state. Success in this context is likely to depend on the strength of a broad-based, pro-reform coalition and a powerful permanent external anchor. In this respect, the nature of Turkey-EU relations is likely to exercise a decisive influence over the evolution of the Turkish political economy in the coming years.

NOTES

The author would like to thank Fikret Şenses and Hakan Tunç for their valuable comments on an earlier draft of this essay and Doğan Aşık and Evren Tok for their able assistance.

1. For detailed investigations of Turkey's postwar development experience, including discussions of different policy phases and the nature of the crises leading to major policy shifts, see Yakup Kepenek and Nurhan Yentürk, *Türkiye Ekonomisi* [Turkish Economy] (Istanbul: Remzi Yayınevi, 2000); Roger Owen and Şevket Pamuk, *A History of Middle East Economies in the Twentieth Century* (London: I.B. Tauris, 1998); Ziya Öniş and James Riedel, *Economic Crises and Long-Term Growth in Turkey* (Washington DC: The World Bank, 1993).
2. In a recent comparative study, Şevket Pamuk demonstrates that Turkey's average growth rate of real GDP per capita in the postwar period was higher than the Middle Eastern and Latin American averages. See Şevket Pamuk, "Economic Growth in Turkey in Comparative Perspective, 1880–2000," Paper presented at the 6th METU International Conference in Economics, Middle East Technical University, Ankara, Sept. 2002.
3. Five decades of continuous growth have helped generate a large and diversified economy. Recent evidence suggests that Turkey is the 22nd largest economy in the world. Yet its standing on a per-capita income basis is much less impressive, with Turkey occupying only the 89th position. This information is based on figures in World Bank, "Entering the 21st Century," *World Development Report 1999/2000* (New York: Oxford University Press for the

World Bank, 2000). These figures suggest growth has not been sufficient to pull standards of living up to developed country standards in the presence of rapid and sustained population growth. For recent demographic trends in Turkey, see TÜSIAD, *Türkiye'nin Fırsat Penceresı: Demografik Dönüşüm ve İzdüşumleri* [Turkey's Window of Opportunity: Demographic Transformation and Projections for the Future] (Istanbul: Türk Sanayicileri ve İşadamları Derneği, 1999). A striking trend in this context concerns the slowdown of population growth during the 1990s. Nonetheless, Turkey enjoys a disproportionately high share of young people, which has major social and political ramifications. Furthermore, we observe a country characterized by a striking dualistic structure with a rather developed western part coexisting with the underdeveloped east. It is a country highly developed by the standards of the majority of countries in its surrounding regions and yet one significantly lagging behind the EU standards and even the standards of the late Mediterranean entrants to the Community when judged on a per capita income basis.

4. On the clientelistic nature of Turkish capitalism in the postwar period, see Ayşe Buğra, *State and Business in Modern Turkey: A Comparative Study* (Albany, NY: State University of New York Press, 1994). On the obstacles faced in the transition to a more competitive form of capitalism, see İzak Atiyas and Hasan Ersel, "Some Observations on the Role of Private Sector in Turkey," mimeograph, Sabancı University and Yapı Kredi Bank, Istanbul (1999).

5. This definition is borrowed from David Waldner, *State Building and Late Development* (Ithaca and London: Cornell University Press, 1999), p.34. Waldner uses the term "popular sector incorporation" instead of "populism."

6. One may argue that the military interlude in Turkey has – in a very unintentional manner – contributed to the deinstitutionalization and fragmentation of the party system in Turkey as well as to the rise of political Islam in Turkey during the course of the 1990s. Hence, we have clear evidence suggesting that short-term stability generated by a temporary authoritarian exit has resulted in greater instability in the future. See Ziya Öniş, "The Political Economy of Islamic Resurgence in Turkey: The Rise of the Welfare Party in Perspective," *Third World Quarterly*, Vol.18, No.4 (1997), pp.743–66.

7. For a comparative analysis of the role of the state in the development experience of Turkey and the East Asian NICs, see Ziya Öniş, *State and Market: The Political Economy of Turkey in Comparative Perspective* (Istanbul: Boğaziçi University Press, 1998) and Waldner (1999).

8. One may defend this statement on the grounds that the democratic regime clearly did not collapse in the aftermath of the 1994 crisis as it had done earlier in the context of previous economic crises. Nonetheless, one can form an indirect link between deteriorating economic conditions and the rise of political Islam in the mid-1990s, which subsequently resulted in the quasi-military intervention in February 1997 that toppled the coalition government – dominated by the Islamist Welfare Party – out of office. Hence, one can argue that the decisive break with the past in this respect occurred in 2001 and not in 1994. Clearly, an explicit EU anchor played a central role in this context.

9. On the nature of Argentine neo-liberalism in the 1990s leading to the crisis of 2001, see Werner Baer, Pedro Elosequi, and Andres Gallo, "The Achievements and Failures of Argentina's Neo-liberal Economic Policies," *Oxford Development Studies*, Vol.30, No.2 (2002), pp.63–85.

10. For a detailed and critical investigation of Turkish neo-liberalism in the 1980s, see Tosun Aricanli and Dani Rodrik (eds.), *The Political Economy of Turkey: Debt, Adjustment and Sustainability* (London: Macmillan, 1990). Turkey's growth performance during the 1980–87 period was superior to its performance in the 1988–98 period. Real GNP growth emerged as 4.66 percent for 1980–87 and 4.12 percent for 1988–98 respectively. One also has to take into account the fact that growth recorded during the second phase was an extremely fragile pattern of debt-led growth, which was clearly unsustainable. The validity of this observation is clearly confirmed by looking at the average growth rate for 1999–2001, which has been recorded as -3.3 percent. A fair comparison of the two decades, however, should explicitly recognize the depth of exogenous shocks in the 1990s that exercised a negative influence over the performance of the Turkish economy, taking into account the impact of the Gulf War, the war against the PKK that lasted until early 1999, the earthquake in 1999, and the successive emerging market crises in the late 1990s.

11. On the weaknesses of the Turkish development model during the 1990s, see Ümit Cizre-Sakallıoğlu and Erinç Yeldan, "Politics, Society and Financial Liberalization: Turkey in the 1990s," *Development and Change*, Vol.31, No.1 (2000), pp.481–508; Nurhan Yentürk, "Short-term Capital Inflows and their Impact on Macroeconomic structure: Turkey in the 1990s," *The Developing Economies*, Vols.37–38 (1999), pp.89–113; Mine Eder, "The Challenge of Globalization and Turkey's Changing Political Economy," in Barry Rubin and Kemal Kirişçi (eds.), *Turkey in World Politics: An Emerging Multiregional Power* (London and Boulder, CO: Lynne Rienner, 2001), pp.189–215.

12. On the underlying causes of fiscal disequilibrium in Turkey during the 1990s, see Izak Atiyas and Şerif Sayın, "A Political Economy Perspective on Turkish Budget Deficits," *Boğaziçi Journal*, Vol.12, No.1 (1998), pp.55–80. One should also emphasize that Turkey was in a state of virtual civil war with the PKK between 1984 and 1999. The intensification of the armed conflict naturally resulted in the diversion of resources to defense, contributing to higher fiscal instability and lower economic growth than would otherwise have been the case.

13. Data obtained from the Central Bank's annual reports at <http://www.tcmb.gov.tr/yeni/evds/yayin/yay/eng.html>.

14. For an illuminating study on the nature and limitations of Turkish democracy, see Ersin Kalaycıoğlu, "Turkish Democracy: Patronage Versus Governance," *Turkish Studies*, Vol.2, No.1 (2001), pp.54–70.

15. For the details of the program, see "Turkey: Letter of Intent, December 9, 1999" at <http://www.imf.org/external/NP/LOI/1999/120999.HTM>. For a concise elaboration of the key features of the program, see Gazi Erçel, "The Disinflation Program for the Year 2000," *Insight Turkey*, Vol.2, No.2 (2000), pp.13–18.

16. On the costly nature of "distributive politics" or "populist redistribution"—resulting in heavy interest burden on domestic public debt with an associated squeeze on critical areas of investment during the 1990s—see Atiyas and Sayın (1998), pp.55–79. The key point to emphasize is that distributive politics did not involve a systematic transfer of resources to the poorest segments of society as part of a coherent social policy.

17. On the nature of the political parties in Turkey—emphasizing their role as patronage dispersion mechanisms as well as the lack of intra-party democracy—see Barry Rubin and Metin Heper (eds.), *Political Parties in Turkey* (London and Portland, OR: Frank Cass, 2002). The collection of essays contains detailed information on the ideology, operation and leadership styles of all the major political parties in Turkey.

18. The recent crises in Turkey have already generated a large literature. For a small sample, see C. Emre Alper, "The Turkish Liquidity Crisis of 2000: What Went Wrong," *Russian and East European Finance and Trade*, Vol.37, No.6 (2001), pp.51–71; C. Emre Alper and Ziya Öniş, "Financial Globalization, the Democratic Deficit and Recurrent Crises in Emerging Markets: The Turkish Experience in the Aftermath of Capital Account Liberalization," *Emerging Markets Finance and Trade*, Vol.39, No.3 (forthcoming 2003), pp.5–26; Fatih Özatay and Güven Sak, "The 2000–2001 Financial Crises in Turkey," Paper presented at the Brookings Trade Forum 2002: Currency Crises, Washington DC, May 2002; Erinç Yeldan, "On the IMF-Directed Disinflation Program in Turkey: A Program for Stabilization or A Recipe for Impoverishment and Financial Chaos?," mimeograph, Department of Economics, Bilkent University, Ankara (2001). Specifically on the under-regulation of both public and private banks in the outbreak of the crises, see C. Emre Alper and Ziya Öniş, "Soft Budget Constraints, Government Ownership of Banks and Regulatory Failure: The Political Economy of the Turkish Banking System in the Post-Capital Liberalization Era," *Boğaziçi University Department of Economics Working Papers*, ISS/EC-02-02 (2002[a]).

19. The financial assistance provided by the Fund in December 1999 totaled approximately $4 billion extended over a period of three years. This was clearly not commensurate with the scale of adjustment involved in the banking sector. In retrospect, the severe information problem manifested itself in the Fund's underestimation of the scale of duty losses in public banks and the problem of financing these in the interbank market. See Alper and Öniş, (2002[a]).

20. For an elaboration of some of the points made in this section in the broader context of IMF reform, see C. Emre Alper and Ziya Öniş, "Emerging Market Crises and the IMF: Rethinking

the Role of the IMF in the Light of Turkey's 2000–2001 Financial Crises," *Boğaziçi University Department of Economics Working Papers*, ISS/EC-02-03 (2002[b]).
21. On the problems associated with exchange rate-based anti-inflation strategies and the associated currency board experiments, see Barry Eichengreen, "Crisis Prevention and Management: Any New Lessons from Argentina and Turkey?," mimeograph, Department of Economics, University of California Berkeley (2001).
22. The United Nations Conference on Trade and Development (UNCTAD) has been particularly vocal in this respect. See, *UNCTAD Trade and Development Report, 1999* (Geneva: United Nations Conference on Trade and Development, 1999). For an argument in favor of national-level capital controls with reference to Turkey, see Yılmaz Akyüz and Korkut Boratav, "The Making of the Turkish Financial Crisis," Paper presented at the conference on "Financialization of the Global Economy," PERI, University of Massachusetts, Dec. 2001.
23. On the impact of the 2001 crisis on poverty, see the contribution by Fikret Şenses in this volume (pp.92–119).
24. For a comprehensive attempt to estimate the size of the underground or informal economy in Turkey over time on the basis of a variety of different methodologies, see Fethi Öğünç and Gökhan Yılmaz, "Estimating the Underground Economy in Turkey," *The Central Bank of Turkey Research Department Discussion Paper* (2000). Various estimates suggest that the ratio of underground economy to official economy is of the order of 1:5 to 1:4 in recent years, which is certainly a large figure by international standards.
25. One should note, however, that resistance to reforms both in the economic and political spheres remained intact in the aftermath of the February crisis. Indeed, major clashes occurred between the newly appointed Economy Minister, Kemal Derviş, and the MHP, key members of the coalition, over a number of key issues of reform. One striking example of this kind of conflict occurred in the context of reforming the Telekom board, one of the key conditions for the $15.7 billion IMF financial rescue package. The MHP was determined to maintain its control over the company and insisted on choosing four of the seven board members. The major conflict between Derviş and the Transport Minister, Enis Öksüz, resulted in a certain loss of confidence and led to a delay in the IMF loan. The financial arm of the IMF was decisive in resolving the issue, however. The board was reappointed two weeks later and the episode ended with the resignation of the transport minister. One could identify several other instances, which were similar to this kind of conflict. What is interesting for our purposes is that the strength of the IMF, in line with the scale of assistance it provided post-crisis, played a key role in breaking the resistance to reform.
26. It is interesting to note that almost all of the key pieces of legislation in the economic sphere involving financial sector reform, agricultural reform, and privatization designed to satisfy both IMF conditions and the EU's Copenhagen criteria—both in the short- and medium-term —were accomplished by August 2002. In addition, major reforms have been accomplished in the political arena. For information on this issue, see <http://www.ikv.org.tr/turkiye-ab/guncel/Tablo5.htm>. The proper implementation of these reforms, however, is another issue.
27. The scale of IMF involvement increased after the February 2001 crisis. During the course of 2001 and 2002, Turkey managed to attract a total of $24.5 billion of IMF assistance. This clearly highlights the validity of the earlier criticism that the scale of assistance provided to Turkey as part of the 1999 program was of a rather limited magnitude given the scale of *ex post facto* adjustment involved.
28. Private financial institutions have been placing great emphasis on the achievement of EU-related reforms and—notably—EU-related political reforms in the post-crisis era. See Lehman Brothers report as a typical example: Lehman Brothers, "Cliff Hanger," *Focus Turkey* (Nov. 30, 2001).
29. On the concept of the "competition state," see Ronen Palan, Jason Abbott with Phil Deane, *State Strategies in the Global Political Economy* (London and New York: Pinter, 1996). On Turkey's state tradition and the dichotomy involving the coexistence of a "soft state" in the economic realm with an excessively "strong" and overpowering state in the political realm that is increasingly under challenge, see Metin Heper and Fuat Keyman, "Double-Faced State: Political Patronage and Consolidation of Democracy in Turkey," *Middle Eastern Studies*, Vol.34, No.4 (1998), pp.259–77.

30. On the underlying causes of weak FDI performance in Turkey, see Abdurrahman Arıman, "Foreign Investments in Turkey," *Insight YASED*, Vol.2, No.4 (2001), pp.12–14.

31. On the measurement of defense expenditure in Turkey and the conceptual problems involved in this process, see Gülay Günlük-Şenesen, "Budget Deficits in Turkey: Expenditure Aspects with Reference to Security Expenditures," Paper presented at the Third METU International Conference in Economics, Middle East Technical University Ankara, Sept. 1999. For a valuable analysis of the role of the military as an economic actor in the context of the Turkish neo-liberal experiment, see Fırat Demir, "A Failure Story: Politics, Society and Financial Liberalization in Turkey; The Paths of Transformation in the Post-Liberalization Era," Paper presented at the 2002 Annual Meeting of the European Public Choice Society, Belgirate, Italy, April 4–7, 2002.

32. For a comprehensive investigation of the evolution of Turkey-EU relations in the postwar context, see Meltem-Müftüler-Baç, *Turkey's Relations with a Changing Europe* (Manchester: Manchester University Press, 1997).

33. On the nature of Turkey-EU relations in the 1990s in the context of the Customs Union, see Canan Balkır, "The Customs Union and Beyond," in Libby Rittenberg (ed.), *The Political Economy of Turkey in the Post-Soviet Era: Going West and Looking East* (Westport, CO: Praeger, 1998), pp.51–78.

34. On the impact of the Helsinki summit on Turkey-EU relations and the challenges that lie ahead, see Ziya Öniş, "Domestic Politics, International Norms and Challenges to the State: Turkey-EU Relations in the Post-Helsinki Era," in Ali Çarkoğlu and Barry Rubin (eds.), *Turkey and the European Union: Domestic Politics, Economic Integration and International Dynamics* (London and Portland, OR: Frank Cass, 2003).

2

The Lost Gamble:
The 2000 and 2001 Turkish Financial Crises in Comparative Perspective

HAKAN TUNÇ

On two occasions, first in November 2000 and then in February 2001, foreign and domestic investors pulled out enormous sums of money from the Turkish market within a matter of days. This rush to withdraw funds came about a year after Turkey introduced a disinflation program predicated on an exchange rate-based stabilization (ERBS), which was designed and supported by the International Monetary Fund (IMF). The Turkish government weathered the crisis in November with the financial support of the IMF and was able to hold on to the exchange rate peg. Three months later, however, turmoil in the market forced the government to abandon the peg. In the months that followed, the currency collapsed, bankruptcies became widespread, unemployment soared, and Turkey faced the worst economic contraction it had seen in decades.

This contribution argues that investor panic played a key role in both the November and February financial crises. In the case of the November crisis, panic was caused by the policies of the newly created banking supervision agency and the subsequent liquidity problems of a mid-sized bank. In February, it was the prime minister's statement that Turkey was in the midst of a "political crisis" following his disagreement with the president that triggered financial panic. The argument that financial panic was a prominent cause of both Turkish crises is in contrast to the common *ex post facto* analysis, which claims that the crises were simply disasters waiting to happen because of Turkey's weak economic fundamentals. Without question, certain economic weaknesses—the widening current account deficit, currency overvaluation, and delays in the implementation of certain structural reforms—existed, but they were hardly severe enough to provoke a financial crisis of the magnitude faced by Turkey.

Financial panic does not occur in a vacuum. I argue that the fragility of the banking sector was a key factor shaping the outcome of the "panic attacks" mentioned above. Turkey's bank fragility was associated with what I call "external illiquidity," meaning maturity and currency mismatches between bank assets and liabilities. The December 1999 disinflation program, with its pre-announced exchange rate peg, was introduced against the background of the open capital account and certain bank weakness, which were significantly exacerbated during the first ten months of the program's implementation due to the presumed exchange rate stability. As discussed below, there are serious dangers involved in combining an open financial market, a pegged exchange rate, and a fragile banking sector. Herein lay the gamble in Turkey's disinflation strategy. Yet, despite the risks, the Turkish program need not have failed so soon, if ever.

This contribution compares the making of the Turkish financial crises with three major financial crises in the 1990s—namely, the Mexican peso crisis in 1994, the Thai crisis in 1997 that triggered the Asian turmoil, and the Brazilian crisis in 1999. The comparison will demonstrate that the Turkish crisis is not a unique case among the recent financial crises in emerging market economies. In all four cases, investor sentiment changed suddenly. This was due primarily to the herd behavior of market participants and their self-fulfilling expectations. The fact that Turkey's exchange rate peg collapsed before the IMF's envisaged move to a flexible exchange rate regime requires another line of comparison with similar ERBS strategies that lasted much longer. In this regard, I compare the circumstances under which Turkey adopted the exchange rate peg with those of Brazil's Real plan in 1994 and Russia's ERBS strategy in 1995. Brazil and Russia prove to be fitting comparisons as they, like Turkey, are both countries that experienced a severe banking crisis during the first year of their respective anti-inflation programs. Unlike what happened in Turkey, however, the banking crises in Brazil and Russia did not develop into full-fledged currency crises.

The first section presents an analytical framework of how the coexistence of banking fragility and financial panic intersect under a fixed exchange rate regime, ultimately resulting in a currency collapse. The second section describes the emergence of financial vulnerability in Turkey before and after the introduction of the stabilization program, and contrasts it to the situations in Brazil (1994–95) and Russia (1995–96). The third section discusses the role played by financial panic in Turkey, Mexico, Thailand, and Brazil, and leads to the conclusion.

BANKING FRAGILITY, FINANCIAL PANIC, AND CURRENCY COLLAPSE:
ANALYTICAL CONSIDERATIONS

The episodes of currency turmoil in the 1990s generated a great deal of debate among economists over the determinants of these crises, which were characterized by the sudden and sharp reversal of capital flows and led to the collapse of pegged exchange rate regimes. Explanations of financial crises distinguish between crises caused by deterioration in economic fundamentals and those that result from a prompt change in investors' expectations about the government's ability to maintain a fixed (or semi-fixed) exchange rate.

The first perspective stresses undisciplined fiscal and monetary policies, which eventually become inconsistent with a fixed exchange rate regime. In this so-called "first generation" model of financial crises, the central bank's expansionary monetary policy (usually through monetization of the fiscal deficit) and/or an unsustainable current account deficit are the primary culprits responsible for the liquidation of domestic currency holdings by market participants in anticipation of devaluation. The important point here is that a financial crisis can be anticipated by looking at the deterioration of macroeconomic fundamentals.[1]

In contrast, the second explanation for the onset of a financial crisis— the one adopted in this essay—emphasizes the unanticipated nature of the crisis. This line of argument focuses on the characteristic herd instinct of the market—that is, the sudden reaction of investors to the actions of other investors—rather than on a country's economic fundamentals. Proponents of the latter perspective argue that a financial crisis can be thought of as a shift in investors' expectations about devaluation or default that, in turn, makes the defense of the peg excessively costly for the government. This shift may lead to a financial panic that can be described as an "adverse equilibrium outcome" in which short-term creditors withdraw their loans from a solvent borrower in a very short period of time.[2] Similar to what happens during a run on the banks, the change in market sentiment usually takes the form of a self-fulfilling prophecy in which each creditor believes that other creditors will stop lending, thus validating the negative expectations. A key issue here is that because of informational limitations and the absence of coordination among investors, foreign lenders cannot distinguish between borrowers from the same country and treat them all as equally risky.[3] The implication is that during a financial panic, the financial system of a country as a whole can be illiquid but solvent—that is, it has a positive net worth but cannot obtain funds from elsewhere.

The sudden loss of investor confidence in a country's economy involves some indeterminacy and is usually triggered by an extraordinary event or an extraneous shock. Yet, for such an event to prompt a change in market sentiment, the country must already be in a "crisis zone." In other words, it must already be vulnerable. This vulnerability can be defined as a situation which, following Chang and Velasco, I call "external illiquidity."[4] External illiqudity arises when the short-term foreign currency obligations of a country's financial system exceeds the amount of foreign currency at the central bank. In such circumstances, investors may wonder whether they can convert their domestically denominated currency into foreign currency at the present pegged exchange rate before the central bank loses so many reserves that it stops defending its currency and devalues.

External illiquidity usually originates in the financial system, particularly in the banking sector. As noted in several recent studies, currency and banking crises in developing countries are usually twin events.[5] The key link between banks and currency crises can be seen when banks' temporary liquidity shortages of foreign currency generate vulnerability to a sudden reversal of capital flows. A liquidity shortage in foreign currency occurs when domestic banks borrow in foreign currency (whether in the form of deposits or loans) and use these liabilities primarily to fund longer term and illiquid investments in domestic currency that cannot be readily converted to cash. Banks' liquidity problems are usually characterized by both a currency mismatch (bank liabilities associated with capital flows are denominated in foreign currency, while loans are denominated in domestic currency) and a maturity mismatch (foreign currency deposits by foreign investors are short term, while loans are medium or long term).[6]

External illiquidity emerges when banks "over-borrow" in foreign currency. Over-borrowing usually results from a combination of two factors. The first factor is the liberalization of both the domestic financial system and the capital account. Capital account liberalization entails abandoning the regulations intended to control capital flows in and out of the country. This "twin liberalization" is likely to result in excessive short-term borrowing by both banks and non-bank financial institutions as the amount of resources available to the financial sector surges.[7] As noted by a number of scholars, short-term capital flows are much more volatile than long-term flows and more prone to a sudden reversal during a financial panic. It has been argued that the prudential regulation and supervision of banks' short-term international borrowing can be an effective check on over-borrowing. Establishing effective regulation and supervision, however, may prove to be difficult and incomplete, as institutional change cannot usually keep up with the high levels of international capital flow following capital account liberalization.[8] The second factor that figures in bank over-borrowing in foreign currency is the fixed exchange rate regime. The apparent stability of the exchange rate peg leads banks to overlook currency risk and induces them to borrow heavily in foreign currency without hedging their exposures.[9] Moreover, fixing the exchange rate within the framework of an ERBS program usually leads to a consumption boom during the initial phase which, in turn, triggers a sudden expansion in bank credit and a rapid increase in the stock of short-term foreign currency liabilities.[10]

As noted above, external illiquidity generates financial vulnerability to a sudden change in investors' sentiment, but the vulnerability itself is not enough to trigger a financial crisis, nor does it determine the timing of the crisis. An extraneous event is necessary to trigger a financial panic and cause a "sudden stop," which can be defined as a massive reversal of capital inflows and a refusal by investors to roll over their short-term credits for banks or the government.[11] When a sudden stop of foreign capital takes place, banks are forced to liquidate their long-term investments at highly discounted prices in order to raise the cash needed to pay off their investors. Soon, a systemic risk in the banking system is likely to emerge in which even a well-managed bank can quickly exhaust its cash reserves and become insolvent, thereby validating the initial expectation of a run. Because of systemic links, the run could spread to the entire banking and financial sectors. Under these circumstances, extreme pressure on the exchange rate appears and a rapid loss of official reserves ensues. The collapse of the exchange rate is likely to occur because stabilizing banks and maintaining the exchange rate become mutually incompatible objectives for the government.[12] When the fixed exchange rate is abandoned, it usually overshoots. This, in turn, usually causes widespread bank collapses due to costly asset liquidation, an unnecessarily large credit crunch and a sharp decline in economic activity. The economic and financial costs for external illiquidity and some weak fundamentals (especially real exchange rate overvaluation) are greatly magnified as a result of creditor panic. In other words, the punishment is much greater than the crime.

FROM FINANCIAL LIBERALIZATION TO EXTERNAL ILLIQUIDITY

The financial crises under consideration in this contribution (Mexico 1994, Thailand 1997, Brazil 1999, and Turkey 2000–1) were the result of several interrelated factors, but they all shared two main underlying sources: a surge in capital flows preceding the crisis and the presence of a pegged exchange rate regime.[13] These capital flows were mostly short term and intermediated by the banking system prior to the crisis. The underlying cause of the capital flow surge is fundamentally related to twin liberalization and exchange rate stability. Foreign investors gained full access to the financial markets of these countries as the interest rate ceilings were lifted and various controls and restrictions on capital flows were either abandoned or reduced.

Turkey and Mexico undertook capital market liberalization in the late 1980s. In Turkey, the capital account was fully liberalized by the Turgut Özal government in 1989.[14] Mexico not only removed most of the restrictions on capital flows in 1989–90 but also privatized state-owned banks and lowered their required reserve ratios to zero, thereby giving them a significant incentive to borrow from abroad.[15] In Thailand, capital account liberalization during the early 1990s was accompanied by the introduction of special incentives to encourage foreign borrowing. For instance, Thai banks received special tax breaks when they conducted their business in the Bangkok International Banking Facility, which operated exclusively in foreign currency transactions.

The major outcome of financial opening was frequent maturity and currency mismatches in bank balance sheets. Financial vulnerability, however, became pronounced only when it was coupled with exchange rate inflexibility. Turkey is a case in point. As a result of deregulation, Turkish banks increasingly borrowed short-term foreign currency from abroad in the 1990s. Borrowing, however, peaked only during the periods when the exchange rate became subject to heavy government intervention and thus appeared to be stable. A major example of this was the government's suppression of the value of the Turkish lira (TL) against the dollar in late 1993. The Turkish authorities' aversion to letting the lira depreciate initially led to a substantial increase in banks' borrowing in foreign currency and the explosion in banks' open currency positions (that is, net external borrowing). This eventually resulted in the spectacular collapse of the TL in early 1994. In the five years that followed, Turkish governments maintained a fairly steady policy of devaluation to preserve the real exchange rate. This "managed float" of the TL induced exchange rate uncertainty and, therefore, became a major disincentive for Turkish banks to avoid increasing their foreign currency-denominated liabilities.[16] By the end of 1999, it is estimated that the open positions of private commercial banks amounted to around $13 billion.[17] Even though this was a significant amount—given the flexible exchange rate—the banking sector did not seem to be vulnerable to a reversal of capital flows.

Turkey's Stabilization Program and Rising Financial Vulnerability

In January 2000, with the aim of eliminating high and chronic inflation, the Turkish government launched a stabilization program with the support of the IMF. The key to the disinflation program was the introduction of a new exchange rate regime characterized by a pre-announced exchange rate and a built-in exit strategy, which envisaged a gradual and smooth transition to a flexible exchange rate after the first critical 18-month period. The program entailed tight monetary and fiscal policy as well as the implementation of structural reforms.[18] Of all the structural reforms, the most important was related to the restructuring of the banking system, the timing of which—as will be discussed—had some important consequences for the November crisis.

As noted by several scholars, the major consequence of the stabilization program was that it increased the vulnerability of the banking sector to a capital reversal.[19] The main impact was a sharp decline in interest rates. This fall affected bank balance sheets in two major ways. First, falling interest rates generated a significant rise in credit expansion and aggregate demand. During the first nine months of the stabilization program, banks' consumer credits tripled. At the same time, bank borrowing from foreign sources reached record levels.[20] Second, as interest rates declined, some banks used short-term foreign credits to purchase excessive amounts of longer term government securities before they fell, as expected, parallel to inflation.[21] These banks tried to make use of very short-term foreign funding to lock in longer term domestic yields and, thus, increasingly relied on short-term domestic financing (repos and interbank loans). As a result, maturity and currency mismatches in bank balance sheets deteriorated. As a sign of this deterioration, banks' net open positions nearly doubled during the first nine months of 2000.[22]

With the benefit of hindsight, the major difference between the Turkish ERBS program of 2000 and other similar programs was that the former was launched at a time when the country had already been integrated into the global financial system after a decade of an open capital account.[23] On the other hand, Mexico, Brazil and Russia undertook ERBS programs when their links to global financial markets were limited. In each of these latter cases, external illiquidity emerged at least a few years after stabilization and when inflation was eliminated. Mexico's ERBS program in 1987, for example, preceded capital market liberalization by almost three years. Hence, Mexico attracted very large amounts of short-term capital only after 1990, mostly in the form of portfolio investment, which eventually caused serious vulnerability in the country's financial system.

Similarly, when Brazil and Russia launched their ERBS programs in the mid-1990s, they had not abandoned all the restrictions and regulations on short-term capital flows. Equally important, during the initial phase of stabilization, the authorities in Brazil and Russia resisted the full deregulation of short-term capital flows. Brazil sought to discriminate between long- and short-term capital flows around the time it launched its anti-inflation program (the Real Plan) in 1994. Short-term equity and debt flows became subject to controls because they were suspected of higher volatility. At the same time, the authorities tried to upgrade incentives for foreign direct investment. Beginning in 1993, Brazilian authorities began to regulate bank borrowing from abroad and restricted foreigners' purchase of government securities and numerous other types of non-resident transactions. Evidence suggests that Brazil's efforts to regulate capital flow were effective in changing the composition of capital flow in favor of long-term flows, at least during the critical first year of stabilization. In the long term, however, the capital controls turned out to be ineffective—as demonstrated by the massive surge in flows that Brazil experienced after 1996.[24]

In Russia, the government's attempt to control capital flows centered on the government's debt instruments, despite the ruble's convertibility. With the intention of protecting the program from the possible volatility of short-term capital flows, the Russian government greatly restricted foreign investors' participation in the lucrative GKO (ruble-denominated short-term government securities) market after it initiated its stabilization program in early 1995. Foreign investors were not allowed to purchase more than ten percent of any GKO issue and repatriate the related income. These restrictions were first relaxed in August 1996 and then entirely removed, in part due to IMF insistence but mainly because the government sought to finance its budget deficit at a lower cost by increasing the demand for GKOs.[25] In sum, keeping some of the restrictions on short-term capital flows during inflation stabilization greatly contributed to successful disinflation in Brazil and Russia. These regulations provided authorities with breathing space during the early phases of their anti-inflation strategy. Turkey, on the other hand, was largely deprived of this option in 2000 because it was extremely difficult to undo its ten-year experience of integration with global capital markets.

It is also interesting to note that both Brazil and Russia experienced a banking crisis in 1995—one year into their stabilization programs. These banking crises, however, did not result in the collapse of the currency, as happened in Turkey. The main reason for this appears to be the absence of external illiquidity in the financial sector. Russian and Brazilian banks did not have currency mismatches, mainly due to restrictions imposed on capital flows. In Brazil, during the aftermath of stabilization, the banks' main problem became a large volume of non-performing loans, which was an outcome of a credit squeeze associated with the government's policy of maintaining high interest rates. In Russia, the major factor in the banking crisis was that interest rates remained high relative to the fall in inflation in the first half of 1995, limiting the funds available to some banks.[26] External illiquidity did emerge in Mexico, Brazil and Russia, but only in the later stage of stabilization when capital controls either lost their effectiveness or were abandoned following the elimination of inflation. Also, the stability brought on by the exchange rate peg played an important part in attracting capital flows—a large part of which were short term.

Financial vulnerability characterized by external illiquidity can be observed in the ratio of short-term foreign debt to the central bank's reserves. This measure is frequently used to compare a country's short-term foreign liabilities to its liquid foreign assets available to service those liabilities in the event of a creditor run.[27] In this regard, a ratio above 1.0 indicates vulnerability to a sharp reversal of capital flows. Table 1 shows the ratios of short-term debt to foreign exchange reserves in the crisis and

TABLE 1

RATIO OF SHORT-TERM DEBT TO CENTRAL BANK RESERVES IN CRISIS AND NON-CRISIS EMERGING MARKET ECONOMIES (SELECTED YEARS)

Crisis cases			Non-crisis cases		
Country	Year	Short-term debt/ reserves	Country	Year	Short-term debt/ reserves
Turkey	1993	1.82	Poland	1997	0.17
	1999	0.91			
	2000 (Q3)	1.30	Hungary	1997	0.46
Russia	1997	1.51	Czech Republic	1997	0.56
	1998 (Q2)	3.05			
Thailand	1997 (Q2)	1.51	India	1997	0.31
Korea	1997 (Q2)	2.12	Philippines	1997 (Q2)	0.92
Indonesia	1997 (Q2)	1.78	China	1997	0.22
Malaysia	1997 (Q2)	0.60	Taiwan	1997 (Q2)	0.25
Mexico	1994 (Q2)	1.72	Colombia	1998	0.84
Brazil	1998 (Q4)	1.21	Chile	1998	0.57
Argentina	1999	1.33	Peru	1998	0.78
	2000	1.54	Venezuela	1998	0.43

Notes: Unless otherwise noted, year-end figures are given.
           Q2=End of second quarter.
           Q3=End of third quarter.

Source: Author's calculation from data of Joint BIS-IMF-OECD-World Bank Statistics on external debt. Data available at <http://www1.oecd.org/dac/debt>.

non-crisis emerging market economies; short-term debt refers to a country's debt owed to international banks and due within a year.[28]

As the data in Table 1 reveals, the basic difference between the two groups is that all crisis cases (except Malaysia) had a short-term debt/reserves ratio that was greater than 1.0. All non-crisis countries, on the other hand, had a ratio below 1.0, indicating low vulnerability. Note that in Turkey the debt/reserve ratio was close to 1.0 at the end of 1999, indicating some financial vulnerability prior to the launch of the stabilization program in January 2000. With the program's introduction, financial vulnerability quickly deteriorated and reached 1.30 during the first nine months of 2000. Also note that Turkey's ratio was dangerously high prior to the country's previous crisis in 1994. These results present strong support for the argument that external illiquidity is a precondition for subsequent crisis by making an economy vulnerable to panic.

Yet, financial vulnerability does not, in itself, explain the crisis that follows. Even though these risk indicators imply vulnerability to a financial crisis, they do not guarantee its advent. Thailand, Indonesia, and Korea had short-term debt/reserves ratios well above 1.0 between 1994 and 1997, but they were not hit by the Mexican "tequila" crisis. Similarly, Mexico was already vulnerable to a financial crisis in 1993, but the peso came under attack only in late 1994. These observations imply that short-term debt in excess of reserves renders a country vulnerable to a financial crisis, but does not necessarily cause it. It is only when financial panic is present that vulnerability is converted into a currency collapse. I now turn to the analysis of financial panic during the recent financial crises in Turkey and draw parallels between them and the crises in Mexico, Thailand, and Brazil.

THE ROLE OF FINANCIAL PANIC IN
THE TURKISH CRISES IN COMPARATIVE PERSPECTIVE

The most dramatic aspect of the Turkish crises was the rapid and unanticipated reversal of private capital inflows. During the first ten months of the stabilization program (January–October 2000), net capital inflows to Turkey amounted to $15.2 billion. In November 2000 and February 2001, the net outflow of capital was $5.2 billion and $6.3 billion respectively. This means that the net swing in private capital flows in one year exceeded a remarkable $20 billion—or ten percent of the GDP (gross domestic product).[29] It is very difficult to attribute this massive reversal of capital flows in such a short period of time to changes in economic fundamentals. Therefore, explanations of the Turkish crises that emphasize the growing current account deficit, the appreciation of the lira, and the overshooting of the inflation target are far from satisfactory.[30] Rather, a sudden swing in investors' expectations is a more compelling argument.

Unanticipated Nature of the Crisis

The financial crises in Turkey were a surprise to both market participants and analysts. Until the onset of the crisis, foreign investors maintained confidence in the Turkish disinflation strategy. In fact, one can argue that no other Turkish stabilization program has received as much support from foreign institutional investors as the December 1999 program did. This support was sustained in the face of positive economic developments after January and the government's commitment to the program's key aspects. As inflation began falling, economic growth returned and the Turkish government adhered strictly to the monetary and fiscal policies set out in the program.

The successful implementation of key aspects of the program, particularly concerning fiscal targets, generated an overwhelmingly positive sentiment towards Turkey in foreign markets. This remained the case until the crisis broke out. The positive market sentiment can be observed in the assessments of credit rating agencies, the reports of market analysts, and the risk premiums attached to loans to Turkey in the months leading up to November. For instance, Standard & Poor's and Fitch IBCA—two of the most prominent credit rating agencies—upgraded Turkey's sovereign risk in April from stable to positive. This rating did not change until after the November crisis. During the first three quarters of 2000, Turkey was one of the most trusted countries among the emerging market economies.[31] Analyses published by leading foreign investment banks also indicate positive sentiments towards the Turkish economy prior to the crisis. Above all, these reports did not raise any serious concern about the rising current account deficit or the partial implementation of certain structural reforms, as some *ex post facto* studies claim.[32] Shortly before the November crisis, market analysts praised the fiscal measures adopted by the Turkish government for 2000.[33]

It is true that there was a small increase in Turkey's risk premium after September, which was reflected in the rising Eurobond spread for Turkish government securities. It is also true that there was a slight net capital outflow in September. Both of these developments, however, were related to deepening economic problems in Argentina, which led to an overall increase in the risk premiums of the emerging markets. In any event, the "Argentine effect" on the Turkish market turned out to be temporary and insignificant. Foreign capital returned to Turkey in October and the rise in the country's spreads did not reach significant percentages.[34]

Similarly, in Mexico (1994) and Asia (1997) the financial crises came as a surprise. As was the case in Turkey, the current accounts of Mexico and Thailand deteriorated prior to the crisis, but foreign investors seemed not to mind and rolled over the short-term debt. Moreover, at the onset of each crisis, interest rate spreads remained, by and large, constant. In Mexico, three months before the devaluation in December 1994, forecasters were expecting the Mexican peso to stay more or less the same in the foreseeable future.[35] Prior to the Asian crisis, the risk premiums attached to loans did not change and capital inflows remained substantial. Moreover, the reports of credit-rating agencies, independent firms, and the IMF did not show any predictions of crisis. The financial risk indicators, such as the rise in short-term debts to foreign exchange reserves, were generally ignored.[36]

An unexpected change in investor confidence can also be observed in the events that led to the Brazilian crisis in January 1999. Unlike the crises in Mexico, Thailand, and Turkey, however, this change took place due to the "contagion effect" of the Russian crisis of August 1998. On the eve of the Russian crisis, Brazil had largely overcome the negative effects of the Asian crisis and investor confidence had returned on a massive scale. In early August, central bank reserves were extremely high and the interest rate was lower than that prevailing before the Asian crisis. Even though there were some problems with the current account and fiscal deficits, the situation in Brazil looked tolerable and manageable in the summer of 1998 and no one anticipated the collapse of its currency a few months later.[37]

Triggering Events

While conditions of vulnerability can be identified, it is extremely difficult to predict the actual onset of a crisis "since the crisis requires a triggering event that leads short-term creditors to expect the flight of other short-term creditors."[38] The events that triggered financial panic were different in Turkey, Mexico, Thailand, and Brazil. The triggering event in Turkey's November crisis was the liquidity problems of one bank that quickly spread to the rest of the banking sector. In Mexico and Thailand, it was the modest devaluation of the domestic currency. In Brazil, it was the default announcement of a major state governor set off the panic. These events were preceded by idiosyncratic incidents that took place in each country. In Mexico, the turning point came with the assassination of Donaldo Colosio, the presidential candidate of the ruling Partido Revolucionario Institutional (PRI) in March 1994. In Thailand, the bursting of the real estate bubble caused financial distress for companies that had huge investments in property markets financed by foreign currency loans. In

Brazil, contagion from the Russian crisis had a sharp negative effect on market sentiment. In the Turkish case, the policy of a new banking agency was the primary cause for the beginning of the uneasiness in the financial markets.

The fragility of banks (or bank-like financial companies as in Thailand) played an important role in the run-up to each crisis, except in Brazil where banks had effectively hedged their borrowing in foreign-currency-to-exchange-rate risk. Above all, fragility severely constrained central bank policy following the unfavorable incidents and led to a rundown of foreign exchange reserves. The Mexican and Thai central banks were hindered in their defense of the peg by currency and maturity mismatches in the financial sector. Both central banks resisted devaluation until the last moment, while they simultaneously refused to increase interest rates. Instead, the monetary authorities in each country partially monetized the growing bank losses and increased net domestic credit. During the first half of 1997, the Bank of Thailand lent huge sums of money to illiquid and failing financial companies at a time when these companies were on the brink of bankruptcy due to falling real estate prices. Moreover, the Bank tried to increase its reserves by committing them to forward contracts, thereby exacerbating its liquidity position.[39]

In Mexico, when foreign investors became uneasy following Colosio's assassination, the central bank tried to compensate its reserve losses by converting its short-term liabilities from peso-denominated cetes to dollar-denominated tesobonos, which only helped shift liquidity problems from the private sector to the government. The Turkish central bank also resorted to credit expansion when certain banks were faced with a liquidity squeeze in November. The only difference was that the liquidity injection of the Turkish monetary authorities occurred within a week in late November instead of over several months, as was the case in Thailand and Mexico. Despite this difference, the outcome of each central bank's policy was the same: private agents quickly converted unwanted domestic currency into foreign currency, causing a drain on the central bank's foreign exchange reserves.

Each of these four crises involved a self-fulfilling prophecy whereby panicky foreign investors stampeded to the exits. It is unlikely that the financial crises would have occurred if each investor had believed that the other investors would remain calm. In the Mexican case, investors refused to roll over tesobonos after the devaluation and thus pushed Mexico to the brink of default. When the Thai government devalued the baht in July 1997, market expectations about Thailand suddenly changed from positive to negative—leading to a massive withdrawal of funds. In Brazil, the shift in investor confidence took place alongside the outbreak of the Russian crisis when foreign investors "discovered" that both countries had pegged exchange rate regimes and fiscal deficits.[40] The rush of investors to exit the Brazilian market after August caused Brazil's central bank to lose one-third of its foreign currency reserves in September alone, while interest rates tripled. The IMF program in November temporarily stopped capital outflow, but did not fully restore investor confidence in Brazil. In a vicious circle, the steep rise in interest rates exacerbated the debt burden of the government, weakening investor confidence further. By the end of December 1998, for the first time in years, Brazil's reserves were not adequate to cover the country's short-term foreign exchange liabilities. The collapse of the Brazilian real came in early January when Governor Franco, the governor of Minais Gerais (the second-largest state of Brazil), declared that he would suspend his state's debt payment to Brazil's federal government and some other governors followed suit.[41]

Table 2 summarizes the main points discussed above, including the major incidents that marked the financial difficulties, central bank responses, and the triggering events for financial panic in the cases of Mexico, Thailand, and Turkey.

TABLE 2

MAJOR INCIDENTS, CENTRAL BANK RESPONSE, AND TRIGGERING EVENTS OF PANIC IN THE MAKING OF FINANCIAL CRISES IN MEXICO (1994), THAILAND (1997), BRAZIL (1999), AND TURKEY (NOVEMBER 2000 AND FEBRUARY 2001)

	Incident that marked the onset of financial problems	Central bank response	Triggering event for financial panic
Mexico, 1994	Assassination of presidential candidate (March)	Credit expansion, issuance of tesobonos (March–Dec.)	Devaluation (Dec.)
Thailand, 1997	Bursting of real estate bubble (early 1997)	Bail-out of certain financial companies, forward sales of currency reserves (first half of 1997)	Devaluation (July)
Brazil, 1999	Russian contagion (Aug. 1998)	High interest rate policy	Governor Franco's default on debt (Jan.)
Turkey, Nov. 2000	Policies of newly-created banking agency (Sept.–Nov.)	Massive injection of liquidity in the banking sector (Nov. 22–30)	Liquidity problems of certain banks (Nov.)
Turkey, Feb. 2001	Nov. crisis	N/A	"Political crisis"

The November Crisis

As noted above, a newly created banking agency played a major role in the making of the November crisis in Turkey. Under pressure from the IMF, the banking legislation of 1999 created the Banking Regulation and Supervision Agency (BRSA), which became operational in late August 2000. In hindsight, one can argue that as a new and independent institution, the BRSA acted too quickly and imposed regulations on the banking sector that were too harsh, causing profound anxiety in the sector. One particularly significant step taken by the BRSA was the decision to put an increasing number of banks under receivership. The owners of these banks were arrested and faced criminal investigation. These developments "greatly added to market nervousness, given the potential for repercussions in the remainder of the sector."[42] An equally important BRSA act that intensified anxiety among bankers came in mid November, when the agency asked the banks to reduce their open positions in order to ensure that they be within the legal limits by the end of the year. This generated a growing demand for foreign currency among certain banks.

The most important consequence of the anxiety in the banking sector was a loss of faith among banks towards each other. Emblematic of this loss of confidence was the increasing resistance of banks to lend to those with temporary liquidity shortages in the interbank market.[43] For instance, first-tier banks cut their lines of credit to Demirbank, a middle-sized bank, during the third week of November—when it became obvious that Demirbank faced temporary liquidity problems. Demirbank was not an ordinary bank in the sense that it played the role of market maker in government securities and in that it held a substantial amount of Treasury bonds in its portfolio, which were highly leveraged by short-term funds. Cut-off from the interbank market, Demirbank was forced to sell its government bond holdings at a loss to maintain liquidity in the face of the increasing cost of funds. Banks with a similar leverage problem also began to unload their holdings of government paper at discounted rates. However, the number of purchasers declined sharply, forcing certain banks to raise funds in the overnight interbank market. In only a few days, the liquidity shortage spread to the rest of the banking system.[44] As the price of government securities fell, interbank interest rates rose, as did the demand for foreign currency. As a consequence of these developments, the sentiment of foreign investors towards Turkey shifted dramatically. During the last week of November, foreign investors—who were "unwilling to accept Turkish bank risk"—exited the overnight market by unloading government securities from their portfolios.[45] During the first week of the crisis, the amount of capital outflow reached $5 billion. At the same time, panicky foreign banks curtailed their credit lines to Turkish banks, thereby putting them under enormous financial distress and greatly exacerbating the liquidity squeeze.

Under these circumstances—similar to the situation in Mexico in 1994 and in Thailand in 1997—the Turkish central bank faced a dilemma. Under the fixed exchange rate regime, it could either defend the currency peg at the expense of aggravating banks' problems or it could act as a lender of last resort by supplying liquidity to the banking system. After a brief hesitation, the Central Bank started providing liquidity to troubled banks, breaching its quasi-currency board rules. As a result, the extra liquidity was merely converted into foreign exchange and further drained reserves. On November 31, the Central Bank decided to stop injecting liquidity into the banking system. In the days that followed, the overnight market interest rate soared to over 2,000 percent. The capital outflow stopped only on December 6, when an IMF-led package amounting to over $15 billion was announced. On the same day, Demirbank was taken over by the BRSA and it was announced that all credits of Turkish banks were brought under government guarantee.[46]

In hindsight, several conclusions can be drawn from the November crisis in Turkey. First, it seems that the timing (as well as speed) of banking reform was badly managed by both the IMF and the Turkish authorities. The IMF clearly underestimated the negative effects of overhauling the banking system in the Turkish financial community during the initial critical phase of stabilization. In other words, it was as much the actions of the BRSA as its timing that amplified the liquidity problems in the Turkish banking sector. Most of these negative effects would have been avoided if banking reform were undertaken towards the end of the program's second year—that is, when the fall in inflation was secured and exchange rate flexibility took effect.[47] It is also important to note that the IMF's insistence on banking reform in Turkey during the early stage of an ERBS program was unprecedented in the Fund's history. For instance, when Russia launched its ERBS program in 1995 with the support of the IMF, the Fund's conditions left banking reform to a later stage of the program, and instead focused exclusively on fiscal and monetary policy for disinflation. In this respect, one can speak of an "overload" in the Turkish program, which can be regarded as the crucial mistake of the IMF.

The second lesson to be learned from the November crisis is that at the onset of market turmoil the Turkish banking sector as a whole was highly leveraged and perhaps somewhat undercapitalized, but it was nowhere near being insolvent. The volume of non-performing loans, a major indicator of bank solvency, was insignificant in the overall banking system, particularly in large commercial banks.[48] As discussed above, the fragility of Turkish banks originated from excessive risk taking characterized by maturity and currency mismatches. Given this serious external illiquidity, the demand for large sums of foreign currency could not be met by the central bank during the panic.

The February Crisis

The November crisis had some ramifications for the crisis that occurred three months later. However, as discussed below, the latter crisis was not a natural extension of the former. In the aftermath of the November crisis, confidence in the stabilization program weakened. This was reflected in the rise of Turkey's risk premium, despite the strong support of the IMF. In December and January, this weakened confidence among market participants also manifested itself in the very short-term basis (mostly overnight) of capital flows and investors' demands for higher interest.[49] Financial panic was thus less pronounced during the February crisis because the expectations of market participants were less optimistic about Turkey than they had been prior to November. Nevertheless, prior to the February crisis there were signs of a return to normality. By early February, the situation in the Turkish markets had, by and large, stabilized. The central bank's reserves were at an all time high, interbank interest rates had fallen to their pre-November levels and the stock market was on the rise.[50] At the time, Deutschebank—one of the main participants in the Turkish financial market—was not expecting a "currency event" in Turkey.[51] Thus, only an exogenous shock in the form of an unexpected and extraordinary event could trigger a crisis.

This event came on February 19, when Prime Minister Bülent Ecevit disclosed that he had had a serious dispute with the president during a meeting of the National Security Council and that, as a result, the country was in the midst of a "political crisis."[52] The announcement immediately translated into the perception in the financial markets that the ruling coalition—and hence the stabilization program—could be unraveling. In the two subsequent days, a major speculative attack on the lira took place as panicky investors (first resident and later non-resident) tried to convert their lira-denominated investments into dollars. Rumor-mongering about the IMF's demand for devaluation (which later turned out to be true) exacerbated the panic. The sudden and massive demand for dollars caused a tremendous liquidity squeeze for banks as they rushed to the interbank market to raise liras to be used to buy dollars from the Central Bank. Unlike during the November crisis, this time the Central Bank refused to act as lender of last resort and did not provide liquidity to banks. As a consequence, overnight interest rates skyrocketed. When two public banks were unable to meet their lira obligations to other banks on February 21, the interbank payments system ceased to function altogether. The next day, under pressure from the IMF, the government announced the floatation of the lira, bringing the stabilization program to an early end.[53]

Many studies of the Turkish financial crises claim that any number of exogenous events could have triggered the crisis after November, given Turkey's weak fundamentals.[54] Such deterministic accounts, however, fail to recognize the fact that Ecevit's behavior was neither preordained nor commonplace. At a time when markets had pinned their hopes on the continuity of the coalition government for the success of the stabilization program, a statement about "political crisis" was the worst possible blow to market confidence. It is true that the financial sector was fragile, that two state-owned banks were short of funds, and that uneasiness in the Turkish markets had not entirely subsided.[55] But there was no reason other than a gargantuan policy mistake to convert these weaknesses into a major crisis. Had it not been for Ecevit's irresponsible proclamations, the stabilization program would most likely have survived, at least until the transition to exchange rate flexibility.

CONCLUDING REMARKS

This contribution argued that the 2000–1 Turkish financial crises resulted from a vulnerability to financial panic that was generated by external liquidity problems. The Turkish stabilization program carried certain risks from the outset and contributed to financial vulnerability in significant ways. The most risky element of the program was the adoption of a pegged exchange rate regime against the background of a modestly vulnerable banking system and at a time when the country was highly integrated in global financial markets. By engendering a lending boom financed by short-term capital flows, the program heightened financial vulnerability during the course of 2000. In light of the above, there was little the government could do in the short term to prevent the deepening financial vulnerability. One might think that some sort of temporary control on capital flows could have mitigated the external liquidity problems. Any control, however, would not only have been difficult to implement but also would likely have caused substantial turmoil in the markets and made the implementation of the disinflation program extremely difficult right from the beginning. Pegging the exchange rate may not have been the best choice of disinflation strategy for Turkey, but an alternative one was not clear at the time.

Turkey lost the gamble it took with the stabilization program, but this outcome was not inevitable. Financial vulnerability reached crisis proportions because it was accompanied by a string of policy mistakes and accidents. The November and February crises could have been avoided if these policy mistakes had not been made. Arguments that attribute the causes of the Turkish financial crises solely to macroeconomic imbalances or exclusively to the design flaws of the stabilization program provide only a partial explanation. Certainly, these factors contributed to the vulnerability of the Turkish economy, but they do not explain the timing and magnitude of the crises. The Turkish turmoil is another testament to the deficiencies of international capital markets.

In the year following the two financial crises, the Turkish economy experienced a severe contraction. Mexico and Thailand also experienced a sharp economic decline following their financial crises, and Brazilian growth slowed down substantially in 1999. All four countries received large emergency loan packages from the IMF, repaid their short-term debts and, thereby, were able to avoid a default. In each country, modest-to-high economic growth returned the following year. When all of these statements and arguments are taken into account, it is difficult to understand the market's failure to roll over short-term debts as anything other than panic. As international capital markets are susceptible to panic, the solution to financial crises should be sought in international mechanisms—such as an international bankruptcy court—that can deal with creditors and the borrowing country during a financial crisis.[56]

NOTES

The author would like to thank Dani Rodrik, Ziya Öniş, and Fikret Şenses for their helpful comments on earlier drafts of this essay.

1. Paul Krugman, "A Model of Balance of Payments Crises," *Journal of Money, Credit, and Banking*, Vol.11 (1979), pp.311–25.
2. The standard study on the subject—which is called "multiple equilibria" in the literature of economics—is Maurice Obstfeld, "Rational and Self-Fulfilling Balance-of-Payments Crises," *American Economic Review*, Vol.76 (March 1986), pp.72–91. See also Paul R. Masson, "Multiple Equilibria, Contagion, and the Emerging Market Crises," *IMF Working Paper*, No.164 (Nov. 1999).
3. The classic treatment of financial panic is Charles P. Kindleberger, *Manias, Panics, and Crashes: A History of Financial Crises* (New York: John Wiley & Sons, 1978).
4. Roberto Chang and Andrés Velasco, "Liquidity Crises in Emerging Markets: Theory and Policy," *NBER Working Paper*, No.72/72 (July 1999). Chang and Velasco call it "international liquidity," which sounds somewhat misleading—hence I use the term "external illiquidity."
5. See Graciela L. Kaminsky and Carmen M. Reinhart, "The Twin Crisis: The Causes of Banking and Balance-of-Payments Problems," *American Economic Review*, Vol.89 (June 1999), pp.473–500. One main reason for an emphasis on banks in currency crises is that banks are special actors within the financial sector in almost all countries, but even more so in emerging market economies where banks intermediate most capital flows.
6. For a theoretical discussion of the impact of capital flows on bank balance sheets, see Pierre-

Richard Agénor, *The Economics of Adjustment and Growth* (San Diego, CA: Academic Press, 2000), Ch.6.

7. Short-term foreign debt flows encompass a range of financial transactions, including commercial bank loans and public debt with a maturity of less than a year, trade credits, other loans, and contracts in foreign currency. Banks prefer to borrow short-term loans because of lower interest rate premiums associated with such loans. For the effects of financial liberalization on the behavior of banks and non-bank financial actors, see Ronald McKinnon and Huw Pill, "Credible Economic Liberalization and Overborrowing," *American Economic Review*, Vol.87 (May 1997), pp.189–93, Papers and Proceedings of the 109th Annual Meeting of the American Economic Association.

8. As Rodrik and Velasco note: "putting in place an adequate set of prudential and regulatory controls to prevent moral hazard and excessive risk-taking in the domestic banking system is a lot easier said than done. Even the most advanced countries fall considerably short of the ideal, as their bank regulators will readily tell you." See Dani Rodrik and Andrés Valesco, "Short-term Capital Flows," Paper prepared for the 1999 ABCDE Conference at the World Bank, April 1999.

9. Michael Mussa, Paul Masson, Alexander Swoboda, Esteban Jadresic, Paolo Mauro, and Andy Berg, "Exchange Rate Regimes in an Increasingly Integrated World Economy," *IMF Occasional Paper*, No.193 (2000).

10. Guillermo A. Calvo and Carlos A. Végh, "Inflation Stabilization and BOP Crises in Developing Countries," *NBER Working Paper*, No.6925 (Feb. 1999).

11. Guillermo A. Calvo, "Capital Flows and Capital-Market Crises: The Simple Economics of Sudden Stops," *Journal of Applied Economics*, Vol.1 (Nov. 1998), pp.35–54.

12. See Chang and Velasco (1999).

13. As Furman and Stiglitz write: "There is overwhelming evidence that financial liberalization increases the vulnerability of countries to crises." See Jason Furman and Joseph Stiglitz, "Economic Crises: Evidence and Insights from East Asia," *Brookings Papers on Economic Activity*, Vol.2 (1998), p.17.

14. For a discussion of the Turkish financial opening, see Izak Atiyas and Hasan Ersel, "The Impact of Financial Reform: The Turkish Experience," in Gerard Caprio Jr., Izak Atiyas, and James A. Hanson (eds.), *Financial Reform: Theory and Experience* (New York: Cambridge University Press, 1994), pp.103–37; Erol M. Balkan and A. Erinç Yeldan, "Turkey," in José M. Fanelli and Rohinton Medhora (eds.), *Financial Reform in Developing Countries* (New York: St. Martin's Press, 1998), pp.129–55.

15. Stephany Griffith-Jones, "Causes and Lessons of the Mexican Peso Crisis," in Stephany Griffith-Jones, Manuel F. Montes, and Anwar Nasuton (eds.), *Short-Term Capital Flows and Economic Crises* (New York: Oxford University Press, 2001), pp.144–72.

16. Turkey survived the Russian crisis in 1999 mainly due to such exchange rate flexibility, which acted as a shock absorber.

17. This is the figure of the Central Bank of Turkey cited in Fatih Özatay and Güven Sak, "The 2000–2001 Financial Crisis in Turkey," Paper presented at the Brookings Trade Forum 2002: Currency Crises, Washington DC, May 2002.

18. For details of the program, see the Letter of Intent of the Turkish government to the IMF at <http://www.imf.org/external/np/loi/1999/120999.htm>.

19. For the developments following the launch of the stabilization program, see Emre Alper, "The Turkish Liquidity Crisis of 2000: What Went Wrong?," *Russian and East European Finance and Trade*, Vol.37, No.6 (2001), pp.51–71; Yılmaz Akyüz and Korkut Boratav, "The Making of the Turkish Financial Crises," *UNCTAD Discussion Paper*, No.158 (April 2002); Ferya Kadıoğlu, Zelal Kotan, and Gülbin Şahinbeyoğlu, *Kura Dayalı İstikrar Programı Uygulaması ve Ödemeler Dengesi Gelişmeleri: Türkiye 2000* [Exchange Rate-Based Stabilization Program and Developments in the Current Account: Turkey 2000] (Ankara: Central Bank of Turkey, 2001); OECD, *Turkey, 2000–2001, Economic Survey* (Paris, 2001); Ercan Uygur, "Krizden Krize Türkiye: 2000 Kasım ve 2001 Şubat Krizleri" [From Crisis to Crisis: The Crises of November 2000 and February 2001], *Türkiye Ekonomisi: Tartışma Metni* [Turkish Economy: A Discussion Paper], No.2001/01 (2001); Erinç Yeldan, "On the IMF-Directed Disinflation Program in Turkey: A Program for Stabilization and Austerity or a Recipe for Impoverishment and Financial Chaos?," mimeograph, Department of Economics, Bilkent University, Ankara (2001).

20. During the first months of 2000, short-term bank credits from abroad amounted to $3.6 billion

and long-term bank credits to $3.2 billion. See Akyüz and Boratav (2002), p.16; Uygur (2001).

21. See Alper (2001), pp.55–8.

22. OECD (2001), p.13. Also see European Banks Equity Research "Industry Analysis: Turkish Banking," *J.P. Morgan Securities* (March 28, 2001).

23. It is ironic that a recent IMF study, which was written around the same time as the Turkish disinflation program was formulated, draws attention to "the difficulties and dangers of running pegged or quasi-pegged exchange rate regimes for emerging market economies with substantial involvement in global markets." See Mussa *et al.* (2000), p.21.

24. G.P. Márcio and Marcus Vinicius F. Valpassos, "Capital Flows, Capital Controls, and Currency Crisis: The Case of Brazil in the 1990s," in Felipe Larraín (ed.), *Capital Flows, Capital Controls, and Currency Crises: Latin America in the 1990s* (Ann Arbor, MI: University of Michigan Press, 2000), pp.142–91; Eliana Cardoso and Ann Helwege, "The 1990s Crisis in Emerging Markets: The Case of Brazil," in Dipak Dasgupta, Marc Uzan, and Dominic Wilson (eds.), *Capital Flows Without Crisis?* (London and New York: Routledge, 2001), pp.161–81; Eliana Cardoso and Ilan Goldfajn, "Capital Flows to Brazil: The Endogeneity of Capital Flows," *IMF Staff Papers 45*, No.1 (March 1998), pp.161–202.

25. The opening of the GKO market to foreigners prompted a rush on Russian securities. By late 1997 over one-third of the GKO market became dominated by foreign investors. For details of the developments in Russia between 1995 and 1998, see Brigitte Granville, "The Problem of Monetary Stabilization," in Brigitte Granville and Peter Oppenheimer (eds.), *Russia's Post-Communist Economy* (New York: Oxford University Press, 2001), pp.93–129. The reasons for the initial restrictions on foreign investors in the GKO market appear to be twofold: the Russian authorities were concerned about the adverse effects of hot money and the government's desire "to protect the domestic banking system sector against a rapid fall of yields" (ibid., p.115).

26. For the 1995 banking crisis in Brazil, see Werner Baer and Nader Nazmi, "Privatization and Restructuring of Banks in Brazil," *Quarterly Review of Economics and Finance*, Vol.40 (2000), pp.3–24. For the Russian banking crisis in 1995, see Mikhail Dmitriev, Mikhail Matovnikov, Leonid Mikhailov, Lumila Sycheva, and Eugene Timofeyev, "The Banking Sector," in Granville and Openheimer (2001), pp.213–37.

27. For the use of the measure, see Rodrik and Velasco (1999); Stiglitz and Furman (1998), pp.50–53; Steven Radelet and Jeffrey Sachs, "The Onset of the East Asian Financial Crisis," in Paul Krugman (ed.), *Currency Crises* (Chicago, IL and London: University of Chicago Press, 2000), pp.105–53.

28. A "crisis" is defined as a situation in which one of two conditions is present: 1) there is a reversal in net foreign capital flows of at least five percent; 2) currency is devalued by 25 percent or more.

29. Korkut Boratav, "2000/2001 Krizinde Sermaye Hareketleri" [Capital Flows during the 2000/2001 Crisis], available at <http://www.bagimsizsosyalbilimciler.org>.

30. For such arguments, see Barry Eichengreen, "Crisis Prevention and Management: Any New Lessons from Argentina and Turkey?," Background paper for the World Bank's *Global Development Finance 2002*, Washington DC; Uygur (2001); Kadıǧolu *et al.* (2000).

31. State Planning Organization of Turkey (DPT), *Pre-Accession Economic Programme* (Ankara, 2001), p.10.

32. For example, in an analysis of economic developments in Turkey a major investment firm considered the widening current account only as a "transitional by-product of the stabilization program." See Serhan Çevik, "On the Sustainability of the Current Account Deficit," *Global Economic Forum*, Aug. 15, 2000.

33. For instance, see Riccardo Barbieri and Serhan Çevik, "Turkey: 2001 Budget to Reaffirm Commitment to IMF Program," *Global Economic Forum*, Oct. 10, 2000.

34. See DPT (2001); Kadıǧolu *et al.* (2001).

35. Jeffrey A. Sachs, Aaron Tornell, and Andrés Velasco, "Financial Crises in Emerging Markets: The Lessons from 1995," *Brookings Papers on Economic Activity*, Vol.1 (1996), pp.147–98; see also Ilan Goldfajn and Rodrigo O. Valdés, "Are Currency Crises Predictable?," *European Economic Review*, Vol.42 (1998), pp.873–85.

36. See Radelet and Sachs (2000), pp.118–24.

37. For the effects of the Russian crisis on Brazil, see Ilan Goldfajn, "The Swings in Capital Flows and the Brazilian Crisis," *Texto Para Discussão*, Pontificia Universidade Católica-Rio

de Janerio, No.422 (April 2000), n.p.; Alfonso Ferreira and Giuseppe Tullio, "The Brazilian Exchange Rate Crisis of January 1999," *Journal of Latin American Studies*, Vol.34, No.1 (Feb. 2000), pp.143–65.
38. Radelet and Sachs (2000), p.133.
39. For the role played by bank fragility in the developments leading to the peso crisis in Mexico, see Griffith-Jones (2001), pp.159–64; Nancy Birdsall, Michael Gavin, and Ricardo Hausmann, "Getting the Lessons Right: A View from the Inter-American Bank," in Sebastian Edwards and Moises Naim (eds.), *Mexico 1994: Anatomy of an Emerging-Market Crash* (Washington DC: Carnegie Endowment for International Peace, 1997), pp.275–94. For Thailand, see Peter G. Warr, "Capital Mobility and the Thai Crisis," in Dasgupta, Uzan and Wilson (2001), pp.215–36.
40. There was also some direct and mechanical contagion from Russia to Brazil. The Russian moratorium on its public debt "produced large losses for major Western financial institutions and led them to sell assets in emerging markets to raise funds to cover their losses, thus creating an outflow of capital from those markets. This affected Brazil in particular because the markets for Brazilian equities and Brady bonds [were] the largest and most liquid of emerging markets, and play important roles in global arbitrage strategies." Cited in Luiz Fernando R. de Paula and Antonio José Alves Jr., "External Financial Fragility and the 1998–1999 Brazilian Currency Crisis," *Journal of Post Keynesian Economics*, Vol.22, No.4 (Summer 2000), p.614.
41. Since investors' principal concern about the exchange rate had been Brazil's ability to maintain fiscal balance, to pay its debts, and to resist the temptation to pay them through monetization, Franco's announcement led to the acceleration of capital outflows. See Victor Bulmer-Thomas, "The Brazilian Devaluation: National Responses and International Consequences," *International Affairs*, Vol.75, No.4 (1999), pp.729–41.
42. OECD (2001), p.14.
43. *Radikal* (Turkish daily), Dec. 5, 2000.
44. *Radikal*, Nov. 23, 2000.
45. OECD (2001), p.10. It is estimated that Deutschebank unloaded $750 million worth of government securities in a single day, see Uygur (2001), p.17.
46. OECD (2001), p.11.
47. Some authors argue that banking reform should have been implemented prior to the introduction of the program. See Akyuz and Boratav (2002); C. Emre Alper and Ziya Öniş, "Soft Budget Constraints, Government Ownership of Banks and Regulatory Failure: The Political Economy of Turkish Banking System in the Post-Capital Account Liberalization Era," mimeograph, Koç University (2001). However, since banking reform takes a long time, its earlier launch would necessarily coincide with the critical first year of the stabilization program. One should also note that IMF policies towards the restructuring of financial companies in Thailand and banks in Indonesia in the midst of the 1997 crisis had disastrous economic consequences for both countries. For a critique of this and other policies of the IMF, see Joseph E. Stiglitz, *Globalization and Its Discontents* (New York: W.W. Norton, 2002). For a vivid journalistic account of IMF policies during the Asian crisis, see Paul Bluestein, *The Chastening: Inside the Crisis that Rocked the Global Financial System and Humbled the IMF* (New York: Public Affairs, 2001).
48. See *J.P. Morgan Securities* (March 28, 2001).
49. "Turkey's Crisis," *OECD Observer*, May 3, 2001.
50. Ibid.
51. Remarks by Peter Garber of Deutschebank at the NBER Conference on "Exchange Rate Crises in Emerging Markets: Turkey," Cambridge, MA, July 18, 2001.
52. The apparent reason for the dispute was the president's charge that the Ecevit government was not undertaking the necessary measures to fight corruption among public officials.
53. *Radikal*, Feb. 20, 21, and 22, 2001.
54. Among others, see Yeldan (2001).
55. For a discussion of the weakness of public banks, see Alper and Öniş (2001). The liquidity shortage of the two public banks seems to have originated from the Treasury's failure to cover the quasi-fiscal losses ("duty losses") these banks incurred through directed lending to various sectors, particularly agriculture.
56. A discussion of this issue, however merited, is beyond the scope of this contribution.

3

On the Structural Weaknesses of the post-1999 Turkish Disinflation Program

AHMET ERTUĞRUL and ERINÇ YELDAN

Turkey initiated an extensive disinflation program in December 1999, which was backed and supervised by the International Monetary Fund (IMF). The aim of this program was to decrease the inflation rate to a single digit by the end of 2002. It relied exclusively on a nominally pegged (anchored) exchange rate system for disinflation, which has been a major concern for Turkish policymakers for over three decades. In November 2000, however, one year after introducing the program, the country experienced a very severe financial crisis. More than $6 billion of short-term capital fled the country, creating a severe liquidity shortage and skyrocketing interest rates.

In early December 2000, the government requested access to the Supplemental Reserve Facility of the IMF. The request was granted, with $7.5 billion of additional support provided on December 22, and the revision of the technical targets of the monetary program. Only then could continued implementation of the program be secured, as the markets seemed to have calmed down. However, on February 19, 2001, shortly after this arrangement with the IMF, the public disclosure of a political dispute between the prime minister and the president badly wounded the uneasy markets. The Central Bank was forced to sell a large portion of its foreign reserves in an attempt to support the Turkish lira (TL) as the short-term interest rates rocketed to over 5,000 percent. In the period that followed, the government could not endure the pressures of the markets any further, and declared the surrender of the pegged exchange rate system on February 22, thereby letting the exchange rates free float.

Following the demise of the exchange rate-based disinflation program, the newly appointed Finance Minister, Kemal Derviş (former vice president of the World Bank) submitted a new letter of intent to the IMF. On May 15, Derviş announced the invigoration of a new stabilization effort under the guidance of a program entitled "Turkey's Transition Program: Strengthening the Turkish Economy." As mentioned in its introduction, the new program would be the continuation of the previous disinflation program and would be backed by a series of "structural reforms" aimed at strengthening the banking system and at transforming the "old ways of economic policy making."[1]

However, the September 11 terrorist attack undermined the implementation of this new program, affecting investors' perceptions adversely. The Turkish government requested, in turn, a new three-year, stand-by arrangement for offsetting the detrimental effects of the external shock. The IMF accepted the new letter of intent dated January 18, 2002, by providing a considerable amount of financial support.

The last two stand-by arrangements should clearly be regarded as the continuation of the disinflation program launched at the end of 1999, even though they were implemented after its failure. The main framework of the program itself, as well as the crisis episode, has been a source of debate since its very beginning.[2] In particular, it was alleged by the former deputy managing director of the Fund, Stanley Fischer, that the difficulties in Turkey relate more to the banking sector and to the deterioration of macroeconomic fundamentals rather than any errors in program design.[3] In particular, according to Fischer, "The recent difficulties in Turkey relate more to banking sector problems, and the *failure to undertake corrective fiscal measures* when the current account widened."[4]

This contribution will attempt to examine this assertion given the available macroeconomic evidence for Turkey. In particular, we highlight the structural weakness of the exchange rate-backed disinflation program as manifested in its liquidity creation mechanism in a small and fragile financial system such as Turkey. An analytical inquiry into the structural causes of the Turkish crisis is clearly not limited to a theoretical curiosum; such an inquiry has clear implications for stabilization policy and for the culpability of the IMF-style austerity programs. Given the painstaking financial crises of the 1990s in the developing world, such stocktaking on the theoretical underpinnings of the orthodox stabilization plans is both timely and urgent. The essay is constructed as follows: the next section points to the underlying liquidity generation mechanism of the 2000 Turkish disinflation program; the following section documents the fragility indicators of Turkish banking, and argues that the disinflation program led to increased vulnerability in the banking system throughout 2000/1; we then briefly overview the fiscal fragility indicators of the public sector and study the behavior of the interest rates under the program; finally, we provide a summary and some concluding comments.

THE LIQUIDITY GENERATION MECHANISM
UNDER THE DISINFLATION PROGRAM

The 2000 Turkish disinflation program adopted the monetary approach to balance of payments as its theoretical foundation for the determination of the liquidity generation mechanism and the resolution of the balance of payments equilibrium. This approach, which provides the underlying frame of reference for almost all IMF-style austerity programs, expects the real exchange rate to be in long-run equilibrium at its purchasing power parity level, and maintains that the domestic supply of money be "endogenized" in a regime of open capital account.

Accordingly, the program limited the monetary expansion to changes in the net foreign asset (NFA) position of the Central Bank, and fixed the Bank's stock of net domestic assets (NDA) at its December 1999 level. It was further announced that the Central Bank would be allowed to change its net domestic asset position within a band of ± five percent of the monetary base, to be revised at three-month intervals. The implication of the rule necessitated the following identity:

Monetary Base = Net Foreign Assets + Net Domestic Assets

Consequently, as a result of the restrictions set on the upper ceilings of the net domestic assets, the program limited the monetary expansion to increases in the stock of net foreign assets.[5]

According to this rule, the liquidity generation mechanism available to the Central Bank practically entailed a monetary regime of a semi-currency board reminiscent of its Argentine counterpart. Within this mechanism, the monetary policy is restricted to the direction of the foreign exchange flows, and, as such, the most important element—to be able to sustain the liquidity needs of the economy—would depend upon the proper continuation of the foreign credit flow into the system.

The expansion of the monetary base was ultimately linked to the foreign exchange inflows, indicating that the Central Bank was committed to the strict rule of no-sterilization throughout the program. Therefore, it was expected that the available liquidity in the domestic economy would be managed by the interest signals inherent in smoothly operating financial markets; rising domestic interest rates would invite foreign inflows, allowing for monetary expansion. Excess liquidity would, in turn, be signaled through lower rates of interest, allowing foreign capital outflows to balance the equilibrium level of liquidity in the domestic financial markets.

Figure 1 portrays the evolution of the liquidity mechanism under the first ten months of the program's implementation. The figure discloses the paths of the monetary base, open market operations (OMOs), the net foreign assets (NFA), and the net domestic assets (NDA) of the Central Bank, as measured by the end-of-week observations, January 7 to December 1, 2000. As can be seen, the Central Bank played the role of a currency board quite successfully until November—the first sign of the culminating crisis. Until then, the monetary base had expanded by only 7.6 percent, while the total assets of the Central Bank increased by a total of 15 percent, mostly because of the rise in foreign inflows during the summer months. All along, the Central Bank conducted its open market operations with the intent to steer the NDA within the limits of the program.

The basic message that emerges from the data in Figure 1 is clear: Turkish monetary authorities have successfully implemented the monetary program within the given targets, conditioning the Central Bank operations to net foreign inflows. In this sense, the outbreak of the November crisis— and the ultimate collapse of the program in February 2001—cannot be attributed to any divergence from the monetary targets.

However, with the eruption of the first crisis in November 2000, and then again in February 2001, it was clear that the basic foundations of the liquidity creation mechanism were at fault. In fact, given the shallowness and fragility of the Turkish financial system, the mechanism was always incapable of bringing about such smooth adjustments towards equilibrium as those envisaged by the program designers. In Table 1 we lay out the basic characteristics of the financial system.

FIGURE 1

MONETARY BASE, NET DOMESTIC ASSETS, NET FOREIGN ASSETS
AND NET OPEN MARKET OPERATIONS
(JANUARY 7, 2000–DECEMBER 1, 2000, END-OF-WEEK OBSERVATIONS)

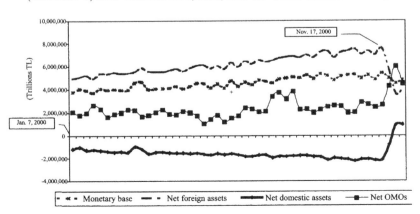

TABLE 1

BASIC CHARACTERISTICS OF THE FINANCIAL SYSTEM

| | Total Assets of the Banking Sector / GNP | Banking Sector Foreign Credits | | Net Short Term Capital Flows (Bill US$) | Current Account Balance / GNP | Total Foreign Debt / GNP | Short Term Foreign Debt / CB Reserves | Currency Sub- stitution* |
		Volume of Inflows (Bill US$)	Volume of Outflows (Bill US$)					
1995	52.2	76,427	75,626	3,713	−1.4	42.8	126.7	54.8
1996	59.4	8,824	8,055	5,945	−1.3	46.2	104.2	50.9
1997	65.9	19,110	18,386	1,761	−1.4	47.8	95.1	48.6
1998	69.4	19,288	19,225	2,601	1.0	50.9	105.4	45.1
1999	92.1	122,673	120,603	759	−0.7	55.7	98.9	45.2
2000	82.8	209,432	204,691	4,035	−4.8	58.3	127.6	44.1

Note: * Rate of Dollarization—Ratio of foreign exchange deposits to total deposits of residents.

Sources: Central Bank Balance of Payments Statistics; State Planning Organization, *Main Economic Indicators*, at <http://ekutup.dpt.gov.tr/teg/2003/02/mei.html>.

As indicators tabulated in Table 1 reveal, the strategy of "public sector deficit financing based on short-term foreign borrowing" led the banking system to be more vulnerable to foreign exchange and interest risks. Increasingly unhedged risk-taking behavior, coupled with a remarkable build-up of the short positions in foreign currency in the banking sector, raised serious doubts about the sustainability of the short-term capital inflow-based public debt management policies.

As manifested in Table 1, the total assets of the banking sector to the ratio of gross national product (GNP) stood at around 80 percent. On the other hand, the sheer volume of short term foreign capital flows intermediated through the banking sector is clearly indicative of their gross volatility and erratic movements. The volume of inflows of banking credits reached $122.7 billion in 1999 and $209.4 billion in 2000. Consequently, the ratio of short-term debt rose abruptly in 2000. Yet, the authors of the Letter of Intent had envisaged that possible increases in Central Bank reserves would be able to match the increase in outstanding short-term foreign debt, and that Turkey would be able to remain sound externally. However, during the course of the year the banking sector succeeded in increasing the net inflows of foreign credit by $4.7 billion. During this process, total short-term debt stock of the banking sector increased to $16.9 billion from its level of $13.2 billion. The lure of the uncontrolled flows of speculative gains clearly grew unchecked throughout 2000, during which the currency risk was eliminated and the entire liquidity generation mechanism was based on the short-term hot money inflows.

As a quantitative indicator of the short-term speculative capital flows, we further report on the behavior of the residents' and non-residents' portfolio purchases and sales of securities, both domestically and abroad. Data on the residents' sales of securities (inflow of foreign exchange) and purchases of securities (outflows) is depicted in Figure 2a. Figure 2b sets out the security purchases (inflows) and sales (outflows) of non-residents. All data are monthly series in millions of dollars and are derived from the Turkish Republic Central Bank's balance of payments statistics.[6]

The volatility of the flows and the disruptive spikes of outflows due to non-residents' operations during November 2000 and February 2001 are clearly visible in Figure 2b. According to Boratav and Yeldan's calculations, before the November 2000 crisis non-residents brought a total of $15.2 billion of "hot money" into the Turkish asset markets, while the residents enabled an outflow of $5.3 billion.[7] Thus, during the course of the program, much of this accumulated short-term debt seems to have financed the flight of residents' capital.

A related indicator of structural fragility present in the system pertains to the degree of dollarization. Measured as the ratio of foreign exchange deposits to total deposits of residents, this ratio—which was as high as 55 percent in 1995—stood at 45 percent just before the inception of the program. The ongoing currency substitution, then, had severely limited the capability of the monetary authority to control the domestic liquidity.

FIGURE 2a

PORTFOLIO INVESTMENTS: SECURITIES SALES (INFLOWS) AND PURCHASES (OUTFLOWS) BY RESIDENTS ABROAD (MILLIONS US$)

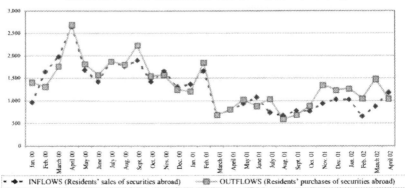

FIGURE 2b
PORTFOLIO INVESTMENTS: SECURITIES PURCHASES (INFLOWS) AND SALES
(OUTFLOWS) BY NON-RESIDENTS IN TURKEY (MILLIONS US$)

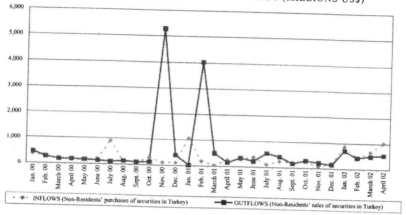

Source: Based on data from the Central Bank, available at <http://www.tcmb.gov.tr>.

Thus, ignoring these historical attributes and structural characteristics of the banking system, the orthodox policy of fully connecting the monetary expansion and liquidity requirements of the domestic economy exclusively to the speculative short-term capital flows was clearly a design flaw—an oversight by the IMF, despite their technical expertise.

DEEPENING THE VULNERABILITY OF THE BANKING SYSTEM

As argued in the preceding section, the underlying cause of the Turkish currency crisis cannot be attributed to the failure of the fiscal and/or monetary authorities in maintaining the main targets of the monetary program. Throughout the year, exchange rate devaluation followed the programmed schedule and the Central Bank successfully controlled the expansion of the monetary base by constraining its net domestic asset position within the program limits.

Similarly, the fiscal operations were in line with both the revenue and the expenditure targets, and the non-interest primary balance on the consolidated budget succeeded in attaining the end-of-year target by as early as September. Consolidated budget data tabulated from the Undersecretariat of Treasury and the Ministry of Finance reveal that budget revenue realizations were actually higher than the targeted values by 3.6 percent in 2000 and by 5.1 percent in 2001. On the other hand, expenditure remained 0.2 percent lower than the 2000 target, and the 2001 targets were exceeded by only 1.7 percent. Consequently, during the years in question public management expenditure and revenue targets were achieved and the primary (budget) surplus as a ratio to national income (including privatization and other non-fiscal revenues) increased to 6.1 percent in 2000 and to 6.7 percent in 2001. This "success" in the public sector balances was attained by restricting expenditure on public services through the extraordinary forced shrinkage of public investments, and by way of extraordinary taxation possibilities particular to 2000.[8]

Clearly, the fiscal austerity objectives reached were far below the program's target. Crisis conditions emerged in due course, mainly as a result of the increasing fragility in the financial system. This fragility was generated by the uncontrolled and excessively volatile capital flows with an exceedingly speculative component. Under the liberalized capital account system, capital inflows intrinsically necessitated a higher rate of return on domestic assets in comparison to the rate of depreciation. This commitment stimulated further foreign capital inflow, and the domestic currency continued to appreciate—inviting an even higher level of speculative capital inflow.[9]

In the context of the Turkish disinflation episode, debt-financed public deficit and rapid acceleration of private expenditure escalated inflows of short-term foreign capital and severely increased the vulnerability of the shallow banking system. As a result, the ratio of the short-term foreign debt to the Central Bank's international reserves rose steadily throughout the program (see Table 1). This ratio is regarded as one of the crucial indicators of external fragility. It could be argued that the value of 60 percent for this ratio is considered a critical threshold from an international speculation point of view.[10] It is alarming to note that in the Turkish case this particular ratio has never fallen below the 100 percent mark since the liberalization of the capital account in 1989. Thus, for the past 12 years the Turkish financial system has been operating constantly in the "danger zone," as far as this indicator is concerned. During the implementation of the disinflation program this ratio rose to 112 percent in June 2000 and to 147 percent by early December 2000.[11]

Thus, the implementation of the program itself increased the financial fragility of the domestic asset market. The combined effect of an easy deficit financing policy and a liquidity-creating mechanism allowing for no-sterilization induced many commercial banks to shift their asset management policies toward bond-financing activities. The share of government debt instruments in total assets rose from 10.3 percent in 1989 (completion of capital account liberalization) to 21.3 percent in 1999, and was 19.8 percent in 2000.[12] The growing willingness of banks to increase their bond-financing activities under these conditions increased the fragility of the financial sector against uncovered interest risk. In addition, the aggressive security management policy of some commercial banks raised further doubts concerning their sustainability.

It must be further noted in this context that—since the liberalization of the capital account in 1989—the asset and liability structures of the banking system have changed substantially. The liability dollarization ratio increased from 25 percent to 48 percent by the end of 1999. In the same period, asset dollarization rose from 26 percent to 38 percent, and the share of the dollar-denominated deposits rose up to 55 percent.[13]

The short-term foreign capital inflow-based deficit financing policy of the government, accompanied by high real rates of interest, incited the commercial banks to extend their short positions in foreign currency, overlooking prudential asset-liability management. Figure 3 depicts the foreign versus domestic (TL) liability and asset structure of the banking system during the 1990s. The steady rise of the open position of the banking system after 1996 is clearly visible. During the implementation of the program—with the elimination of currency risk—the net short position of the banking system nearly doubled, deepening the vulnerability of the banking system against foreign currency risk.[14]

FIGURE 3
FOREIGN ASSETS, LIABILITIES AND OPEN POSITIONS OF
THE BANKING SECTOR

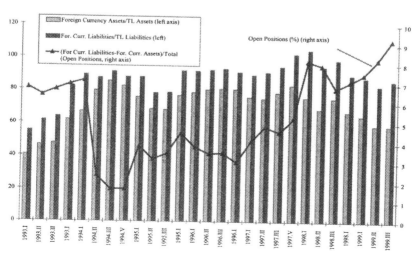

In sum, the program and its liquidity creation mechanism deepened the vulnerability of the banking system to market risks, which have been inflicted since the liberalization of capital movements.

THE STRUCTURE OF FISCAL FRAGILITY
AND THE BEHAVIOR OF INTEREST RATES

Given past experience of exchange rate-based stabilization programs, it is now regarded as an empirical regularity that they initially generate a demand-based expansion accompanied by rising and usually unsustainable trade and current deficits and are followed by a phase of contraction—the magnitude of which depends on the size of the earlier external deficits. During the course of implementation these programs are often associated with the build-up of a bubble in the asset markets. Yet, as the fragility of the banking system against market risks rises and doubts about the program's sustainability are intensified, capital inflows reveal a "sudden stop," heavily squeezing liquidity and sending domestic rates of interest rocketing. This sequence is well matched with the traditional transmission mechanism of exchange rate-based stabilization programs,[15] and in particular the November 2000 and February 2001 crisis episodes in Turkey.

In a financially shallow economy and a fragile banking system, the first disruptive effect of sudden stop and capital reversal is observed in the interest rates. This is because the transmission of any monetary disturbance to the rest of the economy is conducted by interest rates and exchange rates. Yet, since exchange rate-based disinflation programs are explicitly designed to cut off any corrective adjustments of the exchange rates, the full effect of the monetary disturbance is bound to take place in the real interest rates.

In the Turkish context, following a causal relationship serves to summarize this mechanism: the un-sterilized changes in net foreign assets of the central bank induced changes in the monetary base; in turn, those were transmitted to the other real and nominal variables by changes in the interest rates as exchange rates were nominally anchored; under these conditions, the effects of the speculative capital movements on the interest rates would be magnified. The program overlooked this causal relationship and ignored its destructive effects in a fragile banking system.

In fact, the starting conditions of the program openly revealed the structural fragilities of the fiscal accounts and the consequent vulnerability of the financial system against interest rate shocks. The data depicted in Table 2 indicates the deteriorating fiscal stance of the economy. The program took over a financially fragile fiscal position of an 11.6 budget

TABLE 2
FISCAL INDICATORS: TURKEY, 1995–2000

	1995	1996	1997	1998	1999	2000
As Ratio to the GNP (%)						
Public Sector Borrowing Reqs.	5.2	8.8	7.6	9.2	15.1	12.5
Budget Balance	-4.0	-8.3	-7.6	-7.0	-11.6	-10.9
Non-interest Primary Budget	3.4	1.7	0.1	4.7	2.1	5.4
Stock of GDIs*	14.6	18.5	20.2	21.9	29.3	29.1
Interest Payments on:	7.5	10.2	7.7	11.7	13.7	16.4
Domestic Debt	6.2	9.0	6.7	10.6	12.6	15.3
Foreign Debt	1.3	1.2	1.0	1.0	1.1	1.1
Interest Payments / Total Tax Revenues (%)	43.9	59.2	41.7	61.0	66.4	63.7
Interest Payments on Domestic Debt / Net New Domestic Borrowing (%)	78.9	83.1	63.5	97.9	87.5	137.8
Net New Domestic Borrowing / Domestic Debt Stock (%)	52.4	57.8	52.4	49.5	49.3	37.1

Note: Government Debt Instruments (Government Bonds + Treasury Bills), exclusive of Central Bank Advances and Consolidated Debts.

Sources: SPO, *Main Economic Indicators*; Undersecreteriat of Treasury, *Main Economic Indicators, passim.*

deficit/GNP ratio, with interest costs on domestic debt reaching 13.7 percent of the GNP. In addition to the fiscal deterioration, accrued duty losses (quasi-fiscal deficits) of the public banks reached 12 percent of the GNP (more than 50 percent of their total assets) in 2000. These accrued, but unpaid duty losses created very heavy pressure on the liquidity requirement and increased the distorting effect on the rate of interest.

Critical indicators on domestic debt management underscored the sensitivity of fiscal balances to the interest rates: interest payments on domestic debt claimed a rising portion of tax revenues of the consolidated budget in the 1990s. In 1999, this ratio stood at 66.4 percent of the tax revenues. Similarly, the fact that the net new domestic borrowing constituted half of the existing stock of domestic debt in the 1990s clearly revealed the Ponzi-character of unsustainable debt management. Interest payments on domestic debt—as a ratio of net new domestic borrowing—stood at 87.5 percent in 1999 and reached 137.8 percent in 2000 after the implementation of the program.

Given these structural conditions, the program should have envisaged the destructive effects of a possible liquidity squeeze on the interest rates and on the fiscal balance. Under conditions of such interest risk with a pacified central bank, having all macro adjustment mechanisms tied to the interest rates constituted a clear theoretical oversight. The Central Bank was deprived of all of its traditional tools of austerity and crisis management and was left defenseless against possible "speculative attacks" and sudden stops. Under these conditions, it is no surprise that the viability of the program would finally suffer when the "uneasy speculators" shifted focus and decided to reverse their flows, leaving the incipient country illiquid and dried out.

CONCLUSIONS

The Turkish crisis, which came in the aftermath of an exchange rate-based disinflation attempt, followed all the well-documented empirical regularities of such programs: a demand-based expansion accompanied by rising and usually unsustainable trade and current deficits followed by a phase of contraction—in the form of a liquidity squeeze, skyrocketing interest rates, and negative growth. The main weakness of the 2000 disinflation program was its exclusive reliance on speculative short-term capital inflows as the source of the liquidity generation mechanism. Overlooking the existing structural indicators of financial fragility and resting the liquidity generation mechanism on speculative in- and out-flows of short-term foreign capital, the program left the economy defenseless against speculative runs and a sudden stop.

The failure of the program cannot be completely tied to the inability of the government to undertake accurate actions. By deepening the vulnerability of an already shallow and fragile financial system, the underlying liquidity generation mechanism raised doubts concerning sustainability of the program itself.

In sum, muddled with the short-sighted and speculative herd behavior of domestic and foreign financial arbiters, the IMF-directed Turkish disinflation episode spells out all too clearly the dangers of restricting the monetary policy of an economy to speculative in- and out-flows of short-term foreign capital, which, by itself, is excessively liquid, excessively volatile, and its movement subject to herd psychology.

NOTES

1. Başbakanlık Hazine Müsteşarlığı [Undersecretariat of Treasury], *TSEP Document* (2000), p.1.
2. The underlying elements of the disinflation program and the succeeding crises are discussed in detail in Erinç Yeldan, "On the IMF-Directed Disinflation Program in Turkey: A Program for Stabilization and Austerity or a Recipe for Impoverishment and Financial Chaos?," in Nese Balkan (ed.), *The Ravages of Neo-Liberalism: Economy, Society and Gender in Turkey* (New York: Nova Science Club, 2002), pp.1–28; Korkut Boratav and Erinç Yeldan, "Turkey, 1980–2000: Financial Liberalization, Macroeconomic (In)-Stability, and Patterns of Distribution," mimeograph, CEPA and The New School for Social Research (2002) at <http://www.bilkent.edu.tr/~yeldane/crisis.htm>; Ahmet Ertuğrul and Faruk Selçuk, "A Brief Account of the Turkish Economy, 1980–2000," *Russian and East European Finance and Trade*, Vol.10, No.37 (2001), pp.6–28; Barry Eichengreen, "Crisis Prevention and Management: Any New Lessons from Argentina and Turkey?," mimeograph, background paper for the World Bank's *Global Development and Finance* (2001); Ramazan Gençay and Faruk Selçuk, "Overnight Borrowing, Interest Rates and Extreme Value Theory," Bilkent University, Department of Economics Discussion Paper Nos.1–3 (March 2001); Emre Alper, "The Turkish Liquidiy Crisis of 2000: What Went Wrong?," *Russian and East European Finance and Trade*, Vol.10, No.37 (2001), pp.51–71; Erinç Yeldan, *Küreselleşme Sürecinde Türkiye Ekonomisi: Bölüşüm, Birikim, Büyüme* [Turkish Economy in the Process of Globalization: Distribution, Accumulation and Growth] (Istanbul: İletişim Publications, 2001).
3. Stanley Fischer, "Exchange Rate Regimes: Is the Bipolar View Correct?," International Monetary Fund, January, 2001, available at <http://www.IMF.org>. A revised version of the paper later appeared as "Distinguished Lecture on Economics in Government," *Journal of Economic Perspectives*, Vol.15, No.2 (Spring 2001), pp.3–24.
4. Stanley Fischer, "Distinguished Lecture on Economics in Government," *Journal of Economic Perspectives*, Vol.15, No.2 (Spring 2001), p.11 (emphasis added).
5. Yet, it is clear that from the point of view of the Central Bank's analytical balance sheet that expansion of the monetary base would only be possible through increased foreign earnings that would not call for an increase in the foreign liabilities of the Bank. This means that the Central Bank would not be able to increase the stock of money supply by, for example, borrowing foreign exchange from the banking system or by using the IMF's credit facility. Thus, the Central Bank would be able to issue Turkish lira and expand its monetary base only by purchasing foreign currency from the banking sector in a manner where its foreign liabilities would not be increased.
6. See <http://www.tcmb.gov.tr>.
7. Boratav and Yeldan (2002), p.8.
8. For further discussion on the fiscal stance of the Turkish public sector in 2000, see Yeldan (2002).
9. Elements of this vicious cycle are well known and studied extensively in the relevant literature. See, for example, Carlos F. Diaz-Alejandro, "Good-Bye Financial Repression, Hello Financial Crash," *Journal of Development Economics*, Vol.19, Nos.1–2 (Oct. 1985), pp.1–24; Andrés Velasco, "Financial Crises and Balance of Payments Crises: A Southern Cone Experience," *Journal of Development Economics*, Vol.27, Nos.1–2 (Oct. 1987), pp.263–83; Rudiger Dornbsuch, Ilan Godfajn and Rodrigo Valdés, "Currency Crises and Collapses," *Brookings Papers on Economic Activity*, Vol.2, No.2 (June 1995), pp.219–70; Guillermo Calvo and Carlos A. Végh, "Inflation Stabilization and BOP Crises in Developing Countries," in J. Taylor and M. Woodford (eds.), *Handbook of Macroeconomics* (Amsterdam: North Holland, 1999), pp.1531–614; Irma Adelman and Erinç Yeldan, "The Minimal Conditions for a Financial Crisis: A Multiregional Intertemporal CGE Model of the Asian Crisis," *World Development*, Vol.28, No.6 (June 2000), pp.1087–100; Kari Polanyi Lewitt, "Reclaiming the Right to Development," Paper presented at the UNRISD Conference on the Need to Rethink Development Economics, Cape Town, Sept. 2001.
10. Graciela Kaminsky, Saùl Lizondo and Carmen Reinhart, "Leading Indicators of Currency Crises," *IMF Working Papers*, No.97/79 (1997).

11. Türkiye Cumhuriyet Merkez Bankası [Central Bank of Turkey], *Ödemeler Dengesi İstatistikleri* [Balance of Payments Statistics, 2000–2001]. See <http://www.tcmb.gov.tr>.
12. Ibid.
13. Ibid.
14. Eichengreen (2001), p.6.
15. An overview of such exchange rate-based disinflation and stabilization is summarized in Guillermo Calvo, "The Economics of Sudden Stop," mimeograph, University of Maryland (2001); Calvo and Végh (1999), p.1433; Edward J. Amadeo, "The Knife-Edge of Exchange-Rate-Based Stabilization: Impact on Growth, Employment and Wages," *UNCTAD Review*, Vol.1, No.1 (1996), pp.1–26; Pierre-Richard Agenor, *The Economics of Adjustment and Growth* (London: Academic Press, 2000); Yılmaz Akyüz and Anthony Cornford, "Capital Flows to Developing Countries and the Reform of the International Financial System," *UNCTAD Discussion Paper*, No.143, Geneva (1999); Guillermo Calvo, Leonardo Leiderman, and Carmen M. Reinhart, "Inflows of Capital to Developing Countries in the 1990s," *Journal of Economic Perspectives*, Vol.10, No.1 (1996), pp.123–39; Diaz-Alejandro (1985), pp.1–24; Graciela Kaminsky and Carmen Reinhart, "The Twin Crises: The Causes of Banking and Balance-of-Payments Problems," *American Economic Review*, Vol.89, No.3 (June 1999), pp.473–500; Roberto Frenkel, "Capital Market Liberalization and Economic Performance in Latin America," *Center for Policy Analysis, New School for Social Research, Working Paper Series III*, No.1 (May 1998); Agenor and Peter Montiel, *Development Macroeconomics* (Princeton, NJ: Princeton University Press, 1999), Ch.8. For individual country experiences see also Vittorio Corbo, "Reforms and Macroeconomic Adjustments in Chile During 1974–84," *World Development*, Vol.13, No.6 (1985), pp.893–916; S. Edwards and A. Cox Edwards, *Monetarism and Liberalization: The Chilean Experiment* (Chicago, IL: Chicago University Press, 1991); Rudiger Dornbusch and Alexander Werner, "Mexico: Stabilization, Reform, and No Growth," *Brookings Papers on Economic Activity*, No.1 (March 1994), pp.253–315; Don Patinkin, "Israel's Stabilization Program of 1985, Or Simple Truths of Monetary Theory," *Journal of Economic Perspectives*, Vol.7, No.2 (Spring 1993), pp.103–28; Michael Bruno, *Crisis, Stabilization and Economic Reform: Therapy by Consensus* (London: Oxford University Press, 1993); Jose M. Fanelli, Guillermo Rozenwurcel, and Lucia M. Simpson "Argentina," in Rohinton Medhora and Jose M. Fanelli (eds.), *Financial Liberalization in Developing Countries* (London: Macmillan, 1998), pp.31–56; Eichengreen (2001) on Argentina and Turkey.

4

Domestic Needs for Foreign Finance and Exchange Rate Regime Choice in Developing Countries, with Special Reference to the Turkish Experience

C. EMRE ALPER and KAMİL YILMAZ

In the aftermath of the February 2001 crisis, the Central Bank of Turkey followed the advice of the International Monetary Fund (IMF) and adopted an independently floating exchange rate regime. Consistent with this policy stance, the Central Bank has stayed away from active intervention of any sort in the foreign exchange market ever since. Immediately after the floating exchange rate regime was adopted in February 2001, the exchange rate regime choice became an important topic for debate among Turkish economists. However, this debate is not limited to the Turkish context. Indeed, the latter half of the 1990s saw a number of emerging market currency crises that were closely linked to the exchange rate regime choice in one way or another.

The choice of an exchange rate regime is not a trivial issue. The spectrum of exchange rate regimes countries may choose from ranges from a pure float—where the exchange rate is completely market determined—to complete dollarization or membership in a monetary union, the most extreme form of the fixed exchange rate regime. Such a choice has important consequences for a given economy because the movements of the exchange rate provide us with important price signals. In addition, the choice of an exchange rate, together with its anticipated movements, has important repercussions for the inflation rate. Unanticipated movements can cause higher volatility and risk and are associated with higher real interest rates and lower investment. Last but not least, the exchange rate regime may contribute to the outbreak of financial and balance of payments crises, as well as undesirable growth performance.

The literature on the choice of exchange rate regimes has focused mainly on the pros and cons of flexible and controlled exchange rate regimes. As recently summarized by Fischer, this line of research led to an important near-consensus: intermediate exchange rate regimes—those between pure float and hard pegs—do not succeed and do not survive for long.[1] Yet, this conclusion is challenged by the recent crisis in Argentina (2001–2), which followed a currency board arrangement since 1991.

The recent emerging market crises have shown that the focus of the literature is misplaced. Instead of devoting so much time and energy to the impact of exchange rate (ER) regimes on the growth and inflation performance of countries alone, it is important to understand the role of ER regimes in the accumulation of external debt in emerging markets in the post-capital account liberalization era. This shift of focus towards the debt burden will also help us pay more attention to the circumstances influencing the choice of different ER regimes.

This article concentrates on the circumstances that affect the choice of alternative regimes in emerging markets over the last two decades. In particular, we examine the long-ignored political economy dimension of the ER regime choice. Once the political economy dimension is analyzed carefully, it will be possible to reach firm conclusions as to how suitable certain ER regimes are to different countries, as well as the sustainability of the development strategies in a globalized world economy.

EXCHANGE RATE REGIME AND EXTERNAL DEBT DYNAMICS

Following the capital account liberalization decisions taken by the emerging market economies towards the end of the 1980s, large volumes of financial capital moved into these countries. Several factors provided optimal conditions for such large capital flows: higher real interest rates in developing countries relative to industrial countries; higher expected rates of return on investment projects, in part due to the higher growth rates of developing countries; fixed or pegged ER arrangements were followed by most of the developing countries.

These flows led to stock market booms and helped finance current account and budget deficits. However, beginning in 1994, the recipient countries were subjected to sudden stops and/or reversals of capital flows —which proved to be costly to the populations of the countries involved. Research on economic crises and the role of the ER regime choice in this context has picked up in the latter half of the 1990s. This section is an attempt to survey the current literature with a specific focus on the choice of ER regime. Each of the financial crises since 1994 (starting with the crises of Turkey and Mexico in 1994, continuing with the East Asian crisis in 1997, the Russian crisis in 1998, the Brazilian crisis in 1999, the Turkish crisis in 2000–1 and finally the Argentine crisis in 2001–2) were associated with either soft- or hard-pegged rates and resulted in large short-run devaluations and significant real costs.

First, we will address the issue of ER regime classification. While research on policy-related discussions of exchange rate regimes tends to classify the distribution of exchange rate arrangements according to three options—floating, soft pegs and hard pegged rates—a more detailed classification of ER regimes is possible. The IMF's eight-category official exchange rate classification of the member countries—taken from the IMF's Annual Report 2001—is quite useful in this context.[2] The first category is Independent Floating: the category in which the exchange rate is market-determined, with foreign market interventions of the central bank only admissible when there are unjustifiable fluctuations in the exchange rate. The second is Managed Floating: the central bank intervenes to the level of the exchange rate without announcing or specifying a path for it. The third is Crawling Bands: the central bank pre-announces a central rate and adjusts it periodically and does not intervene when the exchange rate fluctuates within a certain margin of that central rate. The fourth is Crawling Pegs: the central bank adjusts the rates in small amounts at a fixed, pre-announced rate or as a result of changes in certain pre-announced selective quantitative criteria. The fifth is Pegged Rates with Horizontal Bands: the central bank maintains the pre-announced central exchange rate within margins that may be wider than one percent around that rate. The sixth is Other Conventional Fixed Peg Arrangements: the central bank maintains the pre-announced central exchange rate within a maximum of one percent margins. The seventh is Currency Board Arrangements: the central bank refrains from any intervention other than buying and selling the foreign currency and does not allow for any fluctuation in the pre-announced fixed exchange rate. The final category is Exchange Rate Regimes with No Separate Legal Tender: these may take place in the event of a complete dollarization or membership in a currency union. To these eight IMF classifications, Bofinger and Wollmerschaeuser add an additional category—which could be considered to be category "zero" in the list—Pure Floating: the exchange rate is completely market-determined and under no circumstance does the central bank intervene.[3]

As of March 31, 2001, out of 186 members of the IMF, 47 countries have an independent floating, 33 have managed floating, five have crawling bands, four have crawling pegs, six have pegged rates with horizontal bands, 44 have other conventional fixed peg arrangements, eight have currency board arrangements and 39 have exchange rate arrangements with no separate legal tender. Many authors, including Collins, Eichengreen, Summers, and Fischer, argue that in the post-capital account liberalization era, countries are moving away from the intermediate exchange rate regimes that are in between the currency board arrangement and the pure float: this trend is coined the "bi-polar view" or the "hollowing out."[4]

Before presenting the literature on the advantages and disadvantages of each exchange rate regime choice, we would like to point out the discrepancy between the official classification, that is, what the countries declare about their exchange rate arrangement category (*de jure* classification) and what category they "ought to be" in (*de facto* classification), based on how they actually behave. Calvo and Reinhart point out heavy foreign exchange market intervention by the declared pure floaters, labeling this the "Fear of Floating."[5] Collins argues that countries that declare themselves under the category "Other Conventional Fixed Peg Arrangements" do maintain the option of nominal adjustments.[6] On the other hand, Levi-Yeyati and Sturzenegger highlight countries running a fixed peg without an official commitment, labeling them under the category "Fear of Pegging."[7] Recent empirical studies by Calvo and Reinhart, Levi-Yeyati and Sturzenegger, and Bofinger and Wollmershaeuser resort to "observed" criteria such as the central bank's foreign exchange reserve volatility, exchange rate volatility, and exchange rate changes volatility to construct their own *de facto* categories, which differ from the official—*de jure*—categories of the IMF.

Having set the stage for a more involved analysis of the exchange rate regimes, we turn to the close link between the exchange rate regime and external debt accumulation over time. Bordo and Flandreau analyze the pre-First World War exchange rate regimes of core and periphery countries and contrast them with today's globalized environment ER regime choices of the developed and the emerging market economies.[8] They argue that there is an important relationship between the choice of an ER regime and the financial maturity of a country. Before the First World War, the core countries that had mature financial systems also had hard currencies and were therefore able to borrow in their own currency in international markets; such countries followed flexible exchange rate policies. However, the peripheral countries that did not have mature financial systems were not able to borrow in international markets in their own currency. As a result, these countries tended to follow pegged ER regimes that would facilitate their ability to borrow internationally and attract foreign investors to their domestic markets.

We developed the main theme of this essay by utilizing Bordo and Flandreau's conclusions regarding the strong link between the choice of the exchange rate regime and the financial maturity of a country. As financial capital flows are expected to be larger for emerging markets relative to the size of domestic financial markets, it might be preferable to have a flexible ER regime that will discourage large capital inflows and destabilize the domestic markets.

In high inflation countries—such as Turkey and many Latin American countries—fixed or pegged exchange rates have primarily been considered to be the main tool of an inflation stabilization plan. The role of exchange rate regimes has been even more important in countries such as Argentina and Brazil, because, despite their initial success in the fight against inflation, they were not able to bring the budget deficit under permanent control. Consequently, controlled ER regimes are preferred by these countries in order to attract foreign capital flows that would help ease the financing of chronic budget deficits. In contrast, in the case of East Asian emerging market economies, most of the capital inflows were used to finance private sector investment projects.

Figure 1 demonstrates the annual external debt to gross national income ratio for the period 1970–2000 for ten emerging market economies: Turkey, four Latin American, and five East Asian countries. The vertical line in each graph indicates the year of capital account liberalization. Note that in all countries apart from Chile and the Philippines, the debt ratio increased following the capital account liberalization. Also note that the countries with an increasing debt burden had either a hard- or a soft-pegged ER regime during the post-capital account liberalization. Chile and the Philippines, on the other hand, had independently floating ER regimes. Mexico, after having used a soft peg in the pre-crisis period, switched to an independent float following the financial crisis at the end of December 1994. The drop in the debt ratio following the ER regime change can easily be discerned from Figure 1. While there were other factors—such as the billions of dollars worth of foreign direct investment from the United States that helped Mexico reduce its debt burden—the ER regime nonetheless played a crucial role.

One of the major arguments in favor of pegged ER regimes under free capital mobility is the discipline that is imposed on the fiscal authority. Lax fiscal policy will lead to foreign exchange reserve losses, eventually leading, in turn, to the abandoning of the peg and devaluation—which will be costly for the country both economically and politically. In such a set up, fiscal discipline is expected to be imposed on the governing authorities—given the eventual political cost—following the

FIGURE 1
EXTERNAL DEBT-GROSS NATIONAL INCOME RATIO (%)

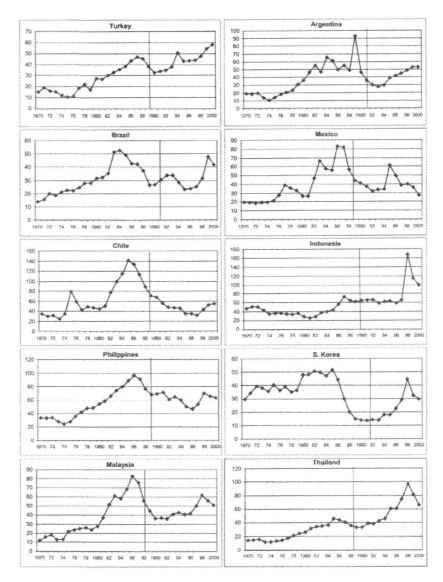

Note: Vertical line indicates year of capital account liberalization.

Source: World Development Indicators Database, The World Bank.

devaluation. However, uncertainty regarding the timing of the devaluation may cause the governing authorities to pursue lax fiscal policies under the assumption that the costs will be incurred only after they are out of office. When we introduce perfect capital mobility to the fixed ER regime and relax the fiscal policy set up, uncertainty about the timing of the eventual devaluation increases since the country is now able to borrow directly or indirectly from international investors. Within such a framework, incremental foreign exchange reserve losses—signaling the unsustainable stance of pursuing such lax policies—will not materialize until it is too late to make changes in the fiscal policy. The sudden capital outflow, triggered by a reversal of the investor sentiment, leads to sudden foreign exchange reserve loss, which leads to devaluation. Within such a framework, the risks taken by the country will become dependent on external borrowing over time. As a result of this over-dependence on controlled exchange rate regimes, the authorities will shy away from devaluing the currency.

Obviously, this fear and inaction can be expected to generate more dependence on foreign savings, which eventually leads to the collapse of the controlled exchange rate regime. As a result of this devaluation and the large share of the foreign currency-denominated debt in total public debt, the debt burden will increase, but once it is realized that the debt burden has reached unsustainable levels, the pegged ER regime will collapse and a crisis will follow. Mexico 1994–95, East Asia 1997, Brazil 1999, Turkey 2001 and Argentina 2001–2 are all examples of the collapse of the pegged ER regimes. Immediately after the financial crises in question, these countries were forced to abandon the soft- or hard-pegged ER regime and move towards more flexibility. Unfortunately, the switch was made too late—only after a huge debt burden had accumulated, forcing a real contraction. This demonstrates once again that the magnitude of the cost that eventually surfaces—coupled with the cost of the devaluation—may render the economy insolvent.

For the reasons noted above, as correctly pointed out by Tornell and Velasco and Larrain and Velasco, fiscal policies are more prudent under flexible—rather than pegged—ER regimes.[9] Under flexible ER regimes it is difficult to stick to lax fiscal policies over a long period, for as the fiscal deficits and financing needs soar the domestic currency is likely to devalue quickly. Such a devaluation of the domestic currency brings about two important political costs: an increasing inflation rate due to the rise in the price of tradable goods; and an increase in the risk premium for domestic assets, which makes the domestic bond market less attractive for international investors—resulting in higher real interest rates, lower investment, and higher unemployment. Furthermore, the funds available for deficit finance are inversely related to the debt burden. Consequently, under a flexible ER regime a government cannot run deficits indefinitely. This fact puts an upper limit on the fiscal deficit determined by the level of external debt.[10]

The flexible ER regime can also push the private sector to display different behavior. As the flexible ER regime releases the government from making a political commitment to maintain the fixed or pegged rate, it simultaneously forces the private sector to either bear or hedge the ER risk inherent in longer term international transactions. Through creating such disincentives against any reckless behavior on behalf of the public and the private sector, flexible ER regimes help keep the debt ratio under control.

One of the most important known disadvantages of floating ER regimes is the difficulty they create in lowering inflation in a country with a depreciating currency. It has long been argued that countries which implement the floating ER regime risk losing control over the inflationary process, since the exchange rate is an important nominal anchor that can be used as a coordinating device when inflation is high and chronic. The pass-through effect is found in general to be stronger in the emerging market economies than in developed countries and is likely to be higher under free float than in managed float or crawling peg.

Casual empirical evidence suggests, however, that developing countries which switched from soft and hard pegs to independent floating ER regimes (whether the switch is preceded by a financial crisis is immaterial) did not have much difficulty in controlling inflation in the medium term.[11] Part of the reason for this lies in the fact that the ER regime switches take place during or after an economic crisis which is accompanied by the collapse of the domestic demand—as in Mexico in 1995, East Asian countries in 1997 and 1998, Brazil in 1999, and Turkey and Argentina in 2001. In the medium term, inflation-targeting policies can effectively replace the loss of the nominal anchor. More importantly, the existence of immediate political costs for lax fiscal policies contributes significantly to the discipline of the fiscal authorities.

East Asian countries differ from Turkey and the Latin American countries because they chose the controlled ER regime—not to use as an anchor to bring inflation down or to attract foreign capital inflows to finance fiscal deficits—but rather to keep the dollar exchange rate stable and hence encourage more trade with the United States, their largest export market. Despite this, they faced risks similar to those of the pegged ER regimes. Hernandez and Montiel demonstrate that the choice of a pegged

TABLE 1
CAPITAL ACCOUNT LIBERALIZATION DATES

Country	Date	Country	Date
Indonesia	Sept. 1989	Argentina	Oct. 1991
S. Korea	Jan. 1992	Brazil	May 1991
Malaysia	Dec. 1988	Chile	Dec. 1988
Thailand	Dec. 1988	Mexico	May 1989
Philippines	Oct. 1989	Turkey	Aug. 1989

Source: International Finance Corporation, *Emerging Market Factbook* (1999), *passim*.

ER regime was critical in attracting foreign capital inflows to the East Asian countries prior to the 1997 crisis.[12] These economies grew rapidly in the second half of the 1980s and the first half of the 1990s, which was mostly due to a very high share—above 30 percent and sometimes close to 40 percent—of investment expenditure in gross domestic product (GDP). Even though these countries also had high savings rates, national savings were not sufficient to finance the rapidly increasing investment expenditures; this financing gap was closed with the help of foreign savings.

The use of pegged ER regimes by East Asian countries provided incentives for both international investors and domestic borrowers to increase the size of the capital inflows to the markets in question. This is why the increase in investment expenditure in the East Asian countries in the post-capital account liberalization era was not necessarily exogenous. Many countries in the region liberalized their capital accounts in the late 1980s and early 1990s (see Table 1), in part because of pressure from the United States and the IMF. Once the capital account was liberalized, commercial banks and corporations began to have access to international financial markets. The lower cost of borrowing and the availability of large sums in the international financial markets made it much easier to finance investment projects that were not possible before, and the availability of large sums of external credit allowed companies to undertake projects with lower rates of return and real estate development projects that had no contribution to the productive capacity.

While the bulk of the literature focuses on the growth and inflation performances under different ER regimes, there are a few studies that analyze these topics from another angle. Using panel data for 95 countries, a study by Domac and Peria analyzes the likelihood of a banking crisis under different ER regimes.[13] Their empirical results indicate that countries with hard- and soft-pegged ER regimes are less likely to experience a banking crisis. However, once a country with a fixed ER regime is struck by a banking crisis, the costs of the crisis are likely to be larger compared to the floating ER regime.

These results are interesting in that they indirectly support the main hypothesis of this contribution. When the ER is fixed, the domestic banks and international investors do not face any ER risk in transferring funds from abroad to the country concerned, and so the banking system relies on a huge open position. As long as the ER is fixed and the fiscal accounts are not completely shambolic, this process continues. However, the process cannot be sustained in the long term. The controlled ER regime leads to a real appreciation of the local currency, which in turn reduces the competitiveness of the country's goods and services. As the external borrowing by the financial, real, and public sectors continues, the external debt to GNP ratio increases. Foreign lenders and investors, looking at such a country, become uneasy about the borrowers' ability to repay. As a result, the more risk-averse foreign investors and banks prefer not to renew loans to the country. Thus, a financial crisis becomes imminent. In such a situation, balance sheet effects will be felt more severely in countries with controlled ER regimes, not only because they have higher debts but also because a significant part of the external debt is a liability for domestic banks and corporations. The maxi-devaluation of the local currency during the crisis will make the debt burden unbearable for the private sector and the government, and bankruptcies in the corporate and the banking sectors will be widespread.

Another study that approached the analysis of ER regimes and their impact from a unique angle is that of Osakwe and Schembri.[14] This study analyzes the output variability under different ER regimes, allowing for the possibility of the collapse of the regime and the ensuing real costs. The theoretical model constructed shows that under the presence of capital flows and export demand shocks, the variability of output will generally be less under a flexible ER regime than under a collapsing fixed ER regime and, in most circumstances, under a permanent fixed ER regime as well. Using simulations, they determine that had Mexico been in a flexible ER regime between 1973 and 1995, the variability of its output would have been half of what it actually was.

THE TURKISH EXPERIENCE

When we analyze the developments during the past two decades in Turkey, we observe a scenario that fits perfectly into the framework described above. Following the acute balance of payments crisis in 1979, Turkey launched a stabilization program on January 24, 1980, which essentially imposed liberalization of the capital account and abandonment of a hard peg, as well as liberalization measures in the financial markets. During the first half of the 1980s, Turkey was able to implement IMF-supported stabilization programs and succeeded in bringing inflation down to less than 40 percent by 1986. Prime Minister Turgut Özal was the driving force behind these measures. However, during the 1980 to 1986 period the government's reform effort focused on external adjustment. Consequently, the internal fiscal adjustment that was desperately needed to bring inflation under permanent control was not accomplished.

The year 1987 was a watershed in the reform process. While the IMF and the World Bank were expecting the fiscal reforms to be implemented, the reform process came to a complete halt. As the democratization process progressed and the public voted for politicians that had been previously banned from politics, "Özal the Reformer" was transformed into "Özal the Populist." The plebiscite of October 1987 was followed by general elections in November 1987, local elections in 1989, and general elections in 1991. Özal's party (ANAP) was eager to harness government resources to its own political wishes. As a result, the budget deficit soared during the intensive electoral competition period of 1987–91 and financing the deficit became a major headache for the government.[15]

By the end of the 1980s, public sector borrowing requirements (PSBR) reached approximately ten percent of the GDP. Before 1986, public deficits were usually financed through monetary finance and direct external borrowing, and only a little by domestic borrowing. In 1986, due to the growing needs for deficit financing, a new law was passed allowing auctions of treasury bills and government bonds in the primary market. However, domestic savings proved insufficient in terms of deficit financing as shown by the rapid rise in the interest rates. In other words, if the government were to have satisfied its borrowing needs from domestic private savings only, it would have had to pay high real interest rates.

In its search for alternative sources of deficit finance, the Özal government decided to liberalize the capital account in August 1989. This was a critical decision, effectively meant to make the Turkish lira (TL) convertible. At the time, there was no external pressure prompting Turkey to liberalize the capital account at such a fast pace. In truth, many analysts at the time found this decision to be premature.[16] The IMF and the World Bank, which had not become staunch advocates of globalization at this point, criticized the government for this premature capital account liberalization. No one emphasized that the government was forced to open the capital account in order to attract foreign financial capital to the secondary market for bonds as well as allowing domestic banks to borrow abroad in order to purchase bonds and treasury bills.

Following the capital account liberalization, the ER regime choice was the most important policy decision. Having set inflation stabilization as its policy priority, the Central Bank decided to follow a pegged ER regime. The TL was pegged to a weighted basket of the US dollar and the German mark. Parenthetically, when there is no adjustment of fiscal balances, the assumption is that a managed float can be very instrumental in keeping inflation under control. True, but only for a while. As long as the fiscal imprudence—the major factor behind the chronic inflation—continued, the Bank's pegged ER policy was doomed to failure. Over a four-year period, the TL appreciated in real terms, thereby increasing the vulnerability of the economy to external shocks and domestic policy mistakes.

The economic crisis of 1994 did not really have any impact on the continuing practice of fiscal imprudence because foreign investors were willing to finance the fiscal deficits as long as they were compensated with a higher rate of return. In the mean time, a new source of financing was found through duty-losses of the state-owned banks. In a non-transparent and politically regulated banking system, these losses could easily be financed through short-term loans. As long as short-term capital inflows continued, the system worked well. However, after the Russian crisis of 1998, matters began to take a turn for the worse. The round of crises in emerging markets and the strong opposition from political elites to genuine economic reform increased the fragility of the economy and the financial sector in particular. One year after an ER-based disinflation program was put into effect, the pegged ER regime era came to an end.

THE ECONOMETRIC ANALYSIS

In this section, we use cross-section time-series data for 57 countries from 1975 to 2000 to analyze the relationship between ER regimes and debt accumulation. Before starting the regression analysis, however, we focus on the classification of ER regimes.

As mentioned before, until recently almost all studies classified ER regimes of different countries according to the claims of the respective governments, that is, using the *de jure* classifications. Recent studies, however, have asserted that governments did not necessarily adopt the ER regime that they announced. As this claim became widespread, researchers strove to develop more reliable classifications of exchange rate regime. One of these studies is that of Levy-Yeyati and Sturzenegger. Using cluster analysis techniques, Levy-Yeyati and Sturzenegger developed a *de facto* classification of ER regimes. They grouped countries according to the behavior of three variables closely related to the ER policy: ER volatility, volatility of ER changes, and volatility of foreign exchange reserves.[17] Since an empirical analysis would yield imperfect results, the analysis required a regrouping of the eight-category *de jure* classification of the IMF into four more distinct groups: independent float, managed float and/or crawling peg, fixed and indeterminate ER regimes. As can be seen in Table 2, in a flexible ER regime the volatility of ER and its changes are expected to be high, whereas the volatility of the foreign exchange (FX) reserves is expected to be low. The reverse is true in a fixed ER regime. Computing these variables for every country-year observation in the data set, the authors used these measures to group countries.

Levy-Yeyati and Sturzengger compared the results of the *de facto* and *de jure* classifications. The two classifications produced very similar results in terms of the total number of observations (country-years) under fixed ER regimes (930 and 927, respectively). However, they differed in terms of the number of observations (country-years) under intermediate (dirty float, crawling peg) and flexible (free float) ER regimes. While *de facto* classification showed more country-year observations (660 vs. 459) to be under the flexible regime category, *de jure* classification put more country-year observations (802 vs. 598) under an intermediate regime. Levy-Yeyati and Sturzenegger further refined their *de facto* classification into five categories with an increasing order from 1 to 5: free float, dirty float, crawling peg, fixed and inconclusive exchange rates. We use their *de facto* ER regime classification along with data from the World Development Indicators database to study the link between the ER regime and the external debt burden.[18]

TABLE 2

VARIABLES USED IN THE *DE FACTO* CLASSIFICATION

	ER Volatility	Volatility of ER Changes	Volatility of FX Reserves
Flexible	High	High	Low
Intermediate	Medium	Medium	Medium
Fixed	Low	Low	High
Inconclusive	Low	Low	Low

Source: Eduardo Levy-Yeyati and Federico Sturzenegger, "Exchange Rate Regimes and Economic Performance," mimeograph, IMF Staff Papers, Vol.47 (2001), pp.62–98.

FIGURE 2
COEFFICIENT OF VARIATION OF DAILY EXCHANGE RATES IN TURKEY

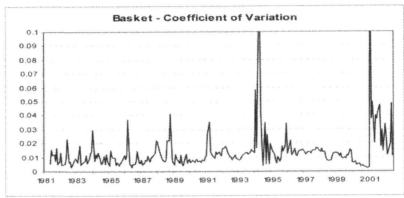

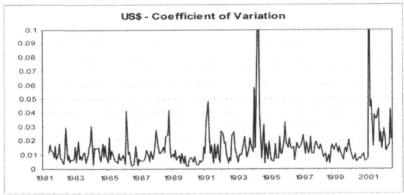

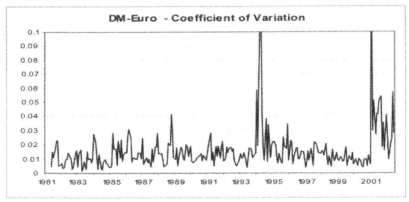

Source: Türkiye Cumhuriyet Merkez Bankası [Central Bank of Turkey]. See <http://tcmb.gov.tr>.

Our data set of 57 countries does not cover all developing countries.[19] Furthermore, not all countries had data for every year from 1975 to 2000. For that reason, we conduct an unbalanced panel regression analysis. In the regression analysis, the dependent variable is the external debt as a percentage of gross national income. In order to test whether the ER regime has any impact on debt accumulation or not, we transformed this variable. We divided the external debt burden (as measured by the external debt to gross national income ratio, defined by the World Bank) at time t with its value at time t-N:

$$DebtBurden(t) / DebtBurden(t-N)$$

This ratio is an indicator of whether the debt accumulation was rapid between t-N and t. For N, we use a value from 1 to 4. Using the lags of ER regime indicator as independent variables enabled us to see whether past ER regimes were significant in terms of debt accumulation or not. All regressions include country-specific dummies. In order not to clutter the results, we dropped the observations with an inconclusive regime classification. Therefore, the ER indicator variable can take on values from 1 to 4.

One can easily find factors—other than the ER regime—that have an impact on debt accumulation over time. Aware of this fact, we gathered data on government budget deficit and gross fixed capital formation (gross investment) as a percentage of GDP and included them as explanatory variables in our cross-section time-series regressions. We would expect the average budget deficit to GDP ratio over the past number of years to lead to an increase in the debt burden of the country over time, since part of the financing will have to originate from external financial sources. The effect of the average investment to GDP ratio over the years in question cannot be clearly determined by theory. As an increase in investment may possibly lead to an increase in the growth rate of GDP, the debt burden is likely to decrease. However, if it is primarily borrowing from abroad that finances the increased investment, the increase in the investment to GDP ratio is likely to cause an increase in the external debt burden.

The results of the cross-section time-series regression are presented in Tables 3a and 3b. Table 3a includes regressions based on the ER regimes in the past two and three years. Average budget deficit to GDP and investment to GDP ratios have positive and significant coefficients for all regressions considered. Next, we look at the coefficients for the ER regime indicators. With N = 2, we first include the lagged ER regime indicator for t-1 on the right-hand side. We then include the indicator for

TABLE 3a

DEBT ACCUMULATION AND EXCHANGE RATE REGIME:
PAST TWO AND THREE YEARS' HISTORY
(EXCHANGE RATE REGIME INDICATOR RANGES FROM 1 TO 4)

Past 2 years' history (N = 2)	Lag 1	Lags 1–2	Lags 1–3	Average 2 lags	Average 3 lags
ER regime-Lag 1	0.028+ [0.015]	0.013 [0.016]	–	–	–
ER regime-Lag 2	–	0.047** [0.017]	–	0.060** [0.019]	–
Investment-GDP ratio (2-year average)	0.008* [0.003]	0.008* [0.003]	–	0.008* [0.003]	–
Budget deficit-GDP ratio (2-year average)	0.018** [0.004]	0.017** [0.003]	–	0.017** [0.004]	–
Constant	0.775** [0.104]	0.665** [0.114]	–	0.663** [0.114]	–
Observations	785	785	–	785	–
Adjusted-R^2	0.05	0.06	–	0.06	–
Past 3 years' history (N = 3)	Lag 1	Lags 1–2	Lags 1–3	Average 2 lags	Average 3 lags
ER regime-Lag 1	0.036+ [0.021]	0.018 [0.021]	0.009 [0.022]	–	–
ER regime-Lag 2	–	0.054* [0.021]	0.041+ [0.021]	0.072** [0.027]	–
ER regime-Lag 3	–	–	0.051* [0.022]	–	0.101** [0.030]
Investment-GDP ratio (3-year average)	0.013* [0.006]	0.012* [0.006]	0.012* [0.006]	0.012* [0.006]	0.012* [0.006]
Budget deficit-GDP ratio (3-year average)	0.035** [0.005]	0.033** [0.005]	0.032** [0.005]	0.034** [0.005]	0.032** [0.005]
Constant	0.649** [0.174]	0.525** [0.185]	0.422* [0.190]	0.524** [0.185]	0.422* [0.190]
Observations	716	716	716	716	716
Adjusted-R^2	0.1	0.11	0.12	0.11	0.12

Notes: Dependent variable is debt/GNI(t) / debt/GNI(t-N).
Terms in parentheses are the standard errors.
**, * and + denote that the estimated coefficient is significant at the one, five and ten percent levels respectively.

TABLE 3b

DEBT ACCUMULATION AND EXCHANGE RATE REGIME: PAST 4 AND 5 YEARS' HISTORY
(SCALED VARIABLE FROM 1 TO 4)

Past 4 years' History (N = 4)	Lag 1	Lags 1-2	Lags 1-3	Lags 1-4	Avg. 2 Lags	Avg. 3 Lags	Avg. 4 Lags
ER regime-Lag 1	0.03 [0.026]	0.011 [0.025]	-0.003 [0.025]	-0.012 [0.026]	—	—	—
ER regime-Lag 2	—	0.067** [0.026]	0.050+ [0.026]	0.038 [0.026]	0.078* [0.034]	—	—
ER regime-Lag 3	—	—	0.068** [0.024]	0.054* [0.024]	—	0.116** [0.037]	—
ER regime-Lag 4	—	—	—	0.073** [0.024]	—	—	0.153** [0.039]
Investment-GDP ratio (4-year average)	0.019* [0.010]	0.018+ [0.010]	0.018+ [0.010]	0.018+ [0.009]	0.018+ [0.010]	0.018+ [0.010]	0.018+ [0.010]
Budget def.-GDP ratio (4-year average)	0.057** [0.008]	0.055** [0.008]	0.054** [0.008]	0.051** [0.008]	0.056** [0.008]	0.054** [0.008]	0.052** [0.008]
Constant	0.491+ [0.266]	0.338 [0.280]	0.198 [0.283]	0.059 [0.286]	0.336 [0.280]	0.2 [0.284]	0.068 [0.287]
Observations	656	656	656	656	656	656	656
Adjusted-R^2	0.13	0.13	0.14	0.15	0.13	0.14	0.15

TABLE 3b (Cont.)

Past 5 years' History (N = 5)	Lag 1	Lags 1–2	Lags 1–3	Lags 1–4	Lags 1–5	Avg. 2 Lags	Avg. 3 Lags	Avg. 4 Lags	Avg. 5 Lags
ER regime-Lag 1	0.03 [0.030]	0.012 [0.029]	-0.003 [0.029]	-0.011 [0.029]	-0.011 [0.029]	–	–	–	–
ER regime-Lag 2		0.064* [0.030]	0.048 [0.030]	0.034 [0.030]	0.027 [0.030]	0.077+ [0.040]	–	–	–
ER regime-Lag 3	–	–	0.074** [0.027]	0.057* [0.027]	0.050+ [0.028]	–	0.120** [0.044]	–	–
ER regime-Lag 4	–	–	–	0.078** [0.028]	0.066* [0.027]	–	–	0.160** [0.046]	–
ER regime-Lag 5	–	–	–	–	0.054* [0.027]	–	–	–	0.190** [0.048]
Investment-GDP ratio (5-year average)	0.025+ [0.013]	0.023+ [0.013]	0.023+ [0.013]	0.023+ [0.012]	0.023+ [0.012]	0.023+ [0.013]	0.023+ [0.013]	0.022+ [0.013]	0.022+ [0.013]
Budget def.-GDP ratio (5-year average)	0.073** [0.010]	0.072** [0.010]	0.070** [0.010]	0.067** [0.009]	0.065** [0.009]	0.072** [0.010]	0.071** [0.010]	0.069** [0.010]	0.067** [0.010]
Constant	0.352 [0.337]	0.208 [0.353]	0.066 [0.356]	-0.084 [0.355]	-0.197 [0.361]	0.206 [0.352]	0.068 [0.357]	-0.074 [0.357]	-0.188 [0.361]
Observations	600	600	600	600	600	600	600	600	600
Adjusted-R²	0.172	0.178	0.186	0.195	0.199	0.178	0.185	0.193	0.198

Notes: Dependent variable is debt/GNI(t) / debt/GNI(t-N).
Terms in parentheses are the standard errors.
**, * and + denote that the estimated coefficient is significant at the one, five and ten percent levels respectively.

both t-1 and t-2 together in the regressions. The results demonstrate that, while previous years' ER regimes does not have a significant impact on debt accumulation in the past two years, the ER regime two years before leads to an increase in the debt burden (see the Lag 1 and Lags 1-2 columns of Table 3a, with $N = 2$). In addition, we include the average of ER regime indicators in the last two years as an explanatory variable. The results are presented under the column headed Average 2 lags. The coefficient estimate for the average of regime indicators in the last two years is 0.06 and statistically different from zero. Actually, this coefficient estimate is equivalent to the sum of the coefficients for the two lagged ER regime indicators under the column Lags 1-2. Even though the fit of the model is not very strong, this is not unexpected. The model with 2 lags does not reflect reality accurately because the ER regime is not likely to make its largest impact on external debt burden in a matter of two years.

For this reason, in the second panel of Table 3a we include the three-year lagged ER regimes as an explanatory variable. When we include this variable separately in the regressions along with three-year averages of the budget deficit and the investment to GDP ratios, the results based upon the coefficient estimates become stronger and the estimated coefficients clearly indicate that the more controlled ER regimes (managed float, crawling peg, and fixed ER) in the past three years contribute to a faster accumulation of external debt. Investment to GDP and budget deficit to GDP ratios also contribute positively to the accumulation of debt.

Next, in Table 3b, we report the same regression results when we include four- and five-year lagged values of ER regime indicators. The 4th and 5th lags of the ER regime indicators have a higher value than previous lags and are more significantly different from zero. We obtain this result irrespective of whether we include each lag separately in the regression or just the average of all past ER regime indicators.

It is worth mentioning that with the inclusion of further lags of the ER regime and the averages of the investment to GDP and budget deficit to GDP ratios, the coefficient estimates for the ER regime indicators increased in magnitude and became statistically more significant. Also, the effect of the investment to GDP ratio on the external debt accumulation turned out to be statistically insignificant, whereas the coefficient estimate on the budget deficit to GDP ratio increased in magnitude and became statistically more significant.

Irrespective of the number of lagged regime indicators, we observed that ER regime has a significant and positive impact on the debt accumulation process. Increase in the regime indicator leads to a faster increase in the external debt to gross national income (GNI) ratio. This result does not change with the number of lags used for the ER regime variable (between 1 and 5), nor does it change when we use the lagged dependent variable as an explanatory variable. We use the lagged dependent variable in order to allow for the possibility of an autoregressive behavior of the speed of debt accumulation over the last five years. The lagged ER regime indicators continue to be significantly different from zero when we allow for an autoregressive behavior in debt accumulation.

Instead of using many lagged ER regime measures that are likely to be highly correlated with each other, it might be preferable to include a single measure of the ER regime over the past few years in the regression. Since the debt-accumulation variable is defined for the past five years, it would be appropriate to include measures of the ER regimes for the past two, three, four and five years. Table 4 presents the results of panel regressions with the regime dummy variables on the right-hand side. Irrespective of the lagged regime measure used, we observe a positive coefficient significantly different from zero at the one percent level. These results are in line with the previous ones reported in Tables 3a and 3b. Altogether, panel regression results support our initial hypothesis that debt accumulation is faster in countries/periods under controlled exchange rate regimes.

MONETARY POLICY UNDER A FLOATING EXCHANGE RATE REGIME

As indicated in the previous section, under current circumstances it seems highly unlikely that Turkey will be able to move away from the floating ER regime. Once this fact is accepted, one should ask "what is the most appropriate monetary policy regime consistent with the floating ER regime?" The answer to this has already been provided. In the absence of a nominal anchor—such as the ER or the monetary base—the Central Bank must adopt inflation targeting as its monetary policy framework and use the target inflation rate as an anchor.

Inflation targeting has been in use in many countries. Recent literature on the experience of different countries using inflation targeting under floating ER regimes clearly shows that it is not possible for the central bank to ignore completely the movements in the ER.[20] This is especially true in the transition to and early phases of inflation targeting. Edwards and Savastano show that in the case of Mexico there was a feedback mechanism from the ER to the monetary policy.[21] During times of "large"

TABLE 4

DEBT ACCUMULATION AND EXCHANGE RATE REGIME (USING A DUMMY FOR EACH REGIME)

Dependent variable: DebtBurden(t) / DebtBurden (t-N)	A) Dummy for managed float, crawling peg and fixed ER regime Number of lagged years (N)				B) Dummy for crawling peg and fixed ER regime Number of lagged years (N)				C) Dummy for fixed ER regime only Number of lagged years (N)			
	2	3	4	5	2	3	4	5	2	3	4	5
Dummy A	0.128* (0.060)	0.260** (0.096)	0.419** (0.125)	0.481** (0.147)	– –	– –	– –	– –	– –	– –	– –	– –
Dummy B	– –	– –	– –	– –	0.116* (0.046)	0.215** (0.075)	0.262** (0.082)	0.356** (0.109)	– –	– –	– –	– –
Dummy C	– –	– –	– –	– –	– –	– –	– –	– –	0.145** (0.046)	0.147* (0.068)	0.348** (0.085)	0.418** (0.104)
Investment-GDP ratio (Average over the history)	0.008* (0.003)	0.012* (0.006)	0.018+ (0.010)	0.023+ (0.013)	0.008* (0.003)	0.013* (0.005)	0.019* (0.010)	0.025+ (0.013)	0.008* (0.003)	0.010* (0.005)	0.013+ (0.007)	0.023+ (0.012)
Budget deficit-GDP ratio (Average over the history)	0.017** (0.004)	0.033** (0.005)	0.054** (0.008)	0.069** (0.010)	0.018** (0.004)	0.035** (0.005)	0.055** (0.008)	0.071** (0.010)	0.017** (0.004)	0.035** (0.005)	0.053** (0.007)	0.065** (0.009)
Constant term	0.787** (0.095)	0.599** (0.161)	0.32 (0.249)	0.15 (0.320)	0.811** (0.086)	0.607** (0.139)	0.444+ (0.240)	0.249 (0.309)	0.831** (0.079)	0.730** (0.121)	0.593** (0.176)	0.357 (0.295)
Observations	785	716	656	600	785	683	656	600	785	647	624	600
Adjusted-R²	0.06	0.11	0.149	0.194	0.06	0.12	0.137	0.187	0.06	0.11	0.163	0.195

Notes: Dependent variable is debt/GNI(t) / debt/GNI(t-N).

Terms in parentheses are the standard errors.

**, * and + denote that the estimated coefficient is significant at the one, five and ten percent levels respectively.

depreciations—hence increased volatility—the Bank of Mexico tightened the monetary base relative to its target. However, the Bank did not directly intervene in the foreign exchange market, nor did it try to defend a specific level for the peso.

In our opinion, such a monetary policy strategy is perfectly sensible in other developing countries with floating ER regimes, including Turkey. First of all, these countries do not have the institutional and market strength of many industrial countries. Thanks to past policies they are highly indebted and, as a result, any form of crisis in another developing country will affect them adversely. Their currencies will depreciate and—given the existing strong pass-through effects—the changes in the ER will have implications for domestic inflation. In such an environment, one is not in a position to claim that the central bank should completely ignore the movements of the ER and not try to adjust its monetary policy in reaction to these developments.

Once the earlier transition phase is successfully completed without worsening the fiscal balances, developing countries can fully implement the inflation-targeting framework. As the inflation subsides and fiscal balances are kept in shape, occurrences in international markets will have a smaller impact on the domestic economy. Consistent with this view, Edwards and Savastano stress that they were able to find evidence of a feedback mechanism between ERs and the monetary policy in Mexico only for the period between 1995 and 1997.[22] After 1997, the Mexican monetary policy resembled a forward-looking, inflation-targeting model. The fact that there may be a feedback mechanism in effect does not mean that developing countries have a "fear of floating."

Calvo and Reinhart claim that many countries with announced floating ER regimes actually have a pegged or fixed ER regime in effect. They conclude that contrary to what many studies suggest, countries are not moving from adjustable and hard pegs to independent floats. They only claim to do so while the peg remains in place, because countries prefer fixed rates that can be obtained best at hard pegs. According to these authors, the central banks use interest rates and otherwise direct FX market intervention to affect the behavior of the ER. As shown by Edwards and Savastano,[23] it is difficult to find evidence in support of Calvo and Reinhart's "fear of floating" hypothesis in the Mexican experience of floating ERs after 1997.[24]

CONCLUSIONS

Each of the recent emerging market financial crises was linked in one way or another to soft- or hard-pegged ER regimes. The relatively high magnitude of the real costs associated with these crises led researchers to find ways to avoid such crises in the future. One could very crudely classify the two broad schools of thought as follows: those who advocate re-establishing restrictions on the capital accounts and those who advocate changes in the ER regimes.

We argue that, in the case of an emerging market economy, if one takes the high public sector borrowing requirement or lax fiscal policies and soft- or hard-pegged exchange rate regime choice as given, capital account mobility—through delaying and magnifying the costs of exchange rate adjustment and fiscal discipline—is not beneficial. However, the short-term political benefits of the ability to acquire foreign finance have provided sufficient incentives for politicians to open capital accounts.

We also claim that, given capital account liberalization, the best type of ER regime is an independently floating one. We discussed three reasons supporting this argument. First, rapid loss of value in a country's currency is politically costly in the case of increased uncertainty, rising inflation, and increased real interest rates. A heavily indebted government cannot put up with higher real interest rates over a long period. Since the political costs are not delayed and accrue immediately, floating ER regimes dictate political and fiscal prudence. Second, in a significantly dollarized economy, loss in the value of domestic currency implies wealth redistribution—which might have undesirable political implications. Third, since the foreign exchange risk will not be borne by the central bank but by foreign investors and domestic financial institutions and corporations, the moral hazard problem will be less likely to occur. Consequently, the magnitude of the short-term capital inflows will also be smaller and hence the likelihood of long durations of real appreciations will be less likely.

Our empirical analysis supports the main hypothesis of this paper about the link between ER regime choice and debt accumulation. Based on a panel regression analysis involving 57 developing countries for the period 1975–2000, and controlling for the budget deficit and investment output ratios, we find clear evidence that countries with lower exchange rate flexibility accumulate debt faster and are more likely to be faced with debt sustainability problems.

Finally, we posit that once the short-term volatility problems following the ER regime switch subsides and the domestic absorption starts to grow,

Turkey needs to implement inflation-targeting policies in order to fill the void in the absence of any nominal anchor. Thus, relinquishing the exchange rate as a nominal anchor does not necessarily imply high inflation if monetary policy focuses on inflation targeting.

NOTES

1. Stanley Fischer, "Exchange Rate Regimes: Is the Bipolar View Correct?," Distinguished Lecture on Economics in Government, delivered at the AEA meetings, New Orleans, Jan. 6, 2001.
2. IMF, "Annual Report of the Executive Board for the Financial Year Ended April 30, 2001," Washington DC, pp.123–31. Available at <http://www.imf.org/external/pubs/ft/ar/2001/eng/index.htm>. The spectrum of the classifications is listed according to the increasing level of control assumed by the central bank.
3. Peter Bofinger and Timo Wollmershaeuser, "Managed Floating: Understanding the New International Monetary Order," *CEPR Discussion Paper*, No.3064 (2001).
4. Susan Collins, "On Becoming More Flexible: Exchange Rate Regimes in Latin America and the Caribbean," *Journal of Development Economics*, Vol.51, No.1 (1996), pp.117–38; Barry Eichengreen, *Globalizing Capital* (New York: Princeton University Press, 1996); Lawrence Summers, "International Financial Crises: Causes, Prevention, and Cures," *American Economic Review*, Vol.90, No.2 (2000), pp.1–16; Fischer (2001).
5. Guillermo A. Calvo and Carmen M. Reinhart, "Fear of Floating," *Quarterly Journal of Economics*, Vol.117, No.2 (2002), pp.379–408.
6. Collins (1996), p.119.
7. Eduardo Levy-Yeyati and Federico Sturzenegger, "Deeds vs. Words: Classifying Exchange Rate Regimes," mimeograph, Universidad Di Tella (2000).
8. Michael Bordo and Marc Flandreau, "Core, Periphery, Exchange Rate Regimes and Globalization," *CEPR Discussion Paper*, No.3077 (2001).
9. Aaron Tornell and Andrés Velasco, "Fixed Versus Flexible Exchange Rates: Which Provides More Fiscal Discipline?," *Journal of Monetary Economics*, Vol.45, No.2 (2000), pp.399–436; Felipe B. Larrain and Andrés Velasco, "Exchange Rate Regimes in Emerging Markets: The Case for Floating," mimeograph, Harvard University (2001).
10. See Larrain and Velasco (2001), pp.9–10.
11. Two relevant studies along the same path are Leonardo Leiderman and Gil Bufman, "Searching for Nominal Anchors in Shock-Prone Economies in the 1990s: Inflation Targets and Exchange Rate Bands," Working Paper 16–96, Foerder Institute for Economic Research, Tel-Aviv University, June 1996, and Larrain and Velasco (2001), pp.20–21. See also Table 4.
12. Leonardo Hernandez and Peter J. Montiel, "Post-Crisis Exchange Rate Policy in Five Asian Countries: Filling in the Hollow Middle?," mimeograph, IMF (2001).
13. Ilker Domac and Maria Soledad Martinez Peria, "Banking Crises and Exchange Rate Regimes: Is there a Link?," mimeograph, The World Bank (2000).
14. Patrick N. Osakwe and Lawrence L. Schembri, "Real Effects of Collapsing Exchange Rate Regimes: An Application to Mexico," *Journal of International Economics*, Vol.57, No.2 (2002), pp.299–325.
15. For a detailed analysis of these issues, among others, see Ziya Öniş and James Riedel, *Economic Crises and Long-Term Growth in Turkey* (Washington DC: The World Bank, 1993).
16. See Hasan Ersel, "The Timing of Capital Account Liberalization: The Turkish Experience," *New Perspectives on Turkey*, No.15 (1996), pp.45–64.
17. See Eduardo Levy-Yeyati and Federico Sturzenegger, "Exchange Rate Regimes and Economic Performance," mimeograph, IMF Staff Papers, Vol.47 (2001), pp.62–98.
18. *De facto* classifications by Levy-Yeyati and Sturzenegger (2001) are not free of problems. For example, applying their classification to Turkey's ER regime in the 1990s, one arrives at the conclusion that it was a free float, which is not true. The stumbling block for this typology

lies in the fact that the authors base their assumptions on the use of the dollar exchange rate. Had they used the weighted basket of the dollar and the mark it would have been possible to classify the ER regime in Turkey throughout the 1990s as a managed float. For a demonstration of the difference, see Figure 2.

19. The list of countries included in the data set is available from the authors on request.
20. See Sebastian Edwards, "Exchange Rate Regimes, Capital Flows and Crisis Prevention," *NBER Working Paper*, No.8529 (2001).
21. Sebastian Edwards and Miguel A. Savastano, "The Morning After: The Mexican Peso in the Aftermath of the 1994 Currency Crisis," *NBER Working Paper*, No.6516 (April 1998).
22. See ibid., p.41.
23. Edwards (2001), pp.35–41.
24. Guillermo Calvo, "Fixed versus Flexible Exchange Rates: Preliminaries of a Turn-of-Millennium Rematch," mimeograph, University of Maryland (1999).

5

Economic Crisis as an Instigator of Distributional Conflict: The Turkish Case in 2001

FIKRET ŞENSES

The transition of Turkish economic policies since January 1980—from an interventionist and inward-looking policy framework to a market-based and outward-oriented neo-liberal model—represented the system's most important transformation. A major pillar of this transition was the capital account liberalization of August 1989. Since then, Turkey has experienced several short-term economic crises, the most notable of which were those erupting in 1994, November 2000, and February 2001.

Short-term crises are nothing new in the Turkish setting, dominated by boom and bust cycles—with periods of rapid growth interrupted by economic crises. Unlike the crises before 1980, which were basically balance of payments crises of different severity, the more recent crises were closely associated with the volatility of short-term capital flows. One must recognize, however, that behind the veil of highly transient capital movements were a number of other important factors. These were headed by current account and public sector deficits of very high proportions and domestic political instability against the background of exogenous events such as the Gulf Crisis in 1990–91, heavy military expenditure during the long-lasting hostilities in the Southeastern and Eastern regions, two major earthquakes in the second half of 1999, and a series of crises in emerging economies—most notably the one in Russia in 1998.

The most recent of short-term crises erupted in February 2001 following the collapse of the exchange rate-based stabilization program introduced in December 1999 with full IMF (International Monetary Fund) support and amidst widespread expectation that it would bring Turkey's high and persistent inflation down to a single digit. This crisis has been regarded as the most severe to date, causing major dislocations in financial markets and spreading quickly, first to the directly producing sectors and then to social sectors. The structural causes and the events that led up to the crisis have been explored in much detail and are beyond the scope of this essay.[1]

The main objective of this study is to assess the initial socio-economic impact of the 2001 crisis, which is still very much a current crisis, with particular emphasis on the year 2001. This covers a wide range of issues comprising labor market indicators—such as unemployment and real wages—and others pertaining to poverty, income distribution, and social sectors such as health and education. The study is based on a qualitative assessment and adopts a "before and after" methodology of comparing the situation before the crisis with the situation afterwards. It makes occasional references to previous crises in other countries, as well as in Turkey itself.

Short-term crises have much in common, but also show a great deal of variation between countries and even in the same country in terms of their causes, duration, recovery, the role played by external agents, and their impact. For example, during the East Asian crisis, the decline in gross domestic product (GDP) in 1998 ranged from nearly 14 percent in Indonesia to only 0.5 percent in the Philippines.[2] Similarly, the recent crises in Turkey and Argentina differed widely: a much higher rate of inflation in Turkey but a much stronger social and political reaction to the crisis in Argentina, to cite but one comparative example. It is hoped that by highlighting the peculiarities of the complex set of effects emanating from the Turkish crisis, this essay will also contribute towards a better understanding of the impact of short-term economic crises in other countries.

The essay is constructed as follows. After a brief discussion of the main conceptual and statistical difficulties encountered during this assessment, the main impact of the crisis will be examined under several headings. This is followed by a discussion of the response of the government, international institutions, and households to the crisis, and, finally, some concluding observations.

CONCEPTUAL AND STATISTICAL DIFFICULTIES

The first of the conceptual difficulties pertains to the dating of the crisis. While most observers would mark February 2001 as the beginning of the current crisis, others, with some justification, would set this date back to November 2000, if not earlier still.[3] At the other end of the time line, while some observers emphasize indicators such as the increase in GDP and the decline in the rate of inflation as signs of the beginning of recovery, others, drawing attention to such indicators as rising unemployment and poverty, regard the crisis as still full blown. On an even more pessimistic note, some observers do not expect an end to the recurrent crises under the present neo-liberal economic policy setting.

Another conceptual difficulty is centered on the question of whether the assessment should be confined to the initial impact of the crisis or broadened to encompass measures taken in response to the crisis and the effects of those measures which are likely to be felt with some delay. Evidence of the effects of economic crises is mixed. On the one hand, there are claims, for example, that the effects of the 1994 crisis were still felt as late as 1998, with large foreign trade and public sector deficits and high rates of inflation.[4] On the other hand, there are those who report that, although the 1994 crisis initially resulted in a rise in poverty, this effect weakened just five months later.[5]

Furthermore, there is the problem of isolating the effects of a crisis from the structural factors that have long dominated the Turkish socio-economic scene and the neo-liberal policies that have emerged as a powerful force since 1980. At the top of the list of structural factors are heavy demographic pressures and the labor market, dominated by agriculture and a large urban informal sector—which is characterized by very large inter-sectoral and interregional productivity differentials and a slow pace of employment creation. Among other noteworthy features of the labor market are high rates of labor market slack—with rates of unemployment and underemployment in 2000 reaching 6.6 percent and 6.9 percent respectively—and the low rate of female participation in urban areas—reaching only 17 percent in the same year.[6]

Also high on the list of structural factors is inequality at all levels, which places Turkey nearer to the Latin American cases of severe inequality rather than the so-called developmental states in East and Southeast Asia. There is some evidence that inequality has been increasing, with the Gini coefficient rising from 0.44 in 1987 to 0.49 in 1994. In 1994, the average income of the highest quintile in income distribution was 9.2 times the level in the bottom quintile in rural areas and 11.9 times in urban areas.[7] Likewise, per capita income in the region of Turkey with the highest income was three times the level of the region with the lowest income, with a six-fold difference in this respect between the richest and the poorest provinces. There were also sharp inequalities in terms of human development indicators, with the differential between the province with the highest and the lowest Human Development Index increasing from 0.324 in 1975 to 0.345 in 1997.[8] The rate of absolute poverty is low overall (7.3 percent in 1994) but very high in some regions and localities, reaching 14.5 percent in the poorest region—as opposed to only 2.3 percent in the richest region in the same year. Vulnerability rate, which is based on a poverty line taking into account basic non-food as well as food spending, is also very high, representing 36.3 percent of the population. A major factor behind these indicators has been the high and volatile rates of inflation during the past 25 years: in the period 1990–2001, for example, inflation averaged a massive 74.1 percent.

The tax structure is regressive in nature and is probably becoming increasingly so as a result of the shift towards indirect taxes.[9] In addition, there is no tax reform in sight. High income groups, especially those deriving income from financial assets, benefit from generous tax exemptions and/or evade the payment of taxes altogether.

Government expenditure on social sectors as a proportion of GDP is lagging much behind the OECD (Organization for Economic Cooperation and Development) countries.[10] Although social insurance coverage is considered wide by the standards of other developing countries, more than one-third (35 percent in 1996) of wage earners and an even larger section of the self-employed are still not covered.[11] Moreover, the provision of health and education services is characterized by large regional inequalities and a growing tendency towards privatization since the inception of the neo-liberal economic model. Two-thirds of the poor in 1995 did not have access to any form of health insurance. Contributing to the problem is the fact that the government does not have a poverty alleviation strategy. Public social assistance programs are ineffective and suffer from lack of funds, poor targeting, lack of coordination, and are regressive in nature. For instance, in 1994 only ten percent of the poor were able to draw state pensions.

There is little doubt that after more than two decades of uninterrupted implementation, neo-liberal economic policies have aggravated this broad picture. The slowdown in the growth of public sector employment—partly as a result of the privatization process, real wage losses accompanied by regressive income transfer mechanisms such as export incentives until 1989, and large interest payments on government debt thereafter, have been among the most prominent instruments in this respect. Financial liberalization as an integral component of the neo-liberal economic model has also been strongly influential, not least through its role—as in other emerging economies—in prompting financial crises.[12]

Compared to the momentum of structural factors and the impact of neo-liberal policies since 1980, the socio-economic effects of the recent crisis can be considered to be small. One should, therefore, guard against exaggerating its effects and recognize at the outset that they are intermingled with the much stronger effects of the two powerful forces mentioned above. In this context, we examine the socio-economic effects of the crisis since its beginning in February 2001, tackling the initial—as well as the likely future—effects and responses.

The conceptual difficulties above are compounded by a dearth of reliable data that is most acute in the sphere of income distribution and poverty. The determination of the incidence and profile of poverty is difficult, and especially so during an economic crisis as there will be new groups moving into poverty. The higher the proportion of the population vulnerable to poverty and the closer they are to the poverty line, the larger the margin of error. In the absence of official statistics and independent studies comparing the situation before and after the crisis, it is not possible to firmly establish the extent of the effect of the crisis on poverty. If there is a rise in poverty, is it the incidence of poverty or its severity or depth, or is what we observe simply a rise in transient poverty? Much of the evidence here must therefore rely on studies of certain localities and circumstantial evidence derived in part from reports in the mass media. Similar difficulties are faced in the context of income distribution as the latest comprehensive income distribution study is based on the 1994 Household Income and Consumption Expenditure Survey.[13]

Although more data is available on the labor market, there is a great deal of divergence among statistics from different sources. This heterogeneity required a number of interviews in order to harmonize the data and draw intelligible conclusions from it. The data on expenditure on social sectors is of better quality, although it doesn't illuminate the incidence of these expenditures on different sections of the population and we are unable to assess the quality changes in the provision of social services during the crisis. Finally, we also face difficulties in accounting for the short- and long-term socio-economic impact of the worsening nutrition level of children, which is likely to affect their school attendance rates and performance at school in the short term and their subsequent performance and status in the labor market in the long term.

THE MAIN IMPACT OF THE CRISIS

Production

The severe depreciation of the Turkish lira (TL) following the abandonment of the currency peg in February was accompanied by a sharp rise in interest rates. The rate of interest on Treasury bills, for example, jumped from 64.9 percent in January to 124.1 percent and 193.7 percent in the following two months, before leveling off at 79.3 percent and 74.1 percent in the last two months of the year.[14] The US dollar/TL parity increased by an average monthly rate of 10.1 percent in February and by another 30.9 percent and 24.9 percent in March and April respectively.[15]

Interest and exchange rate shocks of such severity not only had severe implications for the government's debt-service obligations but also imposed a big burden on the banking sector and on firms.

Although contagion is a very fashionable term in the context of international financial markets, it also has its domestic counterparts. The crisis started in the financial sector, placing many firms in financial distress—resulting in their inability to meet their obligations to the banking sector—and came full circle, increasing the fragility of the banking sector. The sharp rise in interest rates and the severe depreciation of the domestic currency led many small- and medium-sized enterprises to close down. As expected, the hardest hit were firms who had taken foreign currency loans. As a result of the difficulties faced by the banking sector, these firms faced a credit squeeze and were unable to meet their needs for working capital. Furthermore, those in a position to borrow were confronted with exorbitant interest costs in addition to the high costs of imported intermediate goods, most notably petroleum and petroleum-related inputs such as electricity.

After growing by 7.4 percent in the previous year, GDP declined by a massive 7.4 percent in 2001—one of the most severe contractions in Turkish history. The sectors that were hardest hit were manufacturing and services, reflecting mainly the contraction in the financial and construction sectors (see Table 1). Capacity utilization rates in manufacturing declined from 75.9 percent in 2000 to 71.4 percent the following year. As capacity utilization in the public sector during this period actually increased from 79.9 percent to 82.0 percent, this decline was a reflection of the sharp fall in capacity utilization in the private manufacturing sector—from 74.2 percent to 66.9 percent.[16]

There was considerable variation in the pattern of adjustment of different sectors to the crisis. The decline in manufacturing, for example, was much more severe in the private sector, which, unlike the public sector, felt the initial impact of the crisis. Almost all sectors in manufacturing suffered a huge contraction: transport equipment, machinery and equipment, and chemicals were among the sectors most severely hit, but food production was hardly affected by the crisis (Table 1).

Likewise, the crisis also seems to have hit different regions and provinces at different rates. Provinces which are relatively more integrated with the rest of the world and have a higher degree of concentration of financial activities were hit much harder, while others with developed tourism and export sectors even registered some positive growth. Istanbul, for example, seems to have suffered most because of the heavy concentration of financial, manufacturing, and trade activities.[17]

TABLE 1

GROWTH OF PRODUCTION BY BRANCH OF ECONOMIC ACTIVITY, 2000-1

Branch of Activity	2000	I	II	2001 III	IV	Total
GNP	6.3	-3.1	-12.1	-9.0	-12.3	-9.4
GDP	7.4	-0.8	-9.6	-7.4	-10.4	-7.4
Agriculture	3.9	8.5	-2.9	-5.6	-13.6	-6.1
Industry	6.0	0.8	-10.1	-8.9	-10.7	-7.5
Services	8.8	-2.4	-10.3	-7.4	-9.5	-7.6
Food	3.7	2.7	-3.0	-3.7	-1.3	-1.5
Textiles	10.0	-4.2	-8.7	-2.7	-5.6	-5.3
Petroleum Products	-11.4	12.6	5.6	11.5	-3.4	6.0
Chemicals	9.0	-12.0	-15.9	-10.1	-8.1	-11.7
Basic Metals	3.7	2.7	-7.4	-12.6	-7.8	-6.5
Machinery and Equipment	6.7	-7.8	-28.0	-26.4	-17.0	-20.5
Transport Equipment	47.8	-19.7	-48.8	-49.9	-53.9	-45.2
Total Manufacturing Sector	6.4	1.7	-11.0	-9.7	-12.0	-8.1
Public Sector	-6.3	6.9	1.7	-0.4	-7.5	-0.3
Private Sector	9.8	-2.4	-15.3	-12.8	-14.1	-11.5

Source: Türkiye Cumhuriyet Merkez Bankası [Central Bank of Turkey], *Yıllık Rapor 2001* [Annual Report 2001], p.24 (for the manufacturing sector); Başbakanlık Hazine Müsteşarlığı [Undersecretariat of Treasury], *Ekonomik Göstergeler* [Economic Indicators] (July 2002), p.49.

One striking feature of the debate on the impact of the crisis has been its heavy concentration on urban areas. The agricultural sector, which in 2000 accounted for 15.1 percent of GDP and a massive 41.4 percent of employment, has hardly been mentioned despite its heavy loss of production, especially in the final quarter of 2001 (Table 1). The impact of the crisis on agriculture was, however, evident in both the product and factor markets, with the overhaul of the agricultural price support system being accompanied by a sharp rise in prices of key inputs like petroleum and fertilizers.

The Labor Market

The adverse production trends had the most significant impact on the labor market. A distinctive feature of the 2001 crisis was the mass redundancy of labor on a scale hitherto unprecedented in Turkey. Unlike the 1994 crisis, during which reductions in the working week and laying off workers temporarily with or without pay was the common practice, the severity of the 2001 crisis was such that a large number of workers lost their jobs, especially during the first few months of the crisis. This was the combined result of firms under financial strain either reducing their workforce or going out of business altogether.

The evidence on the number of redundancies is rather patchy, with estimates from different sources varying by a wide margin. According to Ministry of Labor data published in February 2002, just one year after the emergence of the crisis, of the 1,567,000 persons who were unemployed, 390,000 were made redundant during the year. At the other extreme, another estimate covering the two years until August 2002 put the total number of enterprises going out of business at 600,000 and the number of workers who lost their jobs as high as 2.3 million.[18]

According to figures given by a trade union, Selüloz-İş, for the largest three provinces (Istanbul, Ankara, and Izmir), in the first few months of the crisis until May, a total of 1,414 enterprises went out of business, resulting in 42,000 workers losing their jobs, with the automotive and machinery sectors hit particularly hard.[19] Estimates for the banking sector alone put the number of workers fired at around 30,000. In mass media, a sector in which labor-shedding reached unprecedented levels by Turkish standards, around 5,000 workers lost their jobs during 2001. Engineers and architects, with nearly 50,000 in their ranks made redundant, represent another major category of workers hardest hit by the crisis.[20]

Detailed information on the profile of workers made redundant during the crisis—in particular their distribution by age, gender, and labor market status—is not available from official sources. A survey conducted by the research team of one of the major opposition parties—the Republican People's Party (RPP)—indicates that 50 percent of these were single, 75 percent male, 25 percent university graduates, 40 percent high school graduates, and a massive 96 percent working in the private sector at the time, mostly in textiles, banking, and construction.[21]

As expected, in the face of the increasing financial difficulties of firms and severely falling domestic demand, the severe contraction in production led—apart from labor shedding—to a virtual halt in recruiting in the private sector. A sharp drop in job openings in the public sector aggravated this. The affect of the crisis on employment, though, was by no means uniform across different production activities. Construction was most severely affected, with employment declining by a massive 18.3 percent during 2001.[22] In the manufacturing sector, for which we have more detailed information, the index of employment (1997 = 100) declined sharply from 89.1 in 2000 to 81.6 in 2001 (see Table 2). The sharpest fall in employment within the manufacturing activities took place in branches such as food, basic metals, and chemicals.[23]

Within the manufacturing sector, employment trends did not always follow production trends. Transport equipment, which suffered the sharpest loss in production in the first few months of the crisis, was also

The Turkish Economy in Crisis

TABLE 2

EMPLOYMENT IN THE MANUFACTURING SECTOR, 1999–2001

	1999	**2000**	**I**	**II**	**2001** **III**	**IV**	**Total**
Total	91.2	89.1	84.0	82.4	81.3	78.8	81.6
Public Sector	89.0	83.6	74.4	80.4	80.0	77.7	78.1
Private Sector	91.7	90.3	86.1	83.1	81.6	79.0	82.5

Note: Figures refer to the index of annual average of production workers, 1997 = 100.

Source: Türkiye Cumhuriyet Merkez Bankası [Central Bank of Turkey], *Yıllık Rapor 2001* [Annual Report 2001], p.230.

the sector in which employment contraction was the slowest. By contrast, in the food industry, which went through only a very mild contraction in production, labor-shedding occurred at the fastest rate. This provides some justification for the observation that some firms used the crisis as an excuse to downsize their labor force. The RPP survey results, indicating that 23 percent of the workers made redundant during the crisis were replaced by new recruits, prove the same point.[24]

Similar to the 1994 crisis, public sector employment served as an instrument of crisis management.[25] The public sector, whose role in employment creation had been in decline due to the process of privatization and trends towards "small government," also cut back its recruitment. This probably hit recent university graduates most severely. On the other hand, with almost perfect job security in the public sector, it was perhaps not surprising to see that this sector did not contribute to the level of unemployment during the crisis. The large number of applicants for public sector jobs, though, indicated greatly reduced job opportunities and the extent of the slack in the labor market increased considerably during the crisis.

As in other countries facing a severe short-term crisis, Turkey experienced a steep rise in unemployment.[26] The data given by the Turkish Employment Service, however, does not reflect this: the number of applicants and the number of those registered as actually unemployed dropped during 2001.[27] However, the Household Labor Force Survey results indicate that the number of unemployed persons increased considerably, from 1,455,000 to 1,892,000 during the same period.[28] Based on the Household Labor Force Survey results, the rate of unemployment increased from 6.3 percent in the last quarter of 2000 to 10.6 percent in the corresponding period in 2001, with the rate increasing further to 11.8

percent in the first quarter of 2002. The rise in unemployment was accompanied by a change in the profile of the unemployed, with the share of young and educated persons increasing sharply.[29]

The effect of the crisis may not, however, be fully reflected in the unemployment rate for at least two reasons. First, some of those who lost their jobs, especially white collar female workers, might have deemed their prospects of re-employment to be rather slim and dropped out of the labor force altogether, joining the ranks of the other "discouraged workers." Second, since persons who worked even one hour during the week before the survey was conducted were considered as employed, the unemployment rate does not capture the full extent of labor market slack.

One would assume that these trends in the labor market might also have swollen the size of the informal sector. However, the share of self-employed persons and unpaid family workers in total employment—which may be taken as an indicator of the size of the informal sector—increased only slightly, from 45.1 percent in 2000 to 45.8 percent in 2001.[30]

As in previous crises, a major effect of the 2001 crisis on the labor market was a sharp drop in real wages. During the 1994 crisis, the real wages and salaries fell in both the public and private sectors to such an extent that it took several years to revert back to the pre-crisis levels in the private sector and even longer in the public sector.[31] The rate of decline in real wages in 2001 was also very large, reaching an average of 14.4 percent in the manufacturing sector (see Table 3).

The effect of the crisis on the working population was by no means confined to those groups discussed above. Although not systematically documented, there were reports of deteriorating working conditions for workers facing threats of redundancy, including longer working hours without pay, reductions in money wages,[32] delays in the payment of wages, and offers to give holidays earlier than usual.[33] In addition, employers encouraged early retirement and resignation. Workers were probably tempted to succumb to these propositions for fear of losing their severance

TABLE 3

GROWTH OF REAL WAGES IN THE MANUFACTURING SECTOR, 2000–1 (%)

	1999	2000			2001		
			I	II	III	IV	Total
Total Manufacturing	11.0	0.5	-3.7	-14.6	-15.4	-20.6	-14.4
Public Sector	19.3	15.1	5.5	-12.5	-14.2	-21.0	-12.0
Private Sector	8.2	-2.1	-5.8	-15.5	-15.9	-20.3	-15.2

Source: Türkiye Cumhuriyet Merkez Bankası [Central Bank of Turkey], *Yıllık Rapor 2001* [Annual Report 2001], p.32.

pay should the firm go bankrupt. The RPP survey showed that only 42 percent of workers made redundant during the crisis could receive their severance pay, and there were reports that many of those who could receive it had payments dispersed over time—thereby eroding their real value severely due to high inflation. Although the quality of the data on trade union membership does not allow us to pass substantiated judgment, most observers agree that trade union effectiveness during the crisis—if not actual membership—was certainly declining.

The Turkish experience has clearly shown that the labor market response to short-term economic crises may take different forms. During the 1994 crisis, for instance, it was more a change in real wages than adjustment in employment.[34] In the 2001 crisis, it was both. Job losses *en masse* were, however, a new phenomenon in the Turkish setting.

Poverty and Income Distribution

There seems to be unanimous agreement among students of the Turkish economy and society at large that both poverty and inequality worsened during the crisis. Yet, at times, proving the obvious is a very difficult task, especially in view of the multiplicity of factors that emanate from the crisis and the heterogeneity of the poor and vulnerable population.

The impact of the crisis on the poor cannot be traced from conventional labor market indicators such as the unemployment rate and real wages, as they can, say, in a Western European economy. The first question here pertains to what extent the profile of workers who lost their jobs during the crisis can be classified as "poor." What little evidence we have on the profile of the workers made redundant during the crisis indicates that it was heavily tilted towards the relatively educated members of the workforce.[35] The fact that a major portion of these workers made redundant were single males—as opposed to being heads of households—may also have greatly reduced the effect of redundancies on poverty. Likewise, the openly unemployed in Turkey generally fit the description of being in "luxury unemployment," hence do not represent the poorest sections of the population.[36] The poor are, therefore, more likely to be found in the ranks of the underemployed in the informal sector and low productivity agriculture. In other words, the "poor" category includes those too poor to be unemployed and the chronically poor outside the labor force. It is likely that the crisis has been instrumental in pushing some of these groups below the poverty line and has increased the plight of others who were poor even before the crisis.

As almost 80 percent of the total income of the poor is derived from labor,[37] trends in real wages can be considered an important indicator of their welfare. In assessing wage trends, an index of real wages based on the formal sector is often used. However, this is inadequate when one wishes to deal with diverse wage trends in different sectors, not only in magnitude but also at times in direction. If self-employment in both the agricultural and urban informal sectors is so widespread, the effect of the crisis on poverty can hardly be discerned from trends in real wages. However, real minimum wages—despite some employers' evasion of implementing them—are a relevant indicator of poverty trend and are at least more accurate than real wages. The real minimum wage declined substantially from an index (1994 = 100) of 145.6 in 1999 to 125.2 in 2000 and 108.0 in 2001.[38] Beyond this, the minimum wage can also be relied on as an implicit poverty indicator given its low level (currently just a little over $100 per month), widespread evasion, and the long line of workers willing to work at that rate. However, those people who fall drastically short of making ends meet for their individual basic needs—let alone those of their dependents—are not considered poor by the World Bank as their income exceeds the one dollar a day international poverty benchmark by a considerable margin.

One has to look even beyond the minimum wage to capture the effects on "invisible" poverty groups in remote agricultural areas, casual workers in the informal sector, and those outside the labor force altogether for which we have no systematic information. In a way, these groups are shielded from the worst direct effects of the financial crisis, such as loss of financial assets and income. In a more fundamental sense, however, these groups may have felt the full brunt of the crisis, most notably through higher prices of food and other essential commodities, and restricted job opportunities. Studies at the community level based on surveys and in-depth interviews may be the most effective means of assessing and monitoring the poverty of these groups. And, in fact, a number of such studies conducted during the crisis have provided ample evidence for the existence of deep pockets of poverty, especially in large urban areas and poor regions.[39]

In this context, the effect of the crisis on poverty—apart from the evidence derived from the trends in minimum wage, along with area studies and press reports—can be gauged from the trends in inflation, social sectors, the number and type of applications to the Social Assistance and Solidarity Fund (SASF—the main public institution in the field of poverty alleviation), and the number of applications to obtain a Green Card—the government's most important instrument aimed at increasing the access of the poor to public health services. According to figures obtained from the Ministry of Health, there has been a sharp increase in both the number of applicants to obtain a Green Card and the number of successful applicants. This number increased by 2.5 million and 2.0 million respectively during the period from September 2000—just before the crisis—and December 2001.[40] Although doubts have been expressed about the effectiveness of this plan as far as the needs of the poor population,[41] the sharp increase in the number of applicants in such a short period of time may be taken as an indication of the effect of the crisis on people with low incomes. The fact that the number of applicants for aid to the municipalities and to the SASF also increased during the crisis augments this view.[42]

Inflation

The sharp rise in interest rates and the exchange rate was accompanied by a large increase in the rate of inflation, with the Consumer Price Index (CPI) rising by a massive 68.5 percent in 2001—as opposed to 39.0 percent in the previous year. The sharpest increase in the CPI during 2001 was in the second quarter, when it rose by 20.6 percent.[43] As interest rates and exchange rates stabilized to some extent, the inflation rate also began to fall towards the end of the year, rising by 4.2 percent in November and 3.2 percent in December.

To get a better idea of the impact of inflation on the poor, one needs to take a closer look at the CPI and examine its individual components—the prices of various food items, fuel, transportation, and public utilities—which account for a major portion of the consumption expenditure of the poor. These manifest a strong tendency to increase faster than the CPI. The food component of the CPI in 2001, for example, increased at a rate of 78.4 percent—as opposed to 68.5 percent for the general index. The list of prices of a number of consumer expenditure categories and essential commodities compiled for this study support this thesis. Individual categories/commodities with special relevance to the consumption of the poor—with the exception of health and education—increased at a rate much higher than the CPI, including the prices determined by the public sector (see Table 4).

Social Sectors

The bulk of tax revenue is used to service government debt. The interest payments on public sector debt (the bulk of which consists of domestic debt) as a proportion of tax revenue, which stood at only 30.7 percent in 1991, increased sharply throughout the decade and reached 77.1 percent in 2000 and 103.3 percent in 2001. With defense constituting another major expenditure category, accounting for 4.5 percent of gross national product (GNP),[44] there was little left for other spending categories.

TABLE 4

CHANGES IN CONSUMER PRICES BY MAJOR CATEGORIES
AND SELECTED ESSENTIAL COMMODITIES, 2000–1 (%)

Category/Commodity	Rate of Change	Category/Commodity	Rate of Change
CPI	68.5	Clothing	65.2
Food	80.2	Cotton Flannel	81.6
Bread	90.5	Printed cotton	82.9
Wheat Flour	136.1	Health	58.4
Macaroni	116.6	Education	52.4
Whole Chicken	68.5	Transportation	77.5
Eggs	116.4	Public	83.3
Margarine	112.1	Other	
Sunflower Oil	218.0	School Uniforms (boys)	52.6
Granulated Sugar	120.8	Electricity	119.1
Leek	164.6	Coal (lignite)	97.8
Spinach	181.0	Kerosene	107.3
Lentils	132.7	Soap	110.4
Haricot Beans	84.1	Notebooks	74.4
Potatoes	78.9	Public Sector Controlled	92.0

Source: State Planning Organization, *Main Economic Indicators* (March 2002), p.119 and databases at <http://www.die.gov.tr>.

A main pillar of the agreement reached between the Turkish government and the IMF in the wake of the crisis was the contraction of government expenditure in order to increase the primary surplus (as a proportion of GDP) from its previous level of 4.9 percent in 2000 to 5.1 percent in 2001.[45] This was accompanied by a sharp fall in public sector consumption, with most of the cutbacks concentrated in the non-wage current consumption categories.[46]

The burden of fiscal adjustment on social sectors like health and education can be traced in part from the share of these sectors in GNP and central budget allocations. These indicators do not reflect a marked change during the crisis. If anything, during the 2000–1 period there was a rise in the share of public spending in GNP for both education and health, increasing from 3.8 percent to 3.9 percent for education and from 0.9 percent to 1.0 percent for health. There was, however, a drop in budget allocations to these sectors during the same period, falling from 10.1 percent to 8.7 percent for education and from 2.4 percent to 2.3 percent for health. Salary payment accounts for the bulk of budget allocations to these sectors, representing 72 percent and 82 percent in the total budget allocations to health and education sectors respectively in 2001.[47]

These aggregate figures do not, however, fully reflect the quality changes in service provision and the incidence of these expenditures. Although we do not have reliable information on the incidence of these expenditure categories, we can safely argue that the provision of both health and education is highly regressive even when the quality of services is disregarded—with the largest provinces and relatively more developed regions among the main beneficiaries. It seems, then, that the government has not changed the priorities of its fiscal policy during the crisis, continuing to give top priority to meeting its obligations to its domestic and foreign creditors and the maintenance of a high defense budget.

Another notable tendency regarding health and education services has been the creeping privatization, in the form of increased provision by the private sector, as well as increased reliance on user charges in the public sector. Likewise, there has been an increased reliance by hospitals, clinics, schools, and universities on non-budgetary means of fund-raising such as setting up *ad hoc* foundations and/or relying on revolving funds, a tendency which may be strengthened during economic crises.[48]

At a microeconomic level, among the most relevant indicators of the effect of the crises in this context are the closely interrelated changes in enrollment rates, school attendance rates, and the burden of educational expenditure on households. Unfortunately, we were unable to get access to data on the first two of these indicators, but data on the third indicator showed that there was an increase in the price of school uniforms and stationery and the cost of transportation (see Table 4)—which probably had the expected effect on the first two indicators.

The discussion above suggests that restricted job opportunities, the rise in the prices of essential commodities, and the developments in relation to the social sectors represent the most direct effects of the crisis on poverty. The emphasis here on the effect of the crisis on the poor sections of the population is not to deny its effects on other sections of the population experiencing a loss of real income and consumption. The sharp drop in consumption goods imports from 7.3 billion dollars in 2000 to 4.1 billion dollars in 2001 and the excess capacity created in private health and education facilities are just some of the many indicators pointing in this direction. The drop in private consumption was particularly severe in consumer durables, followed by light consumption goods—including semi-durables—and services (in that order), with only a slight drop in food consumption.[49] The effect on the poor was of greater concern simply because they had very low incomes even prior to the crisis. This, together with their relatively lower level of education and employment prospects, put them at a severely disadvantaged position when attempting to cope with the crisis.

An important factor in the context of poverty and income distribution was undoubtedly the sudden acceleration in inflation, catching the poor and vulnerable particular unaware. In general terms, it is to be expected that the acceleration in the rate of inflation will benefit groups dependent on financial and interest income rather than those dependent on wage and transfer income and the poor who have a tendency to hold the bulk of their income in cash.[50] In the absence of systematic time-series data, the evidence for major distributional shifts taking place during the crisis can be traced through several factors. Among these, the most prominent are the sharp drop in real wages, the increase in interest payments on government debt, capital flight, and—last but not least—a variety of tax exemptions on financial gains. The rise in the share of indirect taxes in total tax revenue from 58.6 percent in April 2001 to a massive 68.5 percent in April 2002 may also have had an effect in the same direction.[51] What is also certain is that the extreme volatility of interest and exchange rates during the crisis has intensified the distributional imbalances in a haphazard way.[52] People in possession of liquid assets made windfall gains—in some cases overnight, a process fully deserving the description of "casino capitalism." What is perhaps even more important, though, than the actual distributional shifts is the legitimization of this process in society.

Other Effects

The effects of the crisis are by no means confined to the ones discussed above. Socio-economic effects such as the increase in intra-family disputes,[53] petty-theft from handbag snatching to burglaries, various forms of civil disobedience such as having illegal access to public utilities, and other forms of deviant behavior like the increase in crime, bribery, and corruption are beyond the scope of the present study, but should be an integral part of more comprehensive assessments.

Certain other effects of the crisis are also not conducive to quantification. For example, what is the social and economic cost of foreign investors purchasing Turkish assets at "distress prices" following the collapse of the capital market and the Turkish lira?[54] How can we measure, if at all, the trauma that people go through when they face the fear of losing their job and when they actually lose it? How do we account for the short- and long-term impact of a worsening nutrition level for children? What is the social cost of the Prime Minister calling Kemal Derviş of the World Bank in the wake of the crisis and saying, "We are on the brink of a disaster. The country needs you"? What is the cost of Bretton Woods Institutions (BWI) dictating—in the aftermath of the crisis—to a sovereign nation which laws should be passed through parliament and at what speed? How can we measure the cost of the diversion of public attention from such pressing issues as industrialization, employment, poverty, and income distribution to a short-term policy agenda centered on financial markets? What is the cost of the resignation in society to the belief that there is no alternative course to be followed other than that propagated and imposed by the BWI, and the consequent loss in self-confidence and problem-solving ability? Likewise, what is the cost of the state of hopelessness among large sections of the population, blaming the whole social, political, and economic system for their problems and losing confidence in the system's ability to provide them with a secure social and economic life?[55] Finally, how do we measure the socio-economic cost of increased desire for emigration, especially among the younger population—including recent graduates, as a result of declining employment opportunities and real wages and salaries?

THE RESPONSE TO THE CRISIS

The overall effect of the crisis will depend not only on its severity, duration, and the effects covered in this study, but also on the response to the crisis by the government, international organizations, the non-governmental organizations (NGOs), and the households themselves. As in a football match (or in a war), the net effect will be largely determined by the relative strengths of the offensive and defensive mechanisms.

The Turkish Government

There are basically two options for governments in the face of a short-term economic crisis: a) take active steps to protect those who have been hit hardest through various job creation and support mechanisms in the short term and draw-up labor retraining and relocation programs and a poverty alleviation strategy in the medium term; b) let the market take its toll, resulting in massive bankruptcies, closures, lay-offs, and unemployment. At the time of writing the Turkish government seems to have taken the second course. Confronted with a crisis of massive proportions and severe disarray in its finances, the government failed to show any quick and strong response in terms of crisis management and implement appropriate emergency measures, let alone design an anti-poverty strategy.[56]

The government's response compares unfavorably with the response of governments in other countries, not only those in Asia but also in Latin America. In these other cases, governments played a prominent role in paving the way out of the crisis by increasing their expenditure on a variety of social programs to protect the poor and the vulnerable from the harshest results of the crisis. In Asian countries, some of these measures were aimed directly at the labor market, including reduced working time and work sharing, the introduction of labor-intensive public works and other employment creation schemes, and micro credit programs to promote self-employment. In Indonesia, for example, government subsidies on the so-called social safety nets, comprising across-the-board subsidies on food (including such items as rice, sugar, and cooking oil), fuel, medicine, fertilizers, and other essential items, were estimated to be in the range of six percent of GDP.[57] Likewise, in Korea the government extended the coverage of the unemployment insurance scheme, increased the level and duration of benefits, provided training for 250,000 people in 1998, and also subsidized in-house training by private firms. There were certain other steps aimed at increasing social welfare assistance to those insufficiently covered by the unemployment insurance scheme and initiating special loan programs for the unemployed—amounting to 0.6 percent of GDP.[58] The measures taken in Latin American countries facing such crises comprised food assistance programs, unemployment insurance, social funds, extension of health coverage to the unemployed, scholarships for children, and training and retraining programs.[59]

In the Turkish case, apart from weak efforts directed at poverty alleviation (ranging from its efforts through the SASF to the distribution of free milk for school children), the government's efforts seem to be limited to the Employment Protection Act in 2002 and a limited scheme of unemployment insurance to also take effect in 2002, both of which are too little too late. The total state funds allocated for poverty alleviation during 2000–1 rose by 40.4 percent, which represented a large drop in real terms—falling from 0.89 percent of GNP to 0.85 percent.[60] There was an even bigger fall in the real value of funds allocated to the SASF branches and representative offices throughout the country, which increased by only 7.1 percent in nominal terms during the same period.[61] The government's inaction is also reflected in the absence of any concerted attempt on its part to deal with the plight of the large number of people made redundant during the crisis; no comprehensive relocation program is in sight for these people. More strikingly, the government does not even have full information on the actual scale of redundancies and the profile of people made redundant, which is essential for initiating such programs.[62] The scale and effectiveness of poverty-alleviation efforts by some municipalities through the provision of soup kitchens and medical services are also not known.

Although the government's passive attitude in crisis management may be defended on the grounds that it did not have the funds required to implement the necessary social programs, this defense is not well founded. If this had been the case, it is difficult to explain how the government promptly met its obligations to a small group of rentiers who received a substantial proportion of total tax revenue as interest on government debt. Yet, due to public finance difficulties, the government was incapacitated and could not fulfil its basic duties. This created further justification for the proponents of small government and strengthened the position of advocates of pro-market-based reforms. The government was too preoccupied with maintaining good relations with the BWI, and particularly the IMF, to ensure the timely release of funds from these sources in support of the new stabilization program. As in the case of the rest of its economic policies, the government was resigned to expect the major steps in this direction to come from the BWI. It was therefore not surprising that its most important efforts aimed at poverty alleviation should be those introduced in conjunction with the World Bank.

International Institutions

The primary concern of the BWI in Turkey has been the deepening of the market-oriented agenda and the smooth payment of external debt through structural reforms rather than poverty alleviation. Some of their efforts for poverty alleviation were, in fact, directed primarily at relieving the effects of the reform process itself. The program introduced shortly after the outbreak of the crisis with full backing of the BWI was characterized by a striking lack of attention to the socio-economic effects of the crisis. Instead, it reflected the emphasis on financial markets and the optimistic and complacent view that growth would soon resume and all would be well. Consequently, the detailed and stiff conditionality of this agreement—some of which extended well into the political realm—did not include the provision of adequate safety nets. The fact that it did not give sufficient attention to the possible effects of its market-based structural reforms on poverty—most recently in the sphere of agriculture—can be taken as evidence that poverty was not the primary concern of the World Bank either.

The BWI's response in terms of poverty alleviation has been stronger than the Turkish government's but far less than their efforts in countries facing similar crises—where they implemented more comprehensive and effective measures such as support of employment and generating public works programs targeted at the poor households.[63] The main effort by the World Bank in the direction of poverty alleviation has been the introduction of the Social Risk Mitigation Project, which involves a loan of $500 million. Amongst the project's primary aims were providing immediate support to the poorest sections of the population affected by the crisis by increasing income-generating and employment opportunities for the poor, increasing the capacity of state institutions in the sphere of social assistance, and establishing a social assistance system.[64] The actual contribution of this project to poverty alleviation cannot be readily assessed.[65] Although the project, which was implemented in close collaboration with the SASF, may have provided some relief for the distressed population, its real contributions might turn out to be in the development of an institutional base for social policy and also in its association of poverty alleviation with employment creation and education. To the extent that there is a direct link between the BWI-backed structural reforms during the past two decades and the short-term crises as their outcome, the World Bank's efforts are likely to be confined to the mitigation of some of the worst cases of poverty without penetrating the root causes of the problem. This puts the organization in the strange role of attempting to cure a chronic disease it actually contributed to creating.

Other Reactions: Organized Groups and Households

The strongest reactions to the crisis were in the form of a series of demonstrations, some of which involved violence and damage to property. Organized sections of the self-employed, especially those most vulnerable to exchange rate and interest rate shocks, were in the forefront of these demonstrations. Among their concrete demands were the reduction of the interest rate on bank credit and the postponement of the payment of social security contributions and taxes.[66] In perhaps the most violent of these, a demonstration led by furniture manufacturers in Ankara, clashes between the police and demonstrators prompted the banning of all protest meetings and demonstrations for one month. However, these demonstrations, characterized by the absence of the poor, petered out with the announcement of the new economic program under the auspices of the BWI. These demonstrations were unique in that they placed a fair share of the blame on international institutions, including the World Bank. Criticism of the IMF was, of course, nothing new in the Turkish context. Yet, until recently, most of these criticisms had been directed at stand-by programs implemented after the crisis. As in some other countries facing similar crises, the IMF was now blamed for the emergence of the crisis. This may be attributed to the fact that the government had implemented the IMF-backed program with great zest, receiving IMF praise at the highest level just before the onset of the crisis. The weak reaction of trade unions, in sharp contrast to their reaction to the 1994 crisis, presents another notable feature of the response to the current crisis. While there had been a very sharp increase in the number of strikes, the number of workers taking part in strikes, and the number of working days lost through strikes in 1995, there has been a marked decline in all three of these indicators during 2001 and the first nine months of 2002.[67]

One may also be puzzled by the fact that mass redundancies, which would have caused social havoc in the setting of most other countries, have prompted little reaction in the Turkish case. This may be explained in part by the large capacity of the informal sector for labor absorption as well as the workers in this sector possessing a better potential to cope. Perhaps the most important factor in this respect, though, has been the strength of Turkey's tacit social security system, which is based on intra-family and community support systems that may extend to cover close relatives, friends, neighbors, and people originally from the same place of residence meeting in a less-than-secure urban environment after a common migration experience.[68] The fact that nearly two-thirds of families are multigenerational may also have been a major factor in shielding large sections of the population—particularly young couples and the elderly—from the worst effects of the crisis.[69]

The main response of households to the crisis has probably been confined to various types of coping strategies such as cutbacks in inessential consumption expenditure, shifts to cheaper types of food, and increases in the number of household members—with, for example, young couples moving in with their parents. Although there were some reports of reverse migration involving the poor who were unable to cope with the heavy socio-economic pressures in urban areas and returned to their former villages, it is unlikely that this has reached any significant proportions. Various forms of aid to the poor by NGOs and especially by non-poor households probably reach many more households and are more successful in targeting the poor than the official programs. In fact, this pecuniary and/or other aid may also have contributed to dampening the full effects of the crisis on the poor. An important question in this respect pertains to the effect of the crisis and official poverty alleviation measures on these private flows. In the absence of systematic information on this, however, the argument can be constructed in either direction.

It has been reported—in relation to the 1994 crisis—that "although non-anticipated jumps in inflation have unambiguously hurt the poor and worsened income distribution, this effect wears off over time as households *modify their behavior*, indexation mechanisms come into play and nominal incomes adjust."[70] Even if this analysis is correct, one should not overlook the fact that until these "adjustments" take place the poor face a great deal of hardship. What is called "modification of behavior" by households is not a costless process and may involve considerable private and social costs through a diverse set of channels like intra-family disputes, child labor, and the reduced likelihood of children participating in education. Such channels, of course, have repercussions well beyond the short term.

PROSPECTS AND CONCLUSION

The examination of the socio-economic effects of the current crisis in Turkey has shown that it has had far-reaching implications, some visible and easy to quantify, others not so. Although the other sections of the population have also suffered, the burden of the crisis has fallen disproportionately on the low-income population, who were by far the least involved in the events that led up to the crisis. The sharp increase in poverty and destitution during the crisis—as reflected by mass media and independent studies—has also indicated that the traditional complacency of Turkish governments about the extent of poverty is not justified. A major lesson that emerges from this assessment is that equal burden sharing is not easy to accomplish during an economic crisis. This may be attributed to factors in the political realm, and, in particular, the balance of power among different sections of the population. This, in turn, points to the importance of establishing a particular form of democracy to facilitate the political mobilization and organization of the poor and other low-income sectors of the population as a powerful interest group.

It seems that the meager attempts by the government—in close collaboration with international organizations—have fallen short of combating the much more powerful negative effects emanating from the crisis. Instead, the coping strategies of the poor, together with the strength of Turkey's tacit social security system—which are based on various informal support systems, may have shielded a major section of the population from the worst effects of the crisis.

The primary emphasis of policymakers should therefore be on the prevention of such crises. If they occur, the government must take emergency measures if it is to manage them effectively. One important obstacle here stems from the absence of data on poverty and income distribution which would have enabled the link between these indicators and the crisis to be established. There is, therefore, an urgent need to develop a simple official poverty index through which the incidence and profile of poverty can be monitored at short intervals; this should be supplemented by detailed area studies.[71]

However, problems are likely to abound even after official data on these indicators becomes available. There are conflicting conclusions emanating from studies of different countries which assess the effect of short-term stabilization policies and structural adjustment programs. Moreover, the reliability of income- and consumption-based household surveys can often be highly questionable, especially in a developing country dominated by large agricultural and urban informal sectors.[72] Even in the so-called formal sector it is difficult to decipher a true picture of income distribution. One reason for this is that much of the income cannot be traced since it is not declared, partly as a result of a variety of tax exemptions for financial income. This calls for the development of new analytical tools for gauging trends in poverty and income distribution as well as the labor market. Widening the tax base, developing a tax payment culture, and improving tax administration are essential not only because of their positive effects on public finance and income distribution but also for their contribution—as a by-product—to our knowledge of these indicators.

The recent experience has shown that countries also differ in terms of the duration of short-term economic crises. Similar to the situation during the 1994 crisis, Turkey has shown considerable resilience during the current crisis in bringing about a quick turnaround in its key macroeconomic indicators. An important factor in this turnaround was the maintenance of good relations with the BWI, which facilitated the inflow of sizable funds as part of rescue operations. Also assisting the situation was Turkey's special relations with the United States, strengthened further by the September 11 events, which no doubt played a major role. The discussion of poverty and inequality in conjunction with the recent crisis should not lead one, though, to conclude that these are altogether new developments in the Turkish context. The crisis has, however, aggravated these problems, brought them more into the open, and helped to destroy the traditional complacency in Turkish society and government *vis-à-vis* these problems. Nonetheless, this should not lead to a new complacency that once the crisis is over and growth picks up, as recent trends seem to show, all will be well. It is widely recognized that while recessions in general have a negative impact on real wages, poverty, and income distribution, the improvements in these indicators during a recovery may not be nearly as rapid.[73]

Some of the damage of the crisis will be long lasting and some of its effects are bound to make their presence felt in the future. The effects of the government's commitment to extending structural reforms in spheres like privatization, agriculture, and public sector banks in close collaboration with the BWI fall into this category. Furthermore, intra-family and community support systems may be weakened as a result of the erosion of the ability of communities to help each other, particularly while urban living is prolonged. Last but not least, the reaction to the effects of a deep economic crisis may be so severe that it could plunge the country into social and political turmoil, signaling the emergence of a full-scale distributional crisis. Events in Indonesia several years ago and more recently in Argentina have provided important lessons about how economic distress may begin to threaten the very fabric of society. In Turkey, the term "social explosion" (borrowed from the crisis in Argentina) became very fashionable at the height of the crisis but was soon forgotten once a degree of calm was observed in the financial markets and growth started to pick up.

Returning to the title of this contribution, and pointing to short-term economic crises as instigators of distributional crises, it has been argued that such short-term crises may have been instigators of neo-liberal reforms in many countries.[74] The dislocations caused by Turkey's payments crisis in the late 1970s and the introduction of the neo-liberal model early in 1980 is a case in point. One major factor that was responsible for the downfall of import-substitution industrialization in Turkey and elsewhere was the heavy concentration of scarce foreign exchange resources on the small base of the manufacturing sector; the resources subsequently became specific to and "frozen" in that sector without being transformed back to foreign exchange through exports. What we are facing now is a variant of this "capital specificity" argument in the sense that the heavy concentration of income in the top income groups becomes specific to these groups. This income does not return to capital accumulation, as evidenced by poor investment performance— especially in manufacturing, and has obvious connotations for the prospects of growth and industrialization.

"Capital Specificity"—together with the findings of this study— indicates that Turkey may yet face a distributional crisis. Short-term crises along with structural trends and neo-liberal policies since 1980, if continued, may be instrumental in instigating a distributional crisis. To avoid such an outcome, there is an urgent need to construct a plan for emergency assistance to groups most vulnerable to the effects of economic crisis in the short term. Furthermore, there is a dire need to draw-up a development strategy to take the country out of its barren short-term agenda, which is dominated by financial issues and crises, to an agenda dominated by concern for long-term development objectives like growth, industrialization, employment creation, and progress on poverty and income distribution.

NOTES

The author wishes to thank Yıldırım Koç for generously sharing his views and observations on the Turkish labor market, Yasemin Doğan for able research assistance, and Engin San for data collection.

1. See, for example, Yılmaz Akyüz and Korkut Boratav, "The Making of the Turkish Financial Crisis," *Discussion Paper*, No.158 (Geneva: United Nations Conference on Trade and Development, April 2002).
2. See James C. Knowles, Ernesto M. Pernia, and Mary Racelis, "Social Consequences of the Financial Crisis in Asia," Manila Social Forum, Nov. 8–12, 1999, p.1.
3. Increasing distress in the banking sector, two major earthquakes, the sharp increase of public sector deficits, and the decline of GNP by 4.7 percent would also justify the classification of 1999 as a year of crisis.
4. See Ahmet H. Köse and A. Erinç Yeldan, "Turkish Economy in the 1990s: An Assessment of Fiscal Policies, Labor Markets and Foreign Trade," *New Perspectives on Turkey*, Vol.18 (Spring 1998), p.52.
5. World Bank, *Turkey—Economic Reforms, Living Standards and Social Welfare Study* (Ankara: World Bank, 2000).
6. State Planning Organization (SPO), *Main Economic Indicators* (March 2002), p.129; Avrupa Eğitim Vakfı [Europe Education Foundation], *Mesleki ve Eğitim Sistemi Raporu* [Report on Occupation and Education System] (Ankara: Avrupa Eğitim Vakfı, 2002), p.218.
7. Unless otherwise stated, figures given in this section are from World Bank (2000).
8. United Nations Development Programme (UNDP), *İnsani Gelişme Raporu Türkiye 2001* [Human Development Report Turkey 2001] (Ankara: UNDP, 2001), p.3.
9. The share of indirect taxes in total tax revenue increased steadily from 47.8 percent in 1991 to 57.6 percent in 1995 and 59.1 percent in 2000. Başbakanlık Hazine Müsteşarlığı [Undersecretariat of Treasury], *Ekonomik Göstergeler* [Economic Indicators] (June 2002), p.16.
10. Türkiye İşveren Sendikaları Konfederasyonu (TİSK—Turkish Confederation of Employer Associations), *Avrupa Birliği'nin Sosyal Politika Gündemi* [Social Policy Agenda of the European Union] (Ankara: TİSK, 2000), p.10.
11. The corresponding ratio for the self-employed was 42 percent for men and 82 percent for women. See Aysıt Tansel, "Wage-Earners, Self-Employed and Gender in the Informal Sector in Turkey," *METU Economic Research Center Working Papers in Economics*, No.00/15 (Ankara: METU, 2000), p.7.
12. For the role of financial liberalization in the emergence of crises in emerging economies, see Christian E. Weller, "Financial Crises after Financial Liberalisation: Exceptional Circumstances or Structural Weakness?," *Journal of Development Studies*, Vol.38, No.1 (Oct. 2001), pp.98–127; Erinç Yeldan, *Küreselleşme Sürecinde Türkiye Ekonomisi, Bölüşüm, Birikim ve Büyüme* [The Turkish Economy in the Process of Globalization: Distribution, Accumulation and Growth] (Istanbul: İletişim, 2001).
13. The new survey, which was originally scheduled for 2001 but cancelled due to the crisis, is now under way.
14. Türkiye Cumhuriyet Merkez Bankası (TCMB—Central Bank of Turkey), *Yıllık Rapor* [Annual Report] (Ankara: TCMB, 2001), p.96.
15. Başbakanlık Hazine Müsteşarlığı [Undersecretariat of Treasury], *Ekonomik Göstergeler* [Economic Indicators] (June 2002), p.5.
16. TCMB (2001), p.223. In construction, construction permits issued by the municipalities declined from 61,695 in 2000 to 56,046 the following year. (Permits are expressed in units of 1,000m².) TCMB (2001), p.227.
17. Mustafa Sönmez, "Hangi İl, Krizden Nasıl Etkileniyor?" [What is the Effect of the Crisis on Individual Provinces?], *BİA* (May 8, 2001), see <http://www.bianet.org/diger/tartisma2159. htm>. The title of this piece was downloaded from <http://www.bianet.org/diger/tartisma 2159.htm>.
18. See Sinan Aygün, "Türkiye Dönüm Noktasında" [Turkey at a Crossroads], *Zaman* (Aug. 15 2002), <http://www.zaman.com.tr/2002/08/15/yorumlar/default.htmS>.

19. See *Selüloz-İş*, No.68 (May 2001), p.29.
20. Kaya Güvenç, "Türkiye Siyasi İradenin Emekten Yana Tecelli Etmesiyle Kurtulabilir" [Turkey Can be Saved if Political Will manifests itself on the side of Labor], *Tes-İş Dergisi* (June–July 2001), p.26.
21. The report on people who became unemployed as a result of the crisis—prepared by the Science, Management and Culture Platform of the Republican Peoples Party (RPP)—was announced in May 2002 and was widely reported in the Turkish press.
22. SPO (2002), p.129.
23. Ibid., p.131.
24. Similar tendencies were observed during the 1994 crisis when some firms—to shield themselves against the rising severance pay rates of workers with more than five years of service—laid-off experienced workers and substituted them with inexperienced workers soon afterwards. See Özlem Onaran, "Labor Market Flexibility during Structural Adjustment in Turkey," *Discussion Papers in Management Engineering*, No.00/1 (Istanbul: Istanbul Technical University, 2000), p.5.
25. For a list of measures taken during 1994 to restrain and cut back public employment, see Aysıt Tansel, "Public Employment as a Social Protection Mechanism," *Economic Research Center Working Papers in Economics*, No.00/14 (Ankara: Middle East Technical University, 1999), p.10.
26. During the East Asian crisis, for example, the increase in unemployment was estimated at around 20 million.
27. See SPO (2002), p.130. For details of the effects of the Asian crisis on unemployment, see Manila Social Forum (1999). Contrary to the figures of 2001, 2000 showed a very sharp increase in both these indicators. This, coupled with the fact that, compared with informal channels, the Turkish Employment Service is not regarded as the most effective channel for searching for a job—a tendency which may have been strengthened during the crisis when all channels probably lost their effectiveness—leads to the puzzling results shown above.
28. Avrupa Eğitim Vakfı (2002), p.229.
29. The sharpest increase in unemployment was in the 15–24 age group, whose share in total unemployment rose sharply from 26.0 percent to 32.8 percent during 2001 (ibid., p.232.) Furthermore, the rise in unemployment was much more rapid in urban areas, rising from 8.2 percent to 13.2 percent during the same period. See SPO (2002), p.129.
30. Based on Avrupa Eğitim Vakfı (2002), p.218. The underemployment rate, which might be another indicator in this respect, actually declined from 6.9 percent to 6.0 percent during this period.
31. World Bank (2000), p.70. In the manufacturing sector, for example, the real wage index declined by a massive 25 percentage points during the period from the last quarter of 1993 to the second quarter of 1997. See Köse and Yeldan (1998), p.74.
32. See Petrol-İş, *Yeni Gibi Sunulan Eski Bir Program* [An Old Program Presented as New] (Istanbul: Petrol-İş, 2001), p.20.
33. It seems that even large and modern firms such as Brisa have resorted to such practices. See *Selüloz-İş* (2001), p.29.
34. The non-wage adjustments in 1994 were confined largely to the adoption of "flexible" arrangements like part-time work, subcontracting to other firms, and reduction of working hours through paid and unpaid forced holidays. Although there was an increase in unemployment by around 600,000 persons, this was primarily the result of depressed domestic activity rather than mass redundancies—as in 2001. For a discussion of the effect of the 1994 crisis on the labor market, see Onaran (2000), pp.18–19, and Köse and Yeldan (1998), pp.73–5.
35. The Turkish workforce is characterized by a notoriously low average level of schooling. In 2000 only 37.2 percent of workers had received more than five years of schooling. See Avrupa Eğitim Vakfı (2002), p.200.
36. This is confirmed by one recent study which—while accepting the role of unemployment, along with inflation, in increasing poverty—places casual/seasonal workers and the self-employed above the unemployed in the ranking of major poverty groups, with the self-employed constituting 45 percent of the poor. See World Bank (2000), p.ix.

118 The Turkish Economy in Crisis

37. World Bank (2000), p.51.
38. See Mustafa Sönmez, *100 Göstergede Kriz ve Yoksullaşma* [100 Indicators of Crisis and Impoverishment] (Istanbul: İletişim, 2002), p.51.
39. See, for example, Necmi Erdoğan (ed.), *Yoksulluk Halleri, Türkiye'de Kent Yoksulluğunun Toplumsal Görünümleri* [Conditions of Poverty, Social Aspects of Urban Poverty in Turkey] (Istanbul: Demokrasi Kitaplığı Yayınevi, 2002); Sönmez (2002); unpublished studies as widely reported in the press by Sencer Ayata, *Milliyet* (July 6, 7, and 9, 2002); Ayşe Buğra and Çağlar Keyder, *Milliyet*, Oct. 22, 2002. All were quoted in the column by Meral Tamer at <http://www.milliyet.com.tr/>.
40. These numbers increased by a further 1.4 million and 1.0 million respectively by September 2002.
41. According to World Bank (2000) p.61, as a result of the considerable leakage of benefits to the non-poor population, only 4.7 percent of the poor were taking advantage of the scheme in 1995.
42. For the sharp increase in the number of applicants to the Istanbul office of the SASF for aid, see *Milliyet*, Oct. 6, 2002. It seems the number of people utilizing the various soup kitchens operated by different municipalities in Istanbul has also increased substantially. See *Milliyet*, Oct. 12, 2002.
43. TCMB (2001), p.65.
44. Some observers argue that even this may be underestimating the exact figure due to lack of transparency for such expenditures. For a discussion of this issue, see C. Emre Alper and Ziya Öniş, "Finansal Küreselleşme, Demokrasi Açığı ve Yükselen Piyasalarda Yaşanan Sürekli Krizler: Sermaye Hareketlerinin Liberalleşmesi Sonrasında Türkiye Deneyimi" [Financial Globalization, Democratic Deficit and Persistent Crises in Emerging Markets: The Turkish Experience after Capital Account Liberalization], *Doğu Batı*, Vol.4, No.14 (2001), p.215.
45. BHM; *Temel Göstergeler* (June 2002), p.18.
46. In the third quarter of 2001, for instance, non-wage public consumption fell by a massive 29.8 percent—as opposed to 14.3 percent for total public sector consumption. TCMB (2001), p.26.
47. Avrupa Eğitim Vakfı (2002), Tables 1, 2, and 3.
48. The share of the revolving fund earnings in total Ministry of Health expenditure, for example, increased from 14 percent in 1988 to 18 percent in 1994 and increased further to 28 percent in 1998.
49. In the second quarter of 2001, when the drop in consumption was the most severe, expenditure on consumer durables fell by a massive 36.1 percent, light consumption goods by 12.5 percent, food by 4.5 percent, and services by 11.5 percent—as opposed to 11.6 percent for total private consumption. TCMB (2001), p.26.
50. See World Bank (2000), p.26.
51. See Başbakanlık Hazine Müsteşarlığı (June 2002), p.16.
52. On the first day of the crisis, for example, interbank overnight interest rates rose from 45 percent to 6,200 percent. See Alper and Öniş (2001), p.217.
53. The RPP survey showed that in 80 percent of cases family life was negatively affected by the crisis, with nearly one-fifth of the survey respondents reporting intra-family problems resulting in divorce.
54. From the outbreak of the crisis at the beginning of 2001 until March 2002, a total of 45 firms sold more than 50 percent, 31 firms 50 percent, and another 58 firms less than 50 percent of their shares to foreign buyers. See *Milliyet*, May 4, 2002.
55. The fact that opinion polls have consistently shown that a large section of the population is dissatisfied with existing political parties and the rise of political movements known—at least initially—for their challenge of the whole system are pointers in this direction.
56. To be fair to the government, the opposition parties also seemed to have been taken aback by the intensity and scale of the crisis and did not engage themselves in an all-out anti-government campaign based on issues like poverty and income distribution.
57. Manila Social Forum (1999), p.1, and IMF, "Mitigating the Social Costs of the Asian Crisis," *Finance and Development*, Vol.35, No.3 (Sept. 1998), p.20.
58. IMF (1998), p.21.
59. See Nora Lustig and Michael Walton, "Latin American Crisis and Social Costs: What Lessons for Asia?," *International Herald Tribune*, May 29, 1998.

60. See Sosyal Demokrat Halk Partisi (Social Democratic Populist Party), *Yoksulluğu Yenmek için Acil Plan (2003–2005)* [Emergency Plan to Fight Poverty] (Ankara: Sosyal Demokrat Halk Partisi, 2002), p.30.

61. See Başbakanlık Yüksek Denetleme Kurulu [The Supreme Audit Board of Prime Ministry], *Sosyal Yardımlaşma ve Dayanışmayı Teşvik Fonu, 2001 Raporu* [2001 Report on the Social Assistance and Solidarity Encouragement Fund] (Ankara: Başbakanlık Yüksek Denetleme Kurulu, 2002), p.20.

62. A proposal to impose a one-off poverty tax to alleviate the plight of people in distress also fell upon deaf ears. See Fikret Şenses, "Yoksullukla Savaşım için de Yeni Bakış Açıları Gereklidir" [New Perspectives are also Necessary to Fight Poverty], *Cumhuriyet*, Dec. 30, 2001, p.2.

63. See IMF (1998), pp.20–21.

64. For details, see World Bank, *Project Appraisal Document on a Proposed Hybrid Investment/Adjustment Loan in the Amount of US$500 Million to the Republic of Turkey for a Social Risk Mitigation Project/Loan Report No: 22510-TU* (Washington DC: World Bank, 2001), p.2.

65. The same applies to the efforts of the UNDP in Turkey, which cover a wide range of spheres—from supporting poverty studies to the reduction of social, economic, and gender disparities in the least developed regions. For details, see <http://www.undp.org.tr>.

66. For example, in Karaköy, Istanbul, a group of self-employed burned a US dollar note "in protest against its sharp rise against the Turkish lira. In Şanlıurfa, the demonstration was organized at the initiative of the local Chamber of Commerce and Industry with the participation of a total of 29 NGOs. They protested against the erosion of real wages, salaries, and agricultural incomes, unemployment, the closure of businesses, the lack of employment opportunities, and corruption and cronyism. Another demonstration in Narlıdere, İzmir, by public sector employees and workers was remarkable in placing the blame for the crisis squarely on the IMF, the World Bank, and the government's incapacity and neglect of its social responsibilities, in that order.

67. See TİSK, *İşveren*, Vol.40, No.12 (Sept. 2002), p.41.

68. On the strength of these mechanisms, see Oğuz Işık and M. Melih Pınarcıoğlu, *Nöbetleşe Yoksulluk Sultanbeyli Örneği* [Taking Turns in Poverty, The Case of Sultanbeyli] (Istanbul: İletişim, 2001).

69. For multigenerational factors, see World Bank (2000), p.83.

70. Ibid., p.vi (emphasis added).

71. On the issue of a simple poverty index, see Fikret Şenses, "Yoksulluk, Kaygı Veriyor" [Poverty is Worrying], *Milliyet*, Dec. 2, 1997; <http://www.milliyet.com.tr/>.

72. An interesting feature of the Turkish economy—and the labor market in particular—which merits further exploration is what I would call the Summer House Effect (SHE) involving population movements on a large scale over and above the normal population movements through internal tourism and seasonal labor migration. Although it is hard to establish its actual size, judging from the large number of summer homes in a large number of holiday resorts the figures involved are probably very large. The fact that this high level of economic activity lasts up to six months, if not more, reinforces the informality in both the goods and factor markets.

73. In Latin America during the 1980s, for example, poverty increased in 55 of the 58 cases of recession. Conversely, a drop in poverty occurred in only 22 out of the 32 recoveries. See John Gafar, "Poverty, Income Growth, and Inequality in Some Caribbean Countries," *Journal of Developing Areas*, Vol.32 (Summer 1998), p.474.

74. Dani Rodrik, "Understanding Economic Policy Reform," *Journal of Economic Literature*, Vol.34, No.1 (March 1996), pp.9–41.

Social Capital and Corruption during Times of Crisis: A Look at Turkish Firms during the Economic Crisis of 2001

FİKRET ADAMAN and ALİ ÇARKOĞLU

This contribution attempts to unveil the rather intricate relationship between trust and corruption by analyzing the results of a survey conducted in Turkey on the business community during October and November 2001. Our aim was to investigate whether lack of trust among business people towards the business community, as well as towards the general public, is conducive to more corruption in Turkey. As a starting point, we acknowledge that corruptive activities play a role, with varying degrees in different socio-economic conditions, in the emergence of economic and political crises. Accordingly, an inquiry into the relationship between trust and corruption is relevant in any analysis on economic crises, especially the one that hit Turkey most recently.

Perhaps more than any other single factor that attracted public attention, corruption—as expressed under different concepts such as "siphoning of banks," "rent-seeking," and "patronage networks"—occupied the heart of the popular debate in Turkey during the months of economic crisis in 2001. If we abide by the simplest definition of political and administrative corruption—"the use of power by political authorities and/or public servants outside their duties, in order to serve personal interests or the interests of those who, they feel, belong to the same group as themselves"—we cannot avoid noticing its various different reflections in the social and economic life of Turkey.[1]

A quick glance at the vast literature on corruption would indicate that bribery and favoritism are probably the most conspicuous forms of corruption.[2] Other forms include politicians or civil servants abusing their position to perform transactions they should not perform, accelerate some transactions at the expense of others, or act with discretion regarding quality and quantity of work in order to serve their own interests. Besides the forms of corruption that are aimed at personal gain—accepting bribes, nepotism, cronyism, and rent-seeking—there are other types of corruption shaped by political motives. Political clientelism—practiced by politicians who protect and aid their own parties, voters or potential voters—transforms politics into a constant trade between the voting masses ("clients") and the politicians ("patrons") who protect and aid them. Business opportunities provided in return for loyalty to a party rather than in the interests of the public, favoritism in the distribution of services in return for political support, or public support for unproductive sectors of the economy in return for political support—all are frequently encountered examples of corruption in daily life.

Obviously, all incidents of corruption in political life are shaped by decisions made in the public sector—in other words, they form part of a political procedure. All actors in this process—politicians, bureaucrats and electors, as well as interest and pressure groups—become part of these networks of corruption, albeit at different levels. Where political corruption is dominant, ethical norms are violated and social life is pervaded by immorality. In other words, under these circumstances society does not perceive corruption as immoral. Although political corruption tends to be veiled in secrecy at the beginning, the spread of degeneracy through the community can gradually distort social life by encouraging tolerance and a blind eye towards corruption—possibly leading in the end to "kleptocracy."

Political corruption is most often encountered where the public and private sectors meet. In the public sector, political corruption is mostly encountered in fields such as the following: procurement of goods and services; public tenders; market control; the granting of permits and licenses; investment, export and incentive arrangements; the application of quotas; and the collection and supervision of taxes (or tax reductions or deferrals). Elected politicians frequently use their posts to go beyond even self-serving interests in order to provide close relations and family members with jobs or exclusive market positions, and to lend support—especially by providing job opportunities—to wider groups such as people from the same town or province.[3]

Briefly, the concept of corruption we use in the ensuing sections encompasses two essential types of behavior and relationship. The first covers situations where local or central governments abuse their authorities and responsibilities to engage in interest relationships with third parties in the creation and allocation of resources under their control. These situations build patronage relations between the government and interest groups that ultimately result in institutional failures on the government's part.[4] These types of corruption are grouped under the general heading "political corruption" since this kind of favoritism has direct political connotations. It is, moreover, difficult to observe such illegalities, as in the case of a new airport whose location was chosen through partisanship rather than objective assessment. The second type of corruption occurs when individual civil servants violate the principles of public impartiality, justice and equality.[5] We call this "administrative corruption," since what is violated is an administrative disposition of a narrow scope. In these cases it is also easier to observe illegality. It has often been noted that that these two types of behavior—political and administrative corruption—complement each other.

Apart from these two basic categories, we should also define as corruption the case of some local public establishments that are unable to provide regular and satisfactory services due to lack of resources, hence try to create resources by going beyond the regulations. In this case, there is no interest relation but rather a voluntary creation of resources that violates legal arrangements and maybe even the equality clauses of the Constitution. The most typical example of this is the dilemma faced by state schools regarding admissions. In order to provide essential services (like heating the school during the winter), school administrators resort to collecting compulsory fees, called "contributions"—thus violating the principle of free primary education for all. The creation of such irregular funds due to lack of resources is clearly incompatible with the principle of transparency, as well as the principles of equality and justice. It is also possible that not all such funds are returned in the form of services, and that at least some of them are used to serve personal and/or political interests. Households, for their part, perceive this as an irregular way of collecting money and label it as corruption. In any case, the lack of transparency means that there is no reliable information on the use of these irregular funds. Furthermore, personal and/or political gains that may be obtained through use of these funds clearly come under the heading of "administrative corruption," as mentioned above.[6]

The legal classification of the acts cited above as examples of corruption may vary greatly. Some are obviously illegal (bribery, for example), but others are not explicitly forbidden or punishable by law (attempting to gain votes by building an airport or port in a specific region).[7] The former could be termed as the "narrow" meaning of corruption—where illegality is involved. In the "wider" sense, however, corruption can also involve acts that are within the law but against the public interest.

Obviously, the concept of public or social benefit is not always easy to define, and it is therefore difficult to apply to the discussion of corruption. Any action that benefits all individuals in a society will also benefit the public; we can also argue that developments that improve an individual's condition without harming any other individuals also benefit the public. In other situations, though, the public benefit will be less easy to define. In difficult cases, one approach to enable classification would be to consider how the decisionmaking process had operated. Transparency in decisions involving public resources, the functional right to information about them, and freedom of speech will make a classification of public benefit more likely. A retreat from transparency—obstructing sources of information, and especially limits on freedom of speech—will make it easier for individual or group interests to prevail over the public benefit. We classify this latter situation as corruption in the wider sense, although, as noted above, it is impossible for laws to proscribe all situations of this kind. In the end, however, the subordination of public interest to private gain will always be considered illegitimate within the social order, even if laws are not always broken.

All the types of corruption summarized above obviously cause enormous damage to a country's social, economic, and political life. When economic costs are examined, four types become apparent:[8]

1. In the allocation of resources the public benefit is ignored in favor of private (personal and/or political) gain. Since the objectives of public projects will be transformed into maximizing rent, the social contributions of the project in question are bound to remain of secondary importance (for example, having a highway constructed in order to benefit the contractor, without discussing its social benefits).

2. Corruption brings a loss of productivity. On the one hand, resources are used in unproductive fields like lobbying, and on the other hand the loss of transparency and information about these processes increases uncertainty in economic life, while the undermining of general conditions of competition will inevitably lead to a loss of productivity. In the end, gross national product (GNP) will decrease, and so will total investment.

3. The impact of corruption on the distribution of income is an empirical question, since we cannot know enough about the income groups that give and receive corruption-related transfers. However, the resulting change in income distribution occurs mostly outside the legal political process. This factor contributes to constant uncertainty in the system and gives advantage to wealthier income groups. Thus, large-scale corruption is more likely to bring deterioration in the distribution of income.

4. Foreign investors will lose interest in a country with massive corruption, with a likely negative effect on economic growth and development. In addition, local investors may very well prefer to go abroad to find a more secure environment.

In short, corruption brings inefficiency and productivity losses as well as impeding the smooth functioning of the economic governance mechanisms and the flow of goods and services across borders.

The political costs of corruption also vary:

1. Corruption violates equality, a basic principle of any legitimate state, removing the possibility of providing equal service to all citizens.

2. Transparency, a basic principle of democracy, is damaged. Citizens have less chance of obtaining information about the actions of the public administration.

3. As a consequence of (2), the obligation to act accountably is not fulfilled and thus governance becomes more and more difficult.

4. The full functioning of democracy is obstructed. The principle that an unsuccessful party in power will be replaced is undermined, because a party in power can prolong its term through the illegitimate and illegal use of economic power.

5. Corruption may bring populist policies, with short-term concerns replacing long-term ones.

6. Corruption degrades intra-party as well as inter-party politics. There is an important relationship between the problem known as "the leadership hegemony" and the general predominance of corruption.

More importantly for our purposes, when we look at the social costs of corruption we observe a collapse of moral values. This affects future generations as well as present ones. New generations living in a corrupt system will grow-up thinking that these are the normal ways of the world. We also observe that trust in the legal system and the state is weakened. This could clearly encourage the breaking of rules in a number of fields. In other words, the more widely illegality and corruption spread in a certain field, the more often this will be reproduced in other fields in some way.

Although the direction of causation might, at first glance, be unclear, one could take trust relations as the starting point in a chain of events that culminate in corruption networks. Lack of generic interpersonal trust in increasingly complex and competitive socio-economic environments, where state capacity to create and implement the rule of law is low, typically leads to exclusive networks within which a parochial trust bondage is built and maintained. Such networks feed off low satisfaction with public services and low trust in institutions that provide them. These networks multiply into corruption rings and replace the public good provision mechanisms of the state.[9] Informality, together with the tendency to trust only in small exclusive network members, and lack of broad, impersonal or institutional trust, deplete the sources of state legitimacy.

Within a larger theoretical framework, "social capital"—generic interpersonal trust being a major component—is considered an important parameter in explaining society's development and prosperity. Social capital supports the idea that social rules, norms, networks, connectedness and sanctions do play important positive roles. Depleted social capital can thus be seen as a major parameter in explaining the developmental achievements of different countries, the obstacles faced in this process, and long-term potential for overcoming these impediments. It is in this wider framework that trust is understood to make people more willing to interact with others, who are different, in a cooperative way and thereby promote egalitarian values and thus redistributive policies.[10] In a similar vein, "trusting country" contexts involve better governance, effective social programs, and lower crime rates coupled with higher economic growth.[11] More importantly for our purposes, from a purely comparative perspective, as individuals become more trusting the contexts within which they operate tend to become less corrupt.

Trust, in the sense of the major component of social capital, takes individuals' beliefs that other fellow citizens are part of their moral community as its starting point. As people lose this sense of being part of a larger moral community as a component of their social identity, they are expected to replace this general trust with various rings of corruption, which provide a network-specific trust. Corruption then takes the form of misuse of power by political elites and bureaucrats in order to manipulate the affairs of state for private gain. As public sources and capacity are privatized through corrupt deals, a state's capacity cannot be upgraded and thus rationed service distribution opens the public administration for further corruption. The vicious cyclical nature of these interactions leads to a total collapse of the public service delivery mechanisms. These mechanisms thus require restructuring so that the bottlenecks which originally created corruption—thereby depleting trust in the system—can be avoided.

Establishment of a credible and trustworthy institutional framework is extremely important, especially in countries where expectations from the state are high and public resources are very limited. The effectiveness of any economic policy typically involves raising new public funds—either domestically or from international markets—and using them efficiently. However, low trust in institutions leading to small exclusive networks of corruption typically channels these valuable resources into small group interests. As such, the critical issue is to understand how and why low trust in institutions develops, since depleted trust in institutions renders them ineffective in carrying out the task of maintaining social and economic order and policy regulation because they all aim to create private rather than public good. In times of crises, institutional inability to create basic order and policy regulation seriously paralyses the state's power to implement counter-cyclical policies to pull the economy out of crisis. At the risk of sounding simplistic, one might say that lack of trust—a low level of social capital—is conducive to corruptive activities. The prevalence of corruption may play a key role in the occurrence of economic crises, and economic crises would in turn further erode trust among people.

We want to contribute to this debate by testing this hypothesis on the Turkish case using the results of a recent survey study. Questions concerning the dynamics that create low trust in institutions and individuals in general but generate high trust in small exclusive groups that thrive on corrupt deals will be addressed. The answers offered to these questions could change these dynamics to bolster stronger and more credible public authority—an authority that is able to implement policies and build trust within its institutions and deliver the services expected.

In addressing these issues, we focus on the business community in Turkey. Data is from the aforementioned survey analysis conducted with the aim of investigating the corruption problem in Turkey. A total of 1,219 business people—selected randomly from different sectors—were interviewed.[12] We aimed to evaluate a number of hypotheses concerning the intricate relationship between interpersonal trust and trust in institutions and openness to corrupt practices. More specifically, we sought to investigate whether in the Turkish case the lack of trust among business people towards their counterparts as well as towards the general public is conducive to more corruption. This is important for understanding the latest crises that have hit Turkey. If the existence of corruptive activities is one of the elements that contributed to the two crises, then one would like to know whether the trust parameter was effective in explaining corruption. If so, such a parameter can be used to suggest a method to alleviate such corruption and prevent it from continuing to be a relevant factor in economic crises.[13]

After a short review of the relevant literature, this contribution underlines the conceptual relationships evaluated with the empirical data collected. We briefly outline the political and economic context within which we made our empirical observations and point to their conceptual implications on the phenomena of interest. Following a description of the main characteristics of our data set, we present a simple empirical framework for testing the identified hypotheses. The concluding section critically evaluates the findings, offers their implications for our understanding of the relationship between trust and corruption, and emphasizes points of departure for further research.

THEORETICAL BACKGROUND[14]

The term "social capital" has recently received considerable attention among sociologists, economists, and political scientists. It encompasses the idea that social rules, norms, networks, connectedness, and sanctions play important positive roles in societal and economic life in today's developed or developing societies. Social capital is seen to increase productivity, thereby fostering development and alleviating poverty.

Social capital is a concept devised by the Scottish Enlightenment philosophers, who emphasized the significance of friendship in overcoming the negative externalities of industrialization—such as alienation at the workplace and the destruction of cooperation in public life. However, the introduction of the term into sociological literature is usually attributed to James Coleman. Coleman, for his part, defined social capital as "a variety of different entities, with two elements in common: they all consist of some aspect of social structure, and they facilitate certain actors—whether personal or corporate actors—within the structure."[15] In that regard, social capital encompasses the view that it eases "the attainment of certain ends that would not be attainable in its absence."[16] Concomitantly, he proposed to group the entire set of social relations deemed useful for individuals under three different categories: the set of informal insurance arrangements; the information that is communicated through social relations; and the ways in which the existence of norms and effective sanctions facilitates action.

Some well-known examples of social capital provided by Coleman include "the relationships obtaining between merchants in the central market in Cairo (in which 'family relations are important')," and "the greater sense of security felt by a mother of young children in Jerusalem as compared with Detroit, because 'In Jerusalem the normative structure ensures that unattended children will be looked after by adults in the vicinity'."[17] The examples make it possible to grasp Coleman's following claim that: "unlike other forms of capital, social capital inheres in the structure of relations between persons and among persons. It is lodged neither in individuals nor in physical implements of production."[18] These lines indicate that Coleman's conceptualization of social capital is a broad and encompassing one, inhering much of the characteristics of a public good—the kind of good whose provision, though beneficial for all, is so costly such that no rational individual will be willing to undertake its financial burden.

Another view of social capital, put forward by Pierre Bourdieu, hinges on the basics of social-class reproduction. Bourdieu defines social capital as "the aggregate of the actual or potential resources which are linked to possession of a durable network of more or less institutionalized relationships of mutual acquaintance or recognition."[19] With this definition, Bourdieu relates the concept of social capital to that of cultural capital (socially constructed qualifications of one sort or another) and symbolic capital (prestige and honor). These, in turn, are detrimental in the formation and reproduction of class. In that regard, it can be intuited that Bourdieu's conceptualization of social capital can be described by referring to the idea of "connections," which in his terms enables one to grasp "the function of institutions such as clubs or, quite simply, the family, the main site of accumulation and transmission of that kind of capital."[20]

Yet the most famous interpretation of social capital is the one proposed by Robert Putnam. He defined social capital as a set of "horizontal associations" among people who have an effect on the productivity of the community. Putnam, in his empirical investigation of the "networks, norms and trust, and reciprocity that facilitate mutually beneficial co-ordination and co-operation in a community" found that the single most important determinant, both of the performance of democratic local governments and of the differing levels of socio-economic development in the regions of Italy, was the "civic engagement" factor, which is measured by the vibrancy of associational life, newspaper readership, and political participation.[21] Putnam claimed that civic engagement mainly emerges from "weak" horizontal ties. He argued that, "'strong' personal ties (like kinship and intimate friendship) are less important than 'weak ties' (like acquaintanceship and shared membership in secondary associations) in sustaining ... collective action. Dense but segregated horizontal networks sustain cooperation within each group, but networks that cut across social cleavages nourish wider cooperation."[22] Following these lines, Putnam reaches the conclusion that "social trust, norms of reciprocity, networks of civic engagement, and successful co-operation are mutually reinforcing. Effective collaborative institutions require interpersonal skills and trust, but those skills and that trust are also uncalculated and reinforced by organized collaboration."[23] Therefore, the key feature of social capital—in Putnam's conceptualization—is that it facilitates coordination and cooperation in a path-dependent way (*à la* Douglas North).[24]

Following these seminal contributions, much has been added to the literature in subsequent years—a large part at an applied level. These empirical studies aimed to measure social capital and its impact on a set of societal and economic indicators. Social capital, by wide consensus, is accepted as a key factor in development discourse. Attempts at identifying the components of social capital generally agreed that "networks of civic engagement," "norms of generalized reciprocity," "relations of social trust," "norms and sanctions," and "belonging" constitute social capital.[25] "Relations of social trust" between individuals are believed to reduce transaction costs due to the constructed confidence people have in a known social and institutional structure. "Norms of generalized reciprocity" refers to "a continuing relationship of exchange that is at any time unrequited or imbalanced, but that involves mutual expectations that a benefit granted now should be repaid in the future,"[26] and, in that regard, it is attributed to the role of "forming informal insurance arrangements, thus forming security and solidarity among members of a society, as a result of which people will be well-off."[27] The feeling of "belonging" that one has towards a group or society is thought to make an individual explicitly consider the interests of this group or society. In game theory language, it seems that there is an agreement about the "possible" positive impacts of social capital—via its components—on development outcomes such as growth, equity, and poverty alleviation.

Serageldin and Grootaert categorize the useful effects of social capital under three headings, which can be described as follows:

- Sharing information. One would expect to have high degree of information-sharing in a society with high social capital, as individuals would trust each other and would have reciprocal networks. Sharing information will, in turn, reduce uncertainties and increase efficiency.

- Coordinating activities. Uncoordinated actions are usually associated with inefficiencies and transaction costs. In an environment where people do not act in a short-term opportunistic way, but aim at sharing benefits to be accrued in the long run, coordination of activities can be possible. Coordination will cause individuals to interact in a repeated way, thus enhancing trustworthy behavior among them.

- A collective decisionmaking process. Collective actions are usually hampered because of opportunistic behaviors, known as free-riding. The provision of public goods and the management of externalities require individuals to make collective decisions. It is claimed that in an environment with a high social capital level individuals will tend not to free ride but instead contribute to the public cause.[28]

As the above demonstrates, trust should be seen as the main component of social capital. Trust, coupled with the willingness and capacity to cooperate and coordinate and the habit of contributing to a common effort, can be used, arguably, to enhance participatory decisionmaking processes and civic engagement in general and to decrease transaction costs in particular. Yet, there is another side of the coin: the existence of reciprocal interactions, trust, and networks may likewise be a conduit for corruption and bribery. Groups with high social capital able to solve their collective action problems may indeed act as rent-seeking organizations with the aim of lobbying for preferential treatment. It is therefore perfectly possible that only people who are inside the network could share norms and trust.

Mark Warren, with regard to this point, offers clarification by distinguishing two kinds of trust: generalized trust and particularized trust.[29] Although it is commonly believed that the negative externalities of social capital prevail mainly from particularized trust, where trust is felt towards those one personally knows and not to society in general, Warren suggests that a particularized trust could create bad social capital only if the interests encapsulated in the trust relation are not publicly justifiable. Yet, when it comes to generalized trust, one may claim that it is very likely to consolidate good social capital.

The theoretical setting suggests, therefore, that generalized trust—which is attributable to good social capital—is expected to be conducive to a more open, transparent, and accountable public sphere, and, *ipso facto*, a less corrupt society. As a derivative of this link, we anticipate observing a negative relationship between generalized trust and the perceived level of corruption as well as corruption at the attitudinal level. As for the link between corruption and the recurrent economic crises, we took as a given that—especially in the context of a country like Turkey—severe resource shortage within an economic environment characterized by low social capital simply magnifies the negative economic impact of corruption and thus renders the economy more open to crises.[30] By linking the trust factor to corruption and thus to economic crises, our framework provides an alternative to long-term cultural bases of recurrent economic bottlenecks in the context of a developing country. We now turn our attention to the findings of the survey.

THE SURVEY

The questionnaire, through a module of which we attempted to unveil the relationship between trust and corruption, was designed to question the business-state relationship in general and the corruption problem in particular (see note 13). During October and November 2001 the survey was conducted on a total of 1,219 business people, who represented six sectors: industry, construction, trade, transportation and communication, financial institutions, and business and personal services. The survey was conducted in 12 cities categorized as "Large Western," "Small Western," "Large Eastern," and "Small Eastern." It should be noted that the firms from each city were chosen through a random sampling procedure, and each firm in a sector of a city had the same probability of being chosen. It should not, therefore, be surprising that mainly small- and medium-sized firms were chosen and not a single firm from the top 500 largest is represented.

We will continue by presenting our independent and dependent variables—trust and corruption respectively—and then other independent variables we thought may affect corruption.

Measures Used in the Analyses

Trust. Trust constitutes our independent variable. We used four different questions in our survey to tap the issue of trust among the businessmen across our six sectors of activity. The first of these is similar to the standard University of Michigan's Survey Research Center (SRC) (1969) wording: "Generally speaking, would you say that most people can be trusted or that you can't trust most people?"[31] Table 1 shows the distribution of our sample of 1,219 respondents, where we observe that about 58 percent indicated that most people could be trusted. In the second version of this general trust question we again adopted the SRC (1969) wording almost verbatim: "Do you think that most people would try to take advantage of you if they got the chance or would they try to be fair?" In this version of addressing trust, we observe that the number of those trusting people is

TABLE 1

GENERAL TRUST IN PEOPLE

Generally speaking, would you say that most people can or cannot be trusted?		
	Frequency	Percent
Most people can be trusted	705	57.8
Most people cannot be trusted	506	41.5
DN/NA	8	0.7
Total	1,219	100

Do you think that most people would try to take advantage of you if they got the chance or would they try to be fair?		
	Frequency	Percent
Most people would try to be fair	881	72.3
Most people would try to take advantage	327	26.8
DN/NA	11	0.9
Total	1,219	100

	Most people would try to take advantage	Most people would try to be fair	**Total**
Most people cannot be trusted	642 (53.4%)	60 (5%)	702
Most people can be trusted	235 (19.5%)	266 (22.1%)	501
Total	877	326	1,203
Cramer's V	0.494		
Cronbach's alpha	0.66		

significantly higher—about 73 percent of the sample. Similar to SRC's 1964 and 1968 post-election studies that have a 0.5 and 0.48 inter-item correlation, we have a 0.49 inter-item correlation in our study.

Suspecting that trust is domain-specific, we also wanted to question trust in business activity with our businessmen. Our formulation is similar to Burns and Kinder's on trust between neighbors: "Generally speaking, to what degree do people in the business world keep their promises?"[32] Our respondents were offered an 11-point scale, 0 representing "people in the business world never keep their promises" and 10 representing "people in the business world always keep their promises." Table 2 shows that, given a real middle on this new scale, significant numbers of our respondents have opted to stay indifferent or undecided on their answers (31 percent). Only about 28 percent indicated by picking an option in the 6-to-10 range that most people in the business world would keep their promises on our scale, while about 40 percent picked an answer between 0 and 4—indicating a lack of trust in their fellow businessmen.

Our second business domain-specific trust question is as follows: "Do you think that most people in the business world would try to take advantage of you if they got the chance or would they try to be fair?" We again offered an 11-point scale, with 0 representing "most people in the business world always look out for themselves" and 10 representing "most people in the business world always try to be fair." Again, with a real middle on our scale, respondents have predominantly opted to stay indifferent or undecided (25 percent). Only about 25 percent indicated by picking an option in the 6-to-10 range that most people in the business world would keep their promises on our scale, while about 49 percent picked an answer between 0 and 4—indicating a lack of belief in the trust of their fellow businessmen. In both Tables 1 and 2 we observe that few individuals said that they do not have an answer for our four questions or that they do not want to answer them.

TABLE 2
TRUST IN THE BUSINESS COMMUNITY

Generally speaking, to what degree would people in the business world keep their promises?		
	Frequency	Percent
Would not keep their promises (0–4)	491	40.3
Undecided (5)	383	31.4
Would keep their promises (6–10)	341	28.0
DN/NA	4	0.3
Total	1,219	100

Would most people in the business world try to take advantage of you if they got the chance or would they try to be fair?		
	Frequency	Percent
Would try to take advantage of you (0–4)	601	49.3
Undecided (5)	305	25.0
Would try to be fair (6–10)	310	25.4
DN/NA	3	0.2
Total	1,219	100

	Would try to take advantage of you (0–4)	Undecided (5)	Would try to be fair (6–10)	**Total**
Would not keep their promises (0–4)	366 (30.2%)	66 (5.4%)	58 (4.8%)	490
Undecided (5)	151 (12.4%)	171 (14.1%)	61 (5.0%)	383
Would keep their promises (6–10)	83 (6.8%)	67 (5.5%)	190 (15.7%)	34
Total	600	304	309	1,213
Cramer's V	0.394			
Cronbach's alpha	0.63			

The Turkish Economy in Crisis

As a simple index of general trust for people, we gave a score of 1 for each response indicating trust in their fellow man; our scores on each index range from 0 (low trust) to 2 (high trust). For the issue of trust in the business community we aggregated the answers on an 11-point scale into a dichotomous trust-no trust scale. Those answers on our 0-to-10 scale that fall in the range of 0 to 4—indicating that most people in the business community would not keep their promises—are coded as not trusting (0) and those that fall into the 6-to-10 range—indicating that most people in the business community would keep their promises—are coded as trusting (1). Similar coding rules are also applied to recode the second question on trust in the business community into trusting and non-trusting cases. Tables 1 and 2 show that Cronbach's alpha values are barely acceptable. Table 3 shows the distribution of our sample into each one of those categories on the aggregate trust indices ranging from 0 (low trust) to 2 (high trust). Obviously, when dealing with the trust in the business community question—which originally uses an 11-point scale—we are faced with the problem of those who pick the real middle point of the scale (5); these undecided respondents comprise 32 percent of our sample. When we look at the distribution of trust in the business community among those who are decided, we observe higher shares of trusting individuals than is the case for the general trust index. Nevertheless, we should stress that no matter what perspective one adopts when looking at these index figures, it is apparent that the business community neither trusts fellow citizens on the street nor do they trust others in their community of business people.

One question that remains unanswered so far is whether or not trust is domain-dependent and if there are really two separate kinds of trust—one towards general fellow citizens and one towards fellow business community members. One simple indication evidencing two separate dimensions of trust, as captured by our two indices, is that there is a

TABLE 3

DISTRIBUTION OF THE SAMPLE ALONG THE TRUST INDICES (%)

| | | Trust in general | Trust in the business community | |
			Undecided included	Undecided excluded
Low	0	53.4	30.2	44.4
	1	24.5	22.2	32.6
High	2	22.1	15.7	23.0
Undecided			32.0	
Total		100	100	100

TABLE 4

GENERAL TRUST vs. TRUST IN THE BUSINESS COMMUNITY

Trust in general		Trust in the business community		
		Non trusting	Trusting	Total
Not trusting	Count	843	90	933
	% of Total	70.4	7.5	77.9
Trusting	Count	168	96	264
	% of Total	14.0	8.0	22.1
Total	Count	1,011	186	1,197
	% of Total	84.5	15.5	100

significant portion of those trusting in one definition that remains non-trusting according to the other definition. Table 4 below shows the cross-tabulation of our two indices. For example, when we look at general trust we see that 264 respondents out of a total of 1,197 are trusting (22.1 percent), whereas 96 of those are categorized as trusting in the business community (eight percent of the total or 36.4 percent of the trusting 264 people). Similarly, nearly half of those who are trusting in the business community are categorized as non-trusting according to our general trust index.

Corruption. In order to tap respondents' attitudes and behavior *vis-à-vis* corruption the following four sets of questions were asked, which are then used as our dependent variables:

• Perceived intensity of corruption at public institutions. This set of questions is aimed at measuring businessmen's perceptions of the degree of corruption in a number of public institutions. Respondents were asked to reveal their perceived intensity of the degree of corruption on a scale of 0 to 10 for the following institutions: deed offices, municipalities, public hospitals, traffic police, police other than traffic officers, courts, customs, tax offices, army, electric delivery, and public universities. This dependent variable was then simply formulated as the grand total of grades that respondents gave to different institutions.

• Perceived frequency of bribery at service provider public institutions. A variant of the first type of question, this set of questions aimed at measuring the perceived degree of corruption in a set of public institutions that provide services to the business community. The following services were considered: connection to the electric service, wired phone services, permission to open a business, tax payment procedure, customs procedure, courts, health inspection, and fire inspection. This dependent variable was also simply formulated as the grand total of grades that respondents gave to different institutions.

- Total number of illegal payments made to public institutions. Businessmen were asked whether in the last two-year period their firms made any illegal payment to the following institutions: deed offices, municipalities, public hospitals, traffic police, police other than traffic officers, courts, customs, tax offices, electric delivery. This dependent variable was then simply formulated as the total number of institutions to which illegal payments were made.

- Impartiality in the evaluation of credit applications to public banks. With this question businessmen were asked to reveal how they perceive, on a scale of 0 to 10, the impartiality of public banks in evaluating the credit applications of businessmen.

Other Independent Variables.[33] In order to be able to isolate the possible link between trust (both generic and towards the business community) and corruption, a list of independent variables are also incorporated into our econometric estimations. These variables, which are listed below, comprise the demographic characteristics and attitudes of the respondents as well as the firms' characteristics:

- Age (the age of the respondent)
- Education (the education level of the respondent)
- Working abroad (whether or not the respondent has spent time abroad working)
- Position at the firm (owner, partner, CEO, director)
- Pro-freedom (a combined parameter measuring the respondent's attitudes towards expanding democratic rights)
- Readiness for the EU (European Union) accession (a combined parameter measuring the respondent's attitudes towards joining the EU even if this move requires some concessions)
- Number of employees working in the firm
- Sector (the sector in which the firm is positioned: industry, commerce, finance, transportation and communication, construction, or business and personal services)
- Geography (the location of the firm: Large Western cities, Small Western cities, Large Eastern cities, and Small Eastern cities)

To this list one would like to add the magnitude of economic activities that firms have been involved in. Indeed, we attempted to measure this dimension by asking the total revenue of firms, but responses were then discarded as it was felt that most participants tried to avoid responding to this question.

RESULTS

The results of our econometric analyses are presented in a tabular form in Tables 5 through 8.[34] Note that (+) or (-) indicates a 95 percent confidence level, and (++) or (--) indicates a 99 percent confidence level; a plus sign shows that the correlation between the dependent and the independent parameters is in the same direction when all other independent parameters are controlled, and a negative sign shows that the correlation is in the opposite direction.

When we confine ourselves to the relationship between trust and corruption (to simplify matters these entries in the tables are in bold), we observe that the survey conducted with a sample of 1,219 respondents as representative of the business community in Turkey reveals that links do exist and that they are in the expected direction. We further notice that the results indicate segmentation between trust towards the general public and towards business people: when trust towards the general public goes down, businessmen tend to perceive a higher corruption intensity in a set of public institutions (Table 5), a higher prevalence of corruption when the business community is in relation with a set of public institutions (Table 6), and to have paid more bribes to a set of given public institutions in the last two years (Table 7). However, when the issue is impartiality in the evaluation of credit applications to public banks, the results reveal that when trust towards fellow businessmen goes up, the respondents tend to perceive that impartiality increases (Table 8).

RAMIFICATIONS OF THE QUANTITATIVE RESEARCH

The starting point of our analysis was that corruption leads to economic crisis in the context of a developing country like Turkey, one with limited production as well as a limited state capacity to meet the popular demands of the citizenry. One of the long-term bases of corruption is the citizens' lack of trust in people with whom they have had no prior connection. Our survey study on the business community in Turkey revealed two results: the confirmation of the link between trust and corruption, and the high percentage of business people with no trust towards the general public or their fellows as well as the high percentage of corruptive activities.

TABLE 5
PERCEIVED INTENSITY OF CORRUPTION IN PUBLIC INSTITUTIONS

Personal characteristics							Characteristics of the firm		
Demographics				Attitudes					
Age	Position	Education	Work abroad	Trust people/ Trust business	Pro-freedom	Ready for concession to join EU	Number of employees	Sector	Geography
(--)	CEO (-)	University and higher (++)		People (--)	(++)	(++)			Small Western (--) Small Eastern (--) Large Eastern (--)

Note: (+) or (-) indicate a 95 percent confidence interval; (++) or (--) indicate 99 percent confidence interval.

TABLE 6
PERCEIVED FREQUENCY OF BRIBERY AT SERVICE PROVIDER PUBLIC INSTITUTIONS

Personal characteristics							Characteristics of the firm		
Demographics				Attitudes					
Age	Position	Education	Work abroad	Trust people/ Trust business	Pro-freedom	Ready for concession to join EU	Number of employees	Sector	Geography
(--)		University and higher (++)		People (-)				Commerce (-) Transportation and communic- tion (-) Financial Institutions (-)	Small Western (--) Small Eastern (--) Big Eastern (-)

Note: (+) or (-) indicate a 95 percent confidence interval; (++) or (--) indicate 99 percent confidence interval.

TABLE 7

TOTAL NUMBER OF ILLEGAL PAYMENTS MADE TO PUBLIC INSTITUTIONS

Personal characteristics							Characteristics of the firm		
Demographics				Attitudes					
Age	Position	Education	Work abroad	Trust people/ Trust business	Pro-freedom	Ready for concession to join EU	Number of employees	Sector	Geography
(--)	Owner (++) Partner (++) CEO (+)	University and higher (++)	(++)	People (--)			(++)		Small Western (--) Small Eastern (--)

Note: (+) or (-) indicate a 95 percent confidence interval; (++) or (--) indicate 99 percent confidence interval.

TABLE 8

IMPARTIALITY IN THE EVALUATION OF CREDIT APPLICATIONS TO PUBLIC BANKS

Personal characteristics							Characteristics of the firm		
Demographics				Attitudes					
Age	Position	Education	Work abroad	Trust people/ Trust business	Pro-freedom	Ready for concession to join EU	Number of employees	Sector	Geography
	Owner (-) CEO (-)			Business (++)				Construction (+) Commerce (++) Financial Institutions (++)	Big Eastern (++)

Note: (+) or (-) indicate a 95 percent confidence interval; (++) or (--) indicate 99 percent confidence interval.

Empirical results indicated that the more trusting people tend to be less inclined to get involved in immoral and corrupt behavior. Equally importantly, those who trust more tend to perceive that the existing corruption in their societies is declining, thus providing a rational basis for being more trusting. However, when people are losing their trust in people who are unlike them (be they from the general public or the business community), they perceive corruption to be widespread and thus feel less bound by moral obligations to stay away from corruption. As such, they also tend to be more open to corrupt activity.

Furthermore, corruption leads to a depletion of funds for the creation of public goods, which in turn leads to unsatisfactory performance expectations from the government. These disappointed popular demands indicate a government that has fallen behind in its performance in redistributing resources from rich to poor as well as achieving economic growth. As popular dissatisfaction with government performance grows, governmental legitimacy becomes eroded and the credibility of its policy stands no longer exists. In such contexts, a government's ability to effectively follow policies to counteract the impact of economic crises declines. In such a vicious cycle, all relevant factors seem to feed into one another. A lack of trust leads to expansion of corruption, which in turn leads to economic crises by depleting public funds for use in an ineffective way within corrupt deals. Economic crises deplete economic sources for better policy performance, which in turn reduces trust in government to do the right thing. Eventually, governments fail to even protect property rights and to secure the basic provision of public goods, which leads to the creation of a suitable environment in which one relies on corruption to fulfill one's needs and expectations. If public goods cannot be produced and redistributive polices cannot be followed at a satisfactory level, no real tools are left in the hands of the government to counteract the economic crises. Economic crises thus take over, and they lead to a resumption of the cycle of depleting trust.

Our analysis has taken trust as exogenous in the analyses above. An analysis of the determinants of trust is left outside the boundary of our current study. However, we take it for granted that trust, as a moral value, can only change in the long term. If trust in generic or the more domain-specific trust in the fellow business community is low, then expectations of corruptive activity grow, as a result of which openness to corruption is bound to increase.

Our above analyses established that as people-to-people (generic) trust increases, the perceived degree of intensity of corruption in public institutions, the perceived frequency of bribery, and actual illegal payments made to public institutions tend to decline (after controlling for various demographic and attitudinal variables). What is most striking here is the observation that trust in fellow businessmen is also included as a control variable for these analyses. In other words, when it comes to evaluating the performance of the general system of public administration, the domain-specific trust in fellow businessmen does not have a distinct impact. Rather, it is the generic trust in fellow citizens that shapes the evaluations of our interviewed business people concerning the intensity of corruption at public institutions and their perception of the ubiquity of bribery at service provider public institutions as well as the total number of illegal payments made by the business people to public institutions. When, however, the business people are asked to appraise impartiality in the evaluation of credit applications to public banks, we observe that domain-specific trust in the fellow business community—rather than the generic trust in fellow citizens—becomes significant. In other words, when it comes to evaluating the performance of a specific action that would have an impact on the business community, generic trust in fellow citizens is not considered to be impactive.

An important implication of this finding is that system-wide evaluations are shaped by generic trust rather than domain-specific trust in the business community, despite the fact that implied or inherent in all these evaluations is a business activity. The policy relevance of this finding is also not to be underestimated. Despite intense competition and the related difficulty of enlarging the trust base among members of the business community, their evaluations of the overall system depends on their own generic trust in fellow citizens and is unaffected by the degree of competition in their respective sectors or lack thereof—which may be quite hard to create, especially during times of crisis. On a more somber note, the relevance of trust in shaping performance evaluations of the public institutions may limit the effectiveness of any anti-corruption strategy. Since generic trust is expected to be more of a function of long-term change in cultural values, it is quite unlikely to be influenced by the policies that may be pursued in an anti-corruption campaign.

Divergent cultural traits are also evident in some of our analyses (see Tables 5 through 8). For example, attitudes in support of EU membership as well as in support of democratic freedoms are significant in shaping the perceived intensity of corruption in public institutions. However, in no other equation do we observe such an impact on the evaluations.

A potential cultural impact might also be inferred from the differing answers of the respondents in each separate geographical sector. Across different regions of the country, the evaluations of the business community concerning the intensity of corruption, the frequency of bribery, and the actual practice of such acts do vary. Since these impacts are all included as fixed effects of geographic differentiation we cannot attribute them to any specific factor other than geography, which in and of itself is not an interesting variable. Geographic differences might be due to prevalent cultural differentiation across regions. However, they may also be due to contextual differences that are attributable to socio-economic variation, as well as market and state capacity differences across regions. These geographic differences should also be taken into account in the design of an anti-corruption policy. Our results indicate that perceptions in the largest metropolitan provinces are consistently worse than in the rest of the country when it comes to evaluating the performance of public institutions. In smaller western Anatolian provinces or in the East, for example, these evaluations are relatively more optimistic and thus could be easier to influence through a well-designed anti-corruption program. Similarly, we identified sectoral variation in these evaluations, which indicate that a sector-specific anti-corruption strategy will have a positive impact on the perceived effectiveness of the policies pursued.

Education is also diagnosed as playing a role in explaining various dimensions of corruption. More educated people are likely to perceive a higher corruptive intensity but they themselves or their firms also tend to have given more bribes, giving rise to speculation that the perception and attitudes of educated people *vis-à-vis* corruption exacerbate each other. Other parameters, both pertaining to respondent's characteristics—such as age, working abroad, position in the firm—and to firms' employee numbers—seem to affect corruption.

Taken as a whole, then, our analyses suggest that persistent economic crises might have a significant basis in the cultural traits of the societies within which they take shape. Lack of generic trust in unknown others by fellow citizens may simply be feeding the perception of widespread corruption, which in turns helps to justify the tendency to take part in corrupt activities. As a result, economic crises may have a long-term cultural basis in the form of the depleted level of social capital at the time crises hit countries. Obviously, as crises deepen the lack of trust among fellow citizens towards institutions, it becomes a much more difficult task to deal with. Further studies are thus needed to clarify the determinants of generic and domain-specific trust and the extent to which policy initiatives are effective in instilling trust among the target populations. Such studies are also expected to be context-dependent in the sense that they are largely shaped by the economic conditions prevalent at the time of the study. Thus, observations across different time periods would also prove to be effective in discerning the stability of the results obtained over time.

NOTES

The authors would like to thank Ziya Öniş and participants in the seminar at Koç University for helpful comments and criticisms on an earlier version of this study. The authors are also grateful to Burcu Eyigüngör and Tuğçe Bulut for their able assistance.

1. See, among others, Şaban Arslan, *Hortum ve Cinnet* [Syphoning and Insanity] (Istanbul: Om Publications, 2001); Nedim Şener, *Tepeden Tırnağa Yolsuzluk* [Corruption from Top Down] (Istanbul: Metis Publications, 2001); Nedim Şener, *Naylon Holding* [Nylon Holding] (Istanbul: Om Publications, 2002); Serkan Seymen, *Amiral Battı: Sabah Grubunun Öyküsü* [The Admiral has Sunk: The Story of Sabah Group] (Istanbul: Metis Publications, 2001); Ferhat Ünlü, *Sadettin Tantan, Bir Savaş Öyküsü* [Sadettin Tantan, A War Story] (Istanbul: Metis Publications, 2001). The above illustrate in detail how corruption of many different kinds and in many different sectors has led to the collapse of the financial sector in the latest economic crisis.

2. For a detailed exposition, see Susan Rose-Ackerman, *Corruption: A Study in Political Economy* (New York: Academy Press, 1978); Susan Rose-Ackerman, *Corruption and Government: Causes, Consequences and Reform* (Cambridge: Cambridge University Press, 1999). For a review of the literature, see also Arnold J. Heidenheimer, Johnston Michale, and Victor T. LeVine, *Political Corruption: A Handbook* (New Brunswick, NJ: Transaction Publishers, 1989); Salvatore Schiavo-Campo (ed.), *Governance, Corruption and Public Financial Management* (Manila: Asian Development Bank, 1999); Robert Klitgaard, Ronald Maclean-Abaroa, and Lindsey H. Parris, *Corrupt Cities: A Practical Guide to Cure and Prevention* (Washington DC: ICS Press, 2000); Organization for Economic Cooperation and Development (OECD), *No Longer Business as Usual, Fighting Bribery and Corruption* (Paris: OECD Publications, 2000). One can find a similar presentation on Turkey in: Fikret Adaman and Ali Çarkoğlu, *Türkiye'de Yerel ve Merkezi Yönetimlerde Hizmetlerden Tatmin, Patronaj İlişkileri ve Reform* [Satisfaction with Services, Patronage Relations and Reform in Local and Central Governments in Turkey] (Istanbul: TESEV Publications, 2000); Fikret Adaman, Ali Çarkoğlu and Burhan Şenatalar, *Hanehalkı Gözünden Türkiye'de Yolsuzluğun Nedenleri ve Önlenmesine İlişkin Öneriler* [Household View on the Causes of Corruption in Turkey and Suggested Preventive Measures] (Istanbul: TESEV Publications, 2001).

3. There is another dimension to this problem. Officials, whose low salaries do not reflect the power at their disposal, perform small favors for politicians, such as obtaining drivers' licenses or passports, speeding customs procedures, or securing entrance to elite schools. It is a way to repay the politicians who offered them their jobs, which they could not have secured without the political patronage network. Thus, they aim to reach at least a minimum level of material comfort through gifts and money received from this sector. Meanwhile, those outside the political sector are offered a choice: pay a bribe, or suffer through the grinding bureaucratic procedure.

4. See Anne O. Krueger, "Economists' Changing Perceptions of Government," *Weltwirtschaftliches Archive*, Vol.127 (1994), pp.417–31.

5. See Susan Rose-Ackerman, "Bribery," *The New Palgrave: A Dictionary of Economics* (London: Macmillan, 1987), pp.277–9.

6. In the eyes of the public, some instances of bribery and corruption are considered tolerable or "legitimate," while others are considered intolerable or "illegitimate." A household that, for some reason, does not receive a service to which it is entitled might consider the paying of a bribe in order to obtain this service to be "legitimate." For someone who believes that nothing will get done by complaining in a public sector totally devoid of transparency and supervision, the sense of conscientious responsibility over bribery will be relatively low.

7. If one desired to apply the concept of corruption to illegal situations only, the word "degeneration" could be used for the instances that we have named here under "corruption" in a wider sense.

8. For a detailed review, see Pranab Bardhan, "Corruption and Development," *Journal of Economic Literature*, Vol.35, No.3 (1997), pp.1320–46; Jagdish Bhagwati, "Directly-

Unproductive Profit-Seeking (DUP) Activities," *Journal of Political Economy*, Vol.90, No.5 (1982), pp.988–1002; Rose-Ackerman (1987); Krueger (1994); Eric Uslaner, "Trust and Corruption," Paper presented at 2002 Annual Meeting of the American Political Science Association, Boston, 2002[a].

9. See Vito Tanzi, "Corruption around the World: Causes, Consequences, Scope and Cures," *IMF Staff Papers*, Vol.45, No.4 (1998), pp.559–94.

10. See Diego Gambetta, *The Sicilian Mafia: The Business of Private Protection* (Cambridge, MA: Harvard University Press, 1993); Francis Fukuyama, *Trust: The Social Virtues and the Creation of Prosperity* (London: Penguin, 1995); Eric Uslaner, *Moral Foundations of Trust* (Cambridge: Cambridge University Press, 2002[b]); Uslaner (2002[a]); Michael Woolcock, "Social Capital and Economic Development: Toward a Theoretical Synthesis and Policy Framework," *Theory and Society*, Vol.27, No.2 (1998), pp.151–208; Adam B. Seligman, *The Problem of Trust* (Princeton, NJ: Princeton University Press, 1997).

11. See Rafael LaPorta, Florencio Lopes-Silanes, Andrei Schleifer, and Robert W. Vishney, "Trust in Large Organisations," *American Economic Review, Papers and Proceedings*, Vol.87, No.2 (1997), pp.333–8; Uslaner (2002[a]).

12. Apart from the present writers, Burhan Şenatalar was the third member of the team that conducted the survey entitled "Corruption: From the Business Perspective," the main results of which can be obtained at TESEV's website, <http://www.tesev.org.tr>.

13. One should expect a two-way relationship between trust and corruption, but our analysis in this study is unidirectional—from trust to corruption. As we shall discuss later in detail, we probed trust figures under two related but different indices: the first is the index developed by Putnam (see note 21), which aims to measure the intensity of trust or lack of it in fellow citizens; the second consists of a similar set of questions, but this time emphasizes trust towards business people. For corruption, we asked a set of questions that aim at measuring both the perception level of ongoing corruptive activities and the actual act of giving bribes.

14. Some parts of this section are based on Fikret Adaman and Meltem Daysal, "The Dark Side of Social Capital," unpublished mimeograph (2002).

15. See James Coleman, "Social Capital in the Creation of Human Capital," *American Journal of Sociology*, Vol.94, No.94 (1988), pp.S95–S120.

16. See James Coleman, *Foundations of Social Theory* (Cambridge, MA: Harvard University Press, 1990), p.302.

17. Ibid., pp.303–4.

18. Ibid., p.302.

19. Pierre Bourdieu, "The Forms of Capital," in John G. Richardson (eds.), *Handbook of Theory and Research for Sociology of Education* (New York: Greenwood Press, 1986), p.248.

20. Pierre Bourdieu, *Sociology in Question* (London: Sage Publications, 1993), p.33.

21. See Robert D. Putnam, with Robert Leonardi and Raffaella Y. Nanetti, *Making Democracy Work: Civic Traditions in Modern Italy* (Princeton, NJ: Princeton University Press, 1993); Robert D. Putnam, "Bowling Alone: America's Declining Social Capital," *Journal of Democracy*, Vol.6, No.1 (1995), pp.65–78.

22. See Putnam (1993), p.175.

23. Ibid., p.180.

24. Douglas North, *Institutions, Institutional Change and Economic Performance* (Cambridge: Cambridge University Press, 1990).

25. See Joe Wallis and Brian Dollery, "Government Failure, Social Capital and the Appropriateness of the New Zealand Model for Public Sector Reform in Developing Countries," *World Development*, Vol.29, No.2 (2001), p.249.

26. See Putnam (1993), p.172.

27. See Coleman (1990) via İsmail Serageldin and Christiaan Grootaert, "Defining Social Capital: An Integrating View," in Partha Dasgupta and Ismail Serageldin, *Social Capital: A Multifaceted Perspective* (Washington DC: World Bank, 2000), pp.40–58.

28. Serageldin and Grootaert (2000), pp.40–58.

29. Mark E. Warren, "Social Capital and Corruption," unpublished mimeograph (2002).

30. As we underlined in note 1, precisely such a detrimental impact of corruption on the Turkish economy is well documented.

31. The Survey Research Center's exact wording was: "Generally speaking, would you say that most people can be trusted or that you can't be too careful in dealing with people?" See Survey Research Center, *1964 Election Study* (Ann Arbor, MI: Inter-University Consortium for Political Research, University of Michigan, 1969). The second half of the wording was changed in Turkey since a verbatim translation sounded awkward and did not convey the dichotomous sense we wanted to capture.
32. Nancy Burns and Donald Kinder, "Social Trust and Democratic Politics," report to National Election Studies Board Based on the 2000 NES Special Topic Pilot Study, 2000.
33. A description and detailed elaboration of these parameters can be found in Fikret Adaman, Ali Çarkoğlu, and Burhan Şenatalar, *İş Dünyası Gözünden Türkiye'de Yolsuzluğun Nedenleri ve Önlenmesine İlişkin Öneriler* [Business Community View on the Causes of Corruption in Turkey and Suggested Preventive Measures] (Istanbul: TESEV Publications, 2003).
34. Detailed results, as well as the econometric techniques used, are not presented here for reasons of space. Readers may acquire these from the authors.

Towards a Sustainable Debt Burden: Challenges Facing Turkey at the Turn of the New Millennium

O. CEVDET AKCAY and C. EMRE ALPER

Following the failure of the disinflation program initiated in December 1999, Turkey embarked on yet another disinflation program in May 2001, albeit in a radically different environment. In May, the fragility of the financial sector was drastically higher following two interest rate shocks and the consequent devaluation of February 2001.[1] The market participants were also sensitive about the exchange rate regime switch to a free float with virtually no anchor.[2] Besides the fragility of the financial sector and the uncertainty concerning the exchange rates, another issue of concern was Turkey's short- to medium-term debt financing position. In the post-crisis environment, which is characterized by political uncertainty and risks, researchers have been paying particular attention to this issue. Indeed, it is an ongoing consensus that the long-term debt sustainability issue in a low inflation program depends crucially on three factors, which are not necessarily mutually exclusive: 1) consecutive governments that are committed to fiscal discipline; 2) strong real economic growth; 3) lower real interest rates on government securities and lower depreciation rate of the Turkish lira (TL).

According to the International Monetary Fund's (IMF) Staff Report of July 2002, Turkey's net public sector debt to gross national product (GNP) ratio stood at 93.3 percent at the end of 2001. Such a high figure for this ratio—albeit higher that the Maastricht criterion of a 60 percent ceiling value—does not necessarily imply an unsustainable debt financing position, since developed countries such as Belgium, Italy, and Japan display even higher debt/GNP ratios. What is alarming about Turkey's figure is that it stood at 43.7 percent at the end of 1998. In addition, one other issue of concern is the length of the average maturity of the public sector debt, which is very short.[3] The upward trend in the debt/GNP ratio as well as the maturity problem is not a policy choice. In fact, these observations highlight the market participants' reluctance to credit the public sector for longer periods at lower real rates given the political uncertainty and risks as well as the level of the debt/GNP ratio. Figure 1 demonstrates the inverse relationship between the maturity in days and the realized real interest rates on the auctioned government securities since 1990.

In the highly volatile markets of the post-globalization era, debt sustainability emerges as the ultimate criterion for countries that wish to belong in the "fit for investment" class of emerging countries. In contrast, those countries that experience rollover risks see foreign investors flee their markets within 24 hours. Those that do not suffer from such very short-term risks but are exposed to a medium-term insolvency experience, hike up their borrowing costs and predominantly lose access to international markets. Moreover, the multiple equilibria nature of these economies renders them extremely vulnerable to changes in market sentiment, which feeds on medium- to long-term debt financing concerns.[4]

One needs to be aware of the fine line that distinguishes mathematically verifiable unsustainable debt-financing positions from potentially unsustainable positions that could become victims of a self-

FIGURE 1

TURKEY'S AVERAGE *EX-POST* REAL INTEREST RATE
AND MATURITY PRIMARY MARKET AUCTIONS, 1989–2001

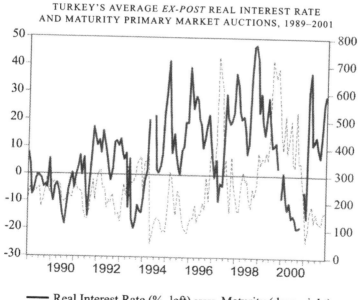

—— Real Interest Rate (%, left) ----- Maturity (days, right)

Source: Türkiye Cumhuriyet Merkez Bankası [Central Bank of Turkey] and the authors' own calculations.

fulfilling prophecy. The first case necessitates proper policy changes with very strong signaling effects; this is a necessary—but not always sufficient—condition for restoration of debt sustainability. It may, though, be a case of "too little, too late," and defaulting on debt might be the only option left for the country. In less serious versions of the first case, a drastic policy change is the only remedy. The implementation of credible policies that involve not only current but also inter-temporal signaling usually ameliorates market dynamics and the market sentiment regarding sustainability then initiates a virtuous circle—but persistence takes care of the rest.

Our conjecture is that Turkey came to a point by 2000 where the above requisite of policy changes decisively imposed itself. With the implementation of the 1999 IMF-sponsored stabilization program, the policy change did indeed come about. The current situation, though, corresponds more or less with the second case, whereby debt sustainability could fall prey to a self-fulfilling prophecy. Due to the February 2001 devaluation, the previous government (1999–2002) paid a very high price for not adhering to the structural reform aspect of the program; the ensuing fiscal tightening and discipline is still evident today. Given that the required shift in fiscal policy was implemented—accompanied by a number of complementary structural reforms (the most important of which is the banking sector reform)—an ever-increasing public debt/GDP ratio could still prevail if other main determinants of sustainability displayed lackluster performances.

This, however, does not seem to be the current outlook in Turkey—even in the face of the political turmoil that erupted in May 2002 and the still-prevalent uncertainty that held the market captive until the November 2002 elections. Fiscal signaling has been forceful, it seems that growth will exceed the targeted three-percent level by a substantial margin, the TL is expected to appreciate in real terms by the end of the year, and—contrary to many people's beliefs—the annual *ex ante* real interest rate is below the threshold value assumed by the IMF program for 2002.

This snapshot of the economy does suggest current sustainability, but it goes without saying that sustainability is an inter-temporal issue *per se*, and mostly a perception problem. The future course of debt dynamic determinants has been disturbing analysts and market participants, namely in the form of the real cost of borrowing, growth rate, non-interest primary surplus, and the exchange rate. These aspects are regarded as susceptible to a number of adverse developments on the political front and vulnerable to a lack of resolution on the part of prospective governments—which would prevent policy implementation. Such concerns, unless eliminated by proper signaling, are potentially destabilizing and are capable of triggering a vicious circle that ultimately could culminate in an increasing public debt/GNP ratio.

Nonetheless, a correction has been achieved in the Turkish economy— not one completed as yet, and not far-reaching enough at this stage to ensure unequivocal solvency in the future, but forceful enough to implicate a strong shift in policy. Central Bank independence law, public borrowing law, public procurement law, and other such laws are revolutionary steps in the economic history of the Turkish Republic and do correspond to a strong shift in public and fiscal policy. The reforms are not completed, but forceful implementation of these laws and the enactment of expenditure and tax reforms will ultimately render the debt dynamics unquestionably sustainable for good. We argue that—notwithstanding the inherent fragility that is bound to persist for some time to come—debt dynamics in Turkey have taken a turn for the better despite the surge in the debt/GDP ratio in 2001 stemming from the state banks' operations. The risks must be assessed as properly and precisely as possible, but sentiment shifts in both directions *should* be commensurate with the direction and forcefulness of policy changes.

Macroeconomic effects of budget deficits, deficit financing, and the consequent debt dynamics have enjoyed substantial attention in macro theory recently, particularly following the recent financial crises experienced by developing countries.[5] The link between political stability, sound fiscal policy, and macroeconomic stability—and consequently to sustainable growth—is now fully recognized. Observers of the Turkish case include Anand and Wijnbergen and Metin, who analyzed the fiscal deficit and inflation relationship in the pre-1986 period when government borrowing from the market was not the major source of financing.[6] Two essays have examined the sustainability of the fiscal policy in Turkey during the post-1986 period: Özatay found that during the 1985–97 period fiscal policy was unsustainable and Akcay *et al.* discovered that the current fiscal outlook is not sustainable by using annual data for the period 1970–2000.[7] These findings should not be interpreted as indicating insolvency, but rather as emphasizing the necessity of a policy change towards fiscal austerity if insolvency is to be avoided in the medium to long term.

This contribution attempts to uncover the roots of the current vulnerable condition of the Turkish economy by analyzing the public sector budget constraint across time from a political economy perspective. Short-term projections on the debt/GNP ratio based on our analytical framework—as well as policy prescriptions—are provided. The discussion is organized as follows. We will first analyze the issues pertaining to understanding the government budget constraint from a political economy perspective. The analytical background to an understanding of the evolution of the debt burden will then be briefly presented. Next, the importance of three variables—domestic and foreign interest rate on public debt, the depreciation rate, and the growth rate of income on fiscal sustainability—will be highlighted. Then, past and present data on public sector balances will be used and simulations regarding the near-future developments of the public sector balances will be presented. Finally, conclusions are given.

THE POLITICAL ECONOMY OF THE GOVERNMENT BUDGET CONSTRAINT

Following the acute balance of payments crisis of the late 1970s, on January 24, 1980, a stabilization and liberalization program was initiated in Turkey. With this program, commercial policy shifted from an import-substitution to an export-led growth strategy. Key elements in this shift occurred as follows: Financial markets were gradually liberalized throughout the 1980s; in 1986, the primary market was opened and the sale of government securities through auctions at the Istanbul Stock Exchange was conducted for the first time; in August 1989, the capital account was liberalized; in January 1990 Turkish lira became fully convertible; finally, by the end of 1991, the secondary market for government securities (as well as the repo market) became fully operational.[8]

The availability of new financial instruments regarding the sources and uses of funds for the public sector has important political economy considerations. This section presents the one-period, inter-temporal government budget constraint and discusses the implications of various forms of financing.[9] We should warn the reader from the outset that there are two important shortcomings in this presentation. First, we shall assume that the public debt is a one-period debt, which means that heterogeneous maturity considerations are ignored. This assumption is taken in order to make the analysis more tractable (the definition of the "period" can be changed to justify the one-period maturity). The second shortcoming has to do with the absence of any unilateral transfers (such as grants and debt relief from international institutions) and privatization receipts from the analysis. At the end of the analysis we shall address these two issues, which may crucially change the implications of the model.

Using national income identities, the simple definition of the budget deficit of the consolidated public sector equals the sum of private sector savings less private sector investment expenditure and the current account deficit. The identity merely states the possibility of the crowding out of private investment in the face of a budget deficit increase in an open economy. A rise in the budget deficit leads to a reduction in private investment for given private savings and the current account deficit.[10] The impact of budget deficits on private investment is unequivocal, mostly with dire repercussions on output growth and further worsening of fiscal balances through reduced tax revenues.

The financing of the deficit can be accomplished through money printing, internal and/or external borrowing, and the use of the central bank's foreign exchange reserves. Each financing mechanism would entail different macroeconomic repercussions: money printing would be linked to inflation, the use of reserves with exchange rate movements and possible balance of payments crises, foreign borrowing with external debt crises, and internal borrowing with higher interest burden and with a potentially explosive public debt/GNP ratio.

The nominal one-period government budget constraint can be written as:

$$G_t - T_t = (M_t - M_{t-1}) + (B_t - (1 + i_{t-1})B_{t-1}) + s_t(B_t^* - (1 + i_{t-1}^*)B_{t-1}^*) \quad (1)$$

The left-hand side of the equation denotes the primary balance, which is the difference between the current nominal public sector expenditure, G_t, and the current nominal conventional tax revenues—such as the income and excise tax—of the public sector, T_t. When the left-hand side is positive, the public sector is said to be running a primary deficit. In other words, current conventional revenues are not enough to cover the current expenditure of the public sector.

The first parenthesis on the right-hand side of the equation gives the change in a money stock definition—such as the monetary base—and denotes the amount of primary deficit that is monetized. When conventional taxes are not sufficient to cover the expenditure, one option available for the authorities is to collect inflation tax, which can be thought of as an "unconventional" tax.

The second parenthesis gives the difference between the newly issued one-period public debt, B_t, and the debt service inherited from the previous period—that is, the nominal principal, B_{t-1}, plus the nominal interest payments, $i_{t-1}B_{t-1}$. The difference is called the "nominal net transfer."

The third parenthesis is similar to the second parenthesis, with one major difference. The terms in the second parenthesis are denominated in domestic currency, whereas the terms in the third parenthesis are denominated in foreign currency. Note that since all else is expressed in nominal domestic prices, the third parenthesis is pre-multiplied by the spot price of one foreign currency in terms of domestic currency, s_t, and hence converted into domestic prices. At this point, the reader should be aware of one important factor. In an environment of capital account openness, the denomination of government debt does not give any information regarding who holds the debt. In other words, the likelihood of a non-resident holding the public debt denominated in domestic currency and a resident holding public debt denominated in foreign currency is not necessarily negligible.

Algebraically, how the public sector primary deficit is financed is irrelevant, meaning whether the deficit is monetized, financed through net transfers denominated in domestic currency, or through transfers denominated in foreign currency makes no difference. However, in terms of political economy considerations, there is a major difference between the monetization of the deficit and financing through borrowing. The monetization of the deficit, as argued earlier, is essentially an inflation tax borne by the domestic money holders of the current generation, which is politically costly for the authorities.[11] On the other hand, financing the public deficit through borrowing transfers the cost of the deficit to future generations, who are unable to vote, and hence this option of financing is not going to entail a huge immediate political cost.

The authorities' decision can be simply stated thus: what is the share of the current primary deficit that should be borne by the current generation and future generations. The answer for a forward-looking authority lies in the composition of government spending. Indeed, if current government spending, G_t, is directed towards the current generation in terms of government consumption and transfers, then the share obtained by the current generation ought to be higher. On the other hand, if the composition of the government spending is such that it is mostly government investment that will be enjoyed by future generations, then shifting a portion of the burden to these generations may be justified. For a myopic authority, which cares only for the short-term political outcome, the solution to the problem is simple: government expenditure should be mostly in the form of government consumption and transfers, which will be enjoyed by the current generation or the voters, and the financing method should be in terms of borrowing, which will shift the burden on to future generations who are not present and cannot vote.

As mentioned previously, the composition of the debt—whether in terms of domestic or foreign currency—does not necessarily provide an important signal regarding whether it is residents or non-residents who are holding the debt in an environment of open capital accounts. However, in terms of political economy considerations, there is one major difference between borrowing in domestic and foreign currency: the importance of the movements on the spot exchange rate, s_t, for foreign currency-denominated debt. Under a floating exchange rate and high capital mobility environment, market agents can immediately punish imprudent behavior or policy mistakes by the authorities. Any capital outflow or relative loss of domestic currency will raise the relative cost of the foreign currency-denominated debt, since s_t increases immediately. Had the public debt been only in terms of the domestic currency or had there been a fixed exchange rate arrangement in effect, the punishment mechanism of the market would have been delayed. The reason for this is that the rise in the interest rates or the cost of a future devaluation and its snowball effect on the domestic debt would have taken a longer time. Hence, we may tentatively conclude that high capital account mobility cum floating exchange rate arrangement works as a market-disciplining mechanism over the political authority.

We may rearrange the equation and collect the interest payments on the left-hand side and thereby gain an insight:

$$PB_t + i_{t-1}B_{t-1} + s_t i_{t-1}^* B_{t-1}^* = \Delta M_t + \Delta B_t + s_t \Delta B_t^* \qquad (2)$$

The primary balance ($G_t - T_t$) plus the interest payments yields the public budget balance. The right-hand side of the equation gives the sources of funds needed to finance the public sector budget deficit: nominal monetization, nominal borrowing in terms of domestic currency, and borrowing in terms of foreign currency converted to current domestic prices.

THE DYNAMICS OF SUSTAINABLE DEBT FINANCING

The macroeconomic effects of budget deficits, their financing, and the ensuing debt dynamics have enjoyed substantial attention in macro theory recently, particularly in the light of the different growth performances displayed by developing countries.[12] The link between sound fiscal policies and macroeconomic stability and ultimately to sustainable growth is now fully recognized and the emerging markets segment of the world economy spares no effort in attempting to construct sustainable growth paths. The size of the budget deficit registered by a country and the means of financing it determine the debt dynamics and the fiscal constraints the country will be subject to in the medium to long term.

Unstable debt financing has dire implications for budgetary policy. When the public perceives the unsustainable nature of the current fiscal policy, it will relinquish its holdings of government debt and necessitate a change in policy. The intention of the governments should be to preempt this and conduct a change of policy before the holders of debt impose the change on them.

The Turkish government has been taking fairly drastic measures since the first half of 2001 following the devaluation in February of that year, but it still remains to be seen if and how these measures will lead to a change in the public's expectations, especially following the change of government after the November 2002 elections. An inference of unsustainability would shift the market sentiment drastically towards a pessimistic outlook and throw the economy into the disequilibrium it tried to avoid to begin with. The interest burden and the length of maturity are the key determinants for debt dynamics. In Turkey, the ratio of the interest payments to the total conventional tax revenue stood at 95 percent in the first eight months of 2002; the budget projections by the Ministry of Finance show that the ratio will stand at 81.5 percent by the end of 2003.

Intuitively, the sustainability of a given fiscal policy is determined by projections of the future path of debt/GNP ratio. It is ultimately the willingness and appetite of the creditors that will determine the sustainability of the ratio. This section will briefly discuss the issue of fiscal sustainability in an analytical framework.[13] Our aim is to use the one-period budget constraint and derive a relationship between the nominal interest rate, the exchange rate depreciation, and the nominal growth rate of the economy. If we divide each term in equation (2) by the nominal income, Y_t, and rearrange the equation, we obtain:

$$pb_t + i_{t-1}b_{t-1}\frac{Y_{t-1}}{Y_t} + i^*_{t-1}b^*_{t-1}\frac{s_t}{s_{t-1}}\frac{Y_{t-1}}{Y_t} = m_t - m_{t-1}\frac{Y_{t-1}}{Y_t} + b_t - b_{t-1}\frac{Y_{t-1}}{Y_t} + b^*_t - b^*_{t-1}\frac{s_t}{s_{t-1}}\frac{Y_{t-1}}{Y_t} \quad (3)$$

In equation 3, the lower-case letters (excluding the interest rate, i_t, and the exchange rate, s_t) denote the corresponding upper case nominal variables as a ratio of the nominal GNP, Y_t. We can simplify this equation by substituting the growth rate of nominal output, g_y, and the depreciation rate of the domestic currency, g_s. Rearranging equation 3 in this manner, we obtain:[14]

$$d_t + b_{t-1} \frac{i_{t-1} - g_y}{1 + g_y} + b_{t-1}^* \frac{i_{t-1}^* + g_s - g_y}{1 + g_y} = \Delta b_t + \Delta b_t^* \quad (4)$$

The right-hand side of the equation gives the sum of the change in the ratios of domestic debt to GNP and foreign currency debt to GNP expressed in foreign currency respectively. The left-hand side of the equation is the sum of three terms. The first term, d_t, denotes the current primary balance less the change in the money supply, scaled by income. In other words, if the primary balance is positive, it denotes the non-monetized portion of the primary deficit. The second term is the previous period's debt stock to income ratio multiplied by the nominal interest rate adjusted for the nominal output growth. Alternatively, this multiplicand can be interpreted as the real interest rate adjusted for the real output growth. The higher the multiplicand, the higher the interest burden of the domestic debt will be. We should point out that the multiplicand increases as the real interest rate goes up and the real output goes down.[15] The third and final term is the previous period's debt stock to income ratio expressed in foreign currency multiplied by the foreign interest plus the depreciation rate of the domestic currency adjusted by the nominal output growth. Similarly, the burden of the foreign-denominated debt rises as the foreign interest rate and the depreciation rate rises and the output growth rate falls. Within such a framework, the sustainability of the fiscal position will depend crucially on the evolution of the debt stock variables, which are the second and the third terms on the left-hand side of the equation. Intuitively, except for these two terms—which are two scaled stock variables—every other term is a flow variable.

To conclude, the sustainable fiscal financing will depend crucially upon the evolution of the public debt stock, which is affected by three factors: the domestic and foreign interest rate on the public debt, the output growth rate, and the depreciation rate of the domestic currency. Finally, we can observe that given the primary balance and the monetization, the lower the fiscal sustainability, the higher the interest rates, the higher the depreciation rate, and the lower the growth rate of income are. Within such a framework, politics matter because perceptions of imprudent political behavior or imprudent behavior by a politician will lead to actions by the market participants such as a capital outflow, which will manifest itself in the form of higher interest rates, higher depreciation rates, and lower economic growth.

THE CASE OF TURKEY

This section will focus on the case of Turkey as an illustration of the political economy of government budget constraint and the analytics of the debt dynamics issues described in the previous sections. First, we turn to the issue of an accurate measurement of the public sector budget balance. Due to the political economy mechanisms of rent distributions, as explained before, finding reliable and consistent time-series data on public sector balances in Turkey is a challenging task, an issue which has been taken up in great detail in a publication by the Turkish Audit Court.[16]

Three different definitions are used to measure the public sector balance. The narrow definition, incidentally, is called the "consolidated budget balance," which consists of the general government budget as well as the annexed institutions. During the 1980s, extra-budgetary funds and the local authorities gained prominence for distributing political rent. The broader definition is the "central budget balance," which includes everything in the consolidated budget balance and also the balances of the local authorities, revolving funds, social security institutions, extra-budgetary funds, and the State Economic Enterprises (SEEs) under privatization. Finally, the broadest definition, the Public Sector Borrowing Requirement (PSBR) includes the balances of central government, the SEEs, and the duty losses of the public banks.

The evolution of these balances as well as the interest payments from the consolidated budget as a percent of Turkey's GNP are presented in Table 1. The striking increase in the ratio of the interest payments, especially after the capital account liberalization of 1990, can be discerned very easily.[17] Furthermore, the consolidated budget balance in the latter half of the 1990s accounts for only half of the PSBR. Other than the difference in terms of the coverage, the major difference between the PSBR and the consolidated public sector balance is that the latter is available monthly but the former is only available annually and announced with a year lag. Findings by Akcay *et al.* suggest that the post-1970 inflationary process in Turkey is closely related to the PSBR and is independent of the evolution of the consolidated budget balance.[18] This is an unfortunate finding since the latter is widely available but does not seem to serve as a good indicator of the public balances.

In terms of debt sustainability and the current situation in Turkey, the following observations can be made. Proper analysis of debt sustainability in any fragile—hence presumably multiple equilibria economy—requires both an utterly positivist and impartial approach to numbers (that is, fundamentals), and a fairly non-quantifiable, sometimes biased (not

TABLE 1

PUBLIC SECTOR BORROWING REQUIREMENT AND ITS COMPONENTS, 1975–2001 (% OF GNP)

Years	Consolidated Balance	Interest Payments	Central Budget Balance	PSBR
1975	0.72	0.43	0.72	4.78
1976	1.15	0.46	1.27	6.80
1977	4.33	0.45	4.15	8.12
1978	1.52	0.49	1.64	3.22
1979	3.13	0.63	3.23	7.20
1980	3.13	0.58	3.92	8.77
1981	1.55	0.93	1.58	3.98
1982	1.48	0.82	1.58	3.52
1983	2.25	1.51	2.76	4.95
1984	4.42	1.99	3.49	5.39
1985	2.26	1.91	1.13	3.58
1986	2.76	2.60	1.07	3.65
1987	3.48	3.02	2.79	6.08
1988	3.09	3.85	2.66	4.83
1989	3.33	3.59	3.41	5.33
1990	3.01	3.52	3.60	7.41
1991	5.28	3.79	7.02	10.16
1992	4.30	3.65	7.28	10.57
1993	6.70	5.83	9.56	12.01
1994	3.91	7.67	6.48	7.89
1995	4.03	7.33	5.39	5.20
1996	8.27	10.00	9.47	8.95
1997	7.62	7.75	7.99	13.10
1998	6.96	11.54	7.71	15.40
1999	12.50	13.69	13.88	24.20
2000	10.93	16.27	10.25	19.60
2001	15.52	22.99	15.32	17.60

Sources: Türkiye Cumhuriyet Merkez Bankası [Central Bank of Turkey] and IMF Staff Report, No.02/137 (July 2002).

necessarily intentional) approach regarding the market sentiment, national mood, and the public's perception of future prospects for the economy— as unsustainable public debt financing can easily be a self-fulfilling prophecy. The vulnerability of such economies stems from the fact that when the sentiment of the investment community is negative, "fundamentals" fail to have an impact in a positive direction even if they are fairly sound, and the setting becomes very conducive for a self-fulfilling crisis. What the economy administrations must do under such tenuous equilibrium conditions is to convey persistently positive policy signals—usually ones pertaining to fiscal discipline, institutional framework, and structural reforms—and openly display ownership of implemented policies. When economic agents feel that they can comfortably confide in the resolute stance of the administration and its consistency (or rather, consistent competence), they will start revising their expectations about the future course of debt dynamics determinants, and the economy could fairly rapidly approach good equilibrium—largely eliminating concerns about deteriorating debt sustainability.

It should be stated at the outset that debt sustainability is ultimately a perception problem, but that the perception will heavily depend on the prevailing and prospective fundamentals of the economy. As stated in the previous sections, the real cost of borrowing (by proxy the real interest rate, though not necessarily the same thing), the growth rate of the economy, and the primary surplus are the classic critical indicators of debt sustainability. In the case of Turkey, the exchange rate might be the most important determinant of debt sustainability due to the large foreign currency component of the total public sector debt (see Figure 2). Any significant depreciation of the TL, *ceteris paribus*, will culminate in an unsustainable debt/GDP ratio due to the explosion in the foreign exchange-denominated and foreign exchange rate-linked debt service. With the numerator of the ratio surging in TL terms due to the depreciating TL and the denominator being in TL by definition—and hence intact in TL terms, the ratio could easily hit the roof and annul all efforts at stabilizing and maintaining the stability of the debt/GDP ratio.

Political turmoil at the end of May 2002 took its toll on the stability of the debt/GNP ratio, undoubtedly due to the surge in the cost of borrowing during the period of uncertainty. However, the final damage was fairly modest thanks to a number of positive developments regarding other debt

FIGURE 2
TOTAL PUBLIC SECTOR DEBT: COMPOSITION BY INSTRUMENT, AUGUST 2002

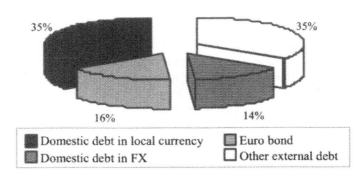

Source: Based on data available from Başbakanlık Hazine Müsteşarlığı [Undersecretariat of Treasury]. See <http://www.hazine.gov.tr>.

dynamics determinants. Limited damage on the real sector (stellar output performance in the second and presumably in the third quarter), extremely stable exchange rates following the surge in the initial phase of the political crisis, and a persistently strong primary surplus showing contributed significantly to damage control on the sustainability front. The surge in nominal interest rates from 54 percent in May 2002 to 80 percent during the climax of the political mayhem corresponded to a significant increase in the servicing of the debt, as inflation expectations virtually remained intact. In the immediate period following the November 2002 elections, there has a been a drastic decline in nominal rates, which is a positive development not only for the purpose of lower borrowing and rollover costs but also for signaling purposes. Whether these objectives can be fully achieved depends crucially on the market's perception of the new government.

The medium- to long-term debt-financing position still remains fragile but manageable thanks to the positive developments on all fronts, especially the drastic initial reduction in the real interest rate and the appreciation of the TL following the November 2002 general elections. The altered composition, ownership, and maturity of the public sector's debt stock throughout 2001 has enabled the Treasury to rollover the debt with relative ease, but during the infamous four months of political uncertainty and turmoil during May–July 2002 the Treasury had to give up its interest rate sensitivity and had to demonstrate its borrowing capability. That was achieved with little difficulty, but the stability of the debt/GDP ratio necessitates lower real cost of borrowing for indisputable sustainability in debt dynamics, and high real rates at some point will serve as an indicator—or even advertisement—of vulnerability and lead to accelerating dollarization. That is a situation to be avoided at all costs by the Treasury, which carries the bulk of the foreign exchange (FX) risk in the system. Although real interest rates are of utmost importance in debt sustainability analysis, one should always take into account the composition of the total public sector debt and the portion that these high real rates apply to (see Figure 2). Currently, that portion is around 37 percent of the total debt, and the appropriate figure for the real cost of borrowing is to be calculated using the weight of different borrowing instruments.

The floating rate notes (FRNs) will help immensely as disinflation continues and (if) real rates decline.[19] As the Treasury will be able to capitalize on these immediately, so will a TL that is appreciating in real terms, reducing the cost of borrowing for the foreign exchange-denominated and foreign exchange-linked portion of internal debt as well as the foreign debt. Bearing in mind that the program entails a fairly generous upward margin regarding *ex ante* average annual real interest rates (the figures in the selected economic indicators section of the original letter of intent for the three years of the program are 33.2 percent, 27.5 percent, and 20.5 percent respectively), there need not be any alarm bells ringing prematurely at this stage as the current *ex ante* real interest rates differ from the assumed figure in the program by an insignificant margin.[20] More importantly, convergence to pre-crisis levels is by no means a remote possibility depending on the post-election outlook, and real rates can come down as fast as they moved up—significantly improving debt-sustainability prospects. The insultingly high real rates on TL borrowing instruments stemmed from perceived political risks in the system, and elimination of these risks will render much more manageable debt dynamics. In this respect, the blow to debt dynamics came from the most exogenous of sources—namely politics—and is the most difficult to avoid and keep under control. Yet, once eliminated, a very rapid convergence to the pre-crisis situation could materialize with minimal economic re-enforcement. With other determinants of debt dynamics mostly in place, the argument outlined above pertaining to the swift possible response of real borrowing rates to an improved political outlook underlies our "workable case scenario." Needless to say, sustained political uncertainty and/or the lack of a resolute stance on policy implementation would be suicidal.

Composition, ownership, and maturity of the public sector's debt stock changed immensely over the course of 2001 (see Figures 2, 3, and 4), and

FIGURE 3
DOMESTIC DEBT STOCK: COMPOSITION BY HOLDERS, AUGUST 2002

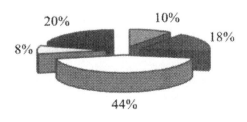

Source: Based on data available from Başbakanlık Hazine Müsteşarlığı [Undersecretariat of Treasury]. See <http://www.hazine.gov.tr>.

FIGURE 4

TOTAL PUBLIC SECTOR DEBT AS PERCENTAGE OF GNP

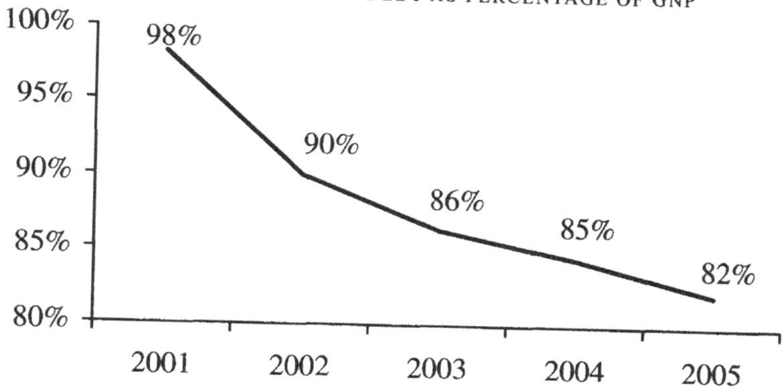

Source: Authors' own calculations.

the Treasury has had an easier task of rolling over the debt compared to the nearly insurmountable difficulties it had in 2001. Most importantly of all, Turkey had a very successful debt-swap in mid-June 2001, which was totally voluntary and mutually beneficial. TL-denominated bonds amounting to approximately $8 billion were swapped, and the banking system was given dollar-denominated bonds in return. The average maturity in the old bonds, which stood at around five months, was extended to more than 36 months in the newly issued ones, providing significant breathing room for the Treasury. The disadvantage is that the entire foreign currency risk is now borne by the Treasury, since the banking system was able to close its open positions with the swap and is hardly exposed to any significant foreign exchange risk at the moment. As mentioned previously, this puts debt dynamics at the mercy of the floating exchange rate, and any implementation slippage will be ticketed with a depreciating TL, which, in turn, will lead to deteriorating debt dynamics. The absence of significant foreign exposure in local markets (that is, foreign investors who could relinquish their TL positions and switch to hard currency) and of banks with open foreign exchange positions makes a rush towards foreign exchange fairly unlikely, providing some breathing space for debt management during trying times. Yet, the very same float will always remind the economic administration during better times that there is no room for complacency until an unequivocally sustainable and robust debt dynamics picture emerges.

Despite the inevitable hike in the debt/GDP ratio due both to the devaluation and the securitization of the duty losses of the state banks, significant achievements regarding debt management can be detected in the aftermath of the February 2001 crisis. The fixed rate component of the debt stock has been reduced drastically, the portion of internal debt to market debt has been halved, state institutions now shoulder a major portion of the debt burden, and the maturity of internal debt stock has been extended considerably. Risk premium theory clearly indicates that the cost imposed on the issuer of debt is positively linked to the percentage of the outstanding debt stock that is being held by the private sector. The greater the portion of the outstanding debt that is held by the public sector—with whom the rollovers will be less problematic by definition, the lower the perceived risk and hence the risk premium on government securities. Such a shift in debt composition by holder is precisely what took place in Turkey, and the market holds only around 45 percent of the total internal debt (see Figure 3 and Table 2) as the remainder is by the public sector and the Central Bank. It should also be noted that the Central Bank's net domestic claims on the Treasury (in other words, its government securities portfolio) is quite sizable. Interest claims constitute the bulk of the Central Bank profits, and these profits are regularly transferred to the Treasury every year, reducing the *ex post* cost of borrowing for the Treasury by a non-negligible margin.

However, due to the inevitable rise in the debt stock/GNP ratio in the aftermath of the recapitalization of state banks and banks under the Savings and Deposit Insurance Fund, while the percentage of debt stock in the hands of the market shrank, the mere size of the debt stock started to become more of a concern in the event of an untoward development which pushes up the servicing costs. In other words, the debt stock is not a problem *per se*, but becomes an overriding one once the servicing cost

TABLE 2

DOMESTIC DEBT STOCK BY HOLDERS (TL, TRILLION) AUGUST 2002

Public Total	76,523
Central Bank	27,999
Public Banks	24,098
SDIF	11,041
Other Public	13,384
Market	60,571
Total	137,093
GNP*	226,018

Note: * The annual GNP figure is for the period June 2001–June 2002.

Source: Başbakanlık Hazine Müsteşarlığı [Undersecretariat of Treasury]. See <http://www. hazine.gov.tr>.

increases dramatically. It should be emphasized that Turkey's problem is mostly a flow problem due to high servicing costs, notwithstanding the extra pressure that the sheer size of the debt itself can exert on the real cost of borrowing and thus on the flow aspect of the problem when risk perception goes sour.

While the change in owner composition enables the Treasury to enjoy a relatively easier time in rolling over its debt, the change in instrument composition facilitates lower borrowing costs in an environment of lower inflation and lower real interest rates. Moreover, the shift to FRNs makes it easier for the Treasury to enjoy the benefits of a reduction in interest rates with minimum delay while the foreign exchange-denominated and foreign exchanged-linked borrowing contributes to the very same evolution of the debt/GNP ratio, provided that the cost of borrowing in terms of foreign currency remains below the cost of securities denominated in domestic currency. The prerequisite for the latter is the appreciation or minor depreciation of the TL in real terms against other currencies. In other words, when the TL appreciates in real terms against foreign currencies, the cost of borrowing on foreign exchange-denominated securities will be even lower in terms of TL. Analogously, when the TL depreciation is modest so will the very same cost in terms of TL, and debt dynamics drastically benefits from stability of the TL *vis-à-vis* other currencies in real terms.

All these have provided the Treasury with some additional ammunition and rendered debt rollovers less problematic under normal circumstances, but the ultimate diagnosis is nevertheless "high fragility." The very same changes could trigger a fast increase in the debt/GNP ratio under adverse conditions, and an analysis of prospective developments on this front is what follows next.

Figures 2–4 illustrate a number of important points pertaining to debt sustainability in Turkey. Some of these have been referred to in the preceding paragraphs, but a major element implicit in the figure deserves further emphasis. Of the public sector's total debt stock, only 35 percent of it is in local currency—which makes debt/GNP ratio very susceptible to exchange rate movements. This is not a "desired" state of affairs but merely the prerequisite of decent debt management in dire straits. Large-scale issuance of dollar-denominated bills instead of local currency bills is a blessing in disguise if you expect local currency not to lose value against foreign currencies, but significant depreciation of the local currency is arguably the perpetrator of insolvency in such a setting. The predicted future course of the real exchange rate is thus a most significant determinant of debt sustainability in the case of Turkey, and our forecasts

The Turkish Economy in Crisis

TABLE 3

WORKING ASSUMPTIONS FOR MEDIUM-TERM PUBLIC DEBT
FINANCING OUTLOOK (%)

	2001	2002	2003	2004	2005
Debt / GDP	98.2	90.0	86.3	84.6	82.2
Real Cost of Borrowing	16.0	14.7	9.6	9.2	8.5
Average Inflation	60.0	60.7	26.2	16.7	12.4
Growth	(7.4)	4.2	6.0	5.0	5.0
Primary Surplus / GDP	5.0	6.5	6.5	5.0	5.0

Source: Authors' own calculations.

indicate slight depreciation of the TL on a Wholesale Price Index basis and slight appreciation on a Consumer Price Index basis. Such differences, however, do not lead to any lack of robustness regarding the sustainability results.

Our working assumption concerning the real rates does not focus on an aggressive downward trajectory, but rather—as noted before—that the TL real rate component is only part of the picture. The overall real cost of borrowing will have to utilize a weighted average real cost, the weights being determined by the share of each instrument in the total public debt stock. These rates are calculated and given in Table 3. Our growth rate assumptions are mostly in line with the IMF's baseline projections for the years 2003 and 2004, and no slippages on the fiscal front are assumed during the remainder of the program. Primary surplus target is an inevitable anchor in the program, and both the growth dynamics and the prospects of success for Turkey's disinflation efforts crucially depend on the unyielding stance of the authorities on the fiscal front. A combination of poor fiscal performance, high real interest rates, low growth, and a depreciating TL is a recipe for disaster. Most importantly, fiscal slippages and inadequate fiscal signaling will inevitably lead to a deterioration in the other determinants and trigger a vicious circle. Shocks to the other determinants could take place, and these could be totally beyond the authorities' control. None of these shocks, however, will—in and of itself—have an impact on debt sustainability as much as a permanent divergence from fiscal targets. Adherence to fiscal targets will indeed reduce the impact of those shocks significantly and help preserve a sustainable path for public debt over the medium and long term.

Using the "centered GDP" approach in order to avoid the exaggeration of the increased debt stock/GDP ratio in 2001,[21] we construct a "working case scenario" that simulates Turkey's debt/GDP path until 2005. Under fairly conservative assumptions regarding the cost of borrowing within the simulation period and conjecturing successful disinflation (with all its by-products, such as respectable growth and non-explosive exchange rate path), Turkey's debt dynamics are indeed fragile but, ultimately, manageable. To claim the opposite without concrete analytical support is merely to initiate the self-fulfilling prophecy feature of debt dynamics. To be aware of the inherent risks is one thing, but to assess the *status quo* with a positivist approach taking into account these risks is another.

There was a desperate need for a regime shift on the fiscal front when the first stabilization program failed in February 2001, and a regime shift seems to be exactly what took place in the last two years. Admittedly, it was a somewhat half-hearted—perhaps even a reluctant—switch, but a switch nevertheless. It needs to be sustained without any compromises and backed up by other structural measures; the transition to a sustainable growth path can then be made with the minimum possible cost in terms of output. Any other route is bound to prove to be excessively costly (monetization, for example, will be excessively costly because of the composition of public debt stock, as illustrated before, or forced debt restructuring due to loss of credibility and difficulties in tapping local and external markets in the next round, and also due to problems concerning the banking sector's balance sheets).

CONCLUSIONS

Following the capital account liberalization of August 1989, the Turkish economy has been subjected to three financial crises: April 1994, November 2000, and February 2001. Currently, due to the combined influence of ongoing political instability, a vulnerable banking sector, and a heavily indebted public sector, the Turkish economy is as prone to financial crisis as ever. This contribution attempted to highlight the causes of the current situation through an analysis of government budget constraint from a political economics perspective. Different forms of deficit financing and the influence of political concerns have been analyzed. We stressed the perverse outcome within the framework of myopic voters, where current deficits are mostly directed for the benefit of the current generation and the burden of these deficits are transferred to future generations through borrowing.

We also underlined the importance of a proper definition of the "fiscal deficit," and that this should also take into account all rent distribution mechanisms, including the balances of extra budgetary funds, state economic enterprises, and the duty losses of the public banks. The weak relation of inflation with the consolidated budget balance, which is the narrow definition of public sector balance, and the strong relation of the inflation with the public sector borrowing requirement, which is a broader definition, highlights the importance of the proper definition to the case of Turkey.

We also established a framework for assessing the medium-term outlook on the fiscal debt burden. In particular, we show that in the absence of privatization and unilateral transfers, debt sustainability crucially depends on the behavior of three variables: the interest rate, the depreciation rate of the domestic currency, and the growth rate. A stable debt/GNP ratio requires a lower domestic and foreign interest rate on the government securities followed by a lower depreciation rate of the domestic currency and a higher growth rate are needed. We argue that political uncertainty worsens medium-term debt sustainability through adversely affecting these three variables. We conclude that borrowing is not a preferred option to finance public deficits in the absence of political stability since this type of financing will adversely affect the future prospects of an economy through causing an increase in the public debt/GNP ratio.

Our working case scenario implies that, with the fiscal regime shift intact and fiscal discipline sustained, Turkey's debt dynamics remain fragile yet manageable. One should bear in mind that while debt dynamics are fairly robust when faced with certain shocks to debt dynamics determinants, there are combinations of shocks that could prove to be extremely dangerous; fatal ones will definitely have fiscal slippages as their key ingredient.

Turkey is a text-book case in untimely liberalization, especially that of the capital account, and very clearly elucidates the misuse, or even abuse, of the borrowing flexibility allowed by the liberalization of the capital account. The current fragile structure of the Turkish economy as well as the ongoing importance of the public debt financing issue on the market and political agenda were rooted in the financing switch of fiscal deficits in 1986 and the capital account liberalization of 1989. With fiscal discipline almost totally non-existent when financial and capital account liberalization were initiated, it became more and more difficult to settle the public sector balances and come up with a non-explosive public sector debt/GDP ratio. Until 2001, the public sector outside central government remained in total disarray and their financing was done through roundabout methods and non-budgetary means. The "true" deficit indicators were overlooked and the "true" debt/GDP ratio did not surface until 2001, when the bold move to register and securitize all hidden losses (duty losses) finally came. All of the factors mentioned above culminated in unsustainable debt dynamics as we illustrated in the main body of the text, and a call was made for a radical fiscal regime shift. With that shift in effect since 2001, there is now a way out of this mess in a fairly fragile setting, but policies leading to that end should be pursued persistently. Options are very limited, stakes are very high, and there is no room for complacency, easy fixes, or cosmetic measures.

NOTES

The authors would like to thank Ziya Öniş for his helpful comments and suggestions.

1. These rates occurred during the Nov. 2000 and Feb. 2001 crises. See C. Emre Alper, "The Liquidity Crisis of 2000: What Went Wrong," *Russian and East European Finance and Trade*, Vol.37, No.6 (2001), pp.54–75.
2. Under the stabilization program of Dec. 9, 1999, the exchange rate was used as a nominal anchor to reduce the inflation rate during the Jan. 2000–Feb. 2001 period. For an extensive review of the issue of the exchange rate regime choice for Turkey, see C. Emre Alper and Kamil Yılmaz, "Domestic Needs for Foreign Finance and Exchange Rate Regime Choice in Developing Countries, with Special Reference to the Turkish Experience," pp.67–91 of this volume.
3. As of Aug. 2002 the domestic debt stock of the public sector in cash basis, which constitutes 56.2 percent of the domestic debt stock of the public sector, has an average maturity of 14.3 "months." Comparable figures are expressed in "years" for developed countries.
4. Economies subject to multiple equilibria are heavily influenced by the changing sentiment of the market. With no discernible change in their economic fundamentals, such economies can be oscillating between the good and the bad equilibria solely because of agents' changing sentiment and expectations, which mostly stem from anticipated policy changes or perceived lack of resolution on the part of economy administrations.
5. For a discussion of these issues for developing countries, see William Easterly, "Growth Implosions and Debt Explosions: Do Growth Slowdowns Cause Public Debt Crises?," *Contributions to Macroeconomics*, Vol.1, No.1 (2001), pp.1–23; John T. Cuddington, "Analyzing the Sustainability of Fiscal Deficits in Developing Countries," *World Bank Policy Research Working Paper*, No.1784 (1997), pp.1–47. For developed countries, see Merih Uçtum and Martin Wickens, "Debts and Deficit Ceilings, Sustainability of Fiscal Policies: An Intertemporal Analysis," *Oxford Bulletin of Economics and Statistics*, Vol.62, No.2 (2001), pp.197–221.
6. See Ritu Anand and Sweder Van Wijnbergen, "Inflation and the Financing of Government Expenditure: An Introductory Analysis with an Application to Turkey," *World Bank Economic Review*, Vol.3, No.1 (1989), pp.17–38; Kıvılcım Metin, "The Relationship between Inflation and Budget Deficit in Turkey," *Journal of Business and Economic Statistics*, Vol.16, No.4 (1998), pp.412–21.
7. See Fatih Özatay, "The 1994 Currency Crisis in Turkey," *Journal of Policy Reform*, Vol.3, No.4 (2000), pp.327–52; O. Cevdet Akçay, C.E. Alper, and Süleyman Özmucur, "Budget Deficit, Inflation, and Debt Sustainability: Evidence from Turkey (1970–2000)," in Aykut Kibritçioğlu, Libby Rittenberg, and Faruk Selçuk (eds.), *Inflation and Disinflation in Turkey* (Aldershot: Ashgate, 2002), pp.77–96.
8. For a review of these developments, among others, see Ahmet Ertuğrul and Faruk Selçuk, "A Brief Account of the Turkish Economy: 1980–2000," *Russian and East European Finance and Trade*, Vol.37, No.6 (2001), pp.6–30; C. Emre Alper and Ziya Öniş, "Soft Budget Constraints, Government Ownership of Banks and Regulatory Failure: The Political Economy of the Turkish Banking System in the Post-Capital Account Liberalization Era," *Boğaziçi University Working Paper*, ISS/EC 02-02 (2002); C. Emre Alper and Ziya Öniş, "Financial Globalization, the Democratic Deficit and Recurrent Crises in Emerging Markets: the Turkish Experience in the Aftermath of Capital Account Liberalization," *Emerging Markets Finance and Trade*, Vol.39, No.3 (2003), pp.5–26.

9. For an elaboration on these issues, see Paul J. Miller, "Higher Deficit Policies Lead to Higher Inflation," *Federal Reserve Bank of Minneapolis Quarterly Review*, Vol.7, No.1 (1983), pp.8–19; William Easterly and Stanley Fischer, "The Economics of the Government Budget Constraint," *World Bank Research Observer*, Vol.5, No.2 (1990), pp.127–42.

10. A rise in the budget deficit could alternatively lead to deterioration in the current account with private investment staying intact. However, in this case the link is a bit ambiguous as the monetary policy accompanying the fiscal expansion becomes crucial. If monetary policy is "contractionary," it increases the interest rate and pushes up the exchange rate, leading to a depreciation of the currency. This depreciation, in turn, improves the current account balance rather than worsening it along with the higher budget deficit.

11. See Thomas Sargent and Neil Wallace, "Some Unpleasant Monetarist Arithmetic," *Federal Reserve Bank of Minneapolis Quarterly Review*, Vol.5, No.3 (Fall 1981), pp.1–17. Sargent and Wallace point to a "seemingly" perverse situation in which tighter monetary policy (implying fiscal deficit financing through borrowing) may actually lead to an increase in the current inflation rate under certain assumptions.

12. See Easterly (2001), pp.1–23.

13. The analysis will be based on Akçay *et al.* (2002), pp.77–96, and Uçtum and Wickens (2001), pp.197–221.

14. Excluding the foreign currency-denominated bond and the exchange rate variables, the derivation is available in Akçay *et al.* (2002), pp.82–3.

15. For the recent cross-country evidence on the relation between growth and public deficits, see Easterly (2001), pp.1–23.

16. Turkish Audit Court, *Year 2000 Fiscal Report*. The report can be accessed (in Turkish) at <http://www.sayistay.gov.tr/rapor/DIGER/2000malirapor.pdf>.

17. For a detailed analysis of fiscal and political developments in the post-capital account liberalization era, see Alper and Öniş (2003).

18. See Akçay *et al.* (2002), p.88

19. Floating rate notes (FRNs) are borrowing instruments which the Treasury uses. In that respect they are similar to discount bonds but, unlike discount bonds—which have fixed rates of return at maturity, FRNs have changing rates and quarterly coupon payments. The payment for each coupon is decided by a reference auction prior to the payment, and market sentiment largely determines the rate of return in these auctions like in any other auction. When an improving market sentiment is in effect, the Treasury can easily capitalize on it and borrow at successively lower rates, and, naturally, exactly the opposite holds when things turn sour.

20. *Ex ante* real interest rate is the expected real interest rate given the current nominal interest rate and expected inflation. More formally, $r = (1 + i)/(1 + e) - 1$, where r is the *ex ante* real interest rate, i is the nominal interest rate, and e is expected inflation.

21. As devaluation and the ensuing rapid depreciation of the currency explodes the FX component of the debt stock and reduces the GDP in real terms at the same time, changes in both the numerator and the denominator of the debt stock/GDP ratio will exert an upward pressure on the ratio. The GDP response and offsetting appreciation of the local currency comes with a lag, and—to avoid the excessive fluctuation in numbers—GDP for any given year is defined with a certain delay, hence part of the following year is included in the current year's GDP. In this case, the delay was chosen as two quarters.

8

The Turkish Banking Sector Two Years after the Crisis: A Snapshot of the Sector and Current Risks

O. CEVDET AKCAY

Turkish banks have been "banking on the government," in other words, lending to the government sometimes at offensively high rates for more than a decade—since 1986 to be precise—and have exposed themselves to significant foreign exchange (FX), interest rate, and asset quality risks in the process. The infamous 2001 crisis indeed stemmed mostly from the fragility of the banking sector, which was not dealt with promptly. The crisis that culminated in the abandonment of the fixed exchange rate regime led to further weakening of the sector through the exchange rate increase and the tarnished equity base. The Banking Sector Reform Act that followed, constructed under the guidance of the Banking Regulatory and Supervisory Agency (BRSA), did ameliorate the situation: the sector is currently much more transparent, and considerably healthier. The structural transformation of the sector, however, is far from over, and cannot actually be completed before transformation in the public sector is complete and the borrowing need of the Treasury is substantially reduced. This contribution aims to describe the situation of the sector before and after the 2001 crisis, and, more importantly, to emphasize the current risks the system still faces two years after the crisis. There seem to be no "quick fixes:" a resolute stance on the part of the government regarding fiscal balances and reduced borrowing needs are perhaps the only way out. Signs of recovery in that direction will lead to increased confidence and improving market sentiment, which will also make it easier for banks to bolster proper banking and financial intermediation.

THE REGULATORY FRAMEWORK AND A BRIEF DESCRIPTION OF THE SECTOR

The Turkish Banking environment suffered deeply from the absence of a prudent regulatory environment. Until the BRSA acted in August 2000, the

Treasury and the Central Bank shared supervisory duties between themselves. Naturally, such supervision should not be the job of these two institutions and can easily create conflicts of interest. Moreover, the Treasury and the Central Bank have always been extremely prone to political meddling and influencing, and it is only very recently that the Central Bank gained legal independence through the Central Bank Law, which was enacted in the first quarter of 2001. As the entity in charge of monitoring banks (state banks assuming particular importance in this regard), the Treasury had always been subject to severe pressure from politicians interested in rent distribution. Similarly, the Central Bank was forced to open advances to the Treasury in financing deficits until 1997 when a law prohibiting the extension of such advances beyond a month was passed. The Central Bank ultimately gained the long-awaited full independence status and is finally free from all political interference, at least in principle. There are still those who advocate a central bank that bases its monetary policy on prospective policies of the government, but proper governance requires precisely the opposite prioritization. Central Bank independence is indeed a prerequisite for the implementation of most modern monetary frameworks.

Poor, lax, and arbitrary regulation as a basic reason for many problems in the sector actually answers quite a number of interesting questions about the sector that had puzzled some economists and led to and/or fed some misleading arguments. These arguments basically pertain to issues of profitability and foreign presence (or lack of it), which will be discussed in detail in the upcoming sections. Startlingly, in the late 1980s and throughout the 1990s, people whose trustworthiness as credit customers would be questionable at best were issued banking licenses and owned banks due to immense demand in the sector.

In the face of all this excess local demand and high profitability,[1] foreign presence had been very limited (profitability has to be assumed one way or another, as growth would not have been observed otherwise). The sector displayed all the characteristics of a "sun rise" industry over the last 15 years, implying the presence of above-normal economic profits.[2] An astonishing question naturally follows: why did foreign entrants who unequivocally had stronger capital bases and an edge in efficiency not exploit the opportunities offered by such high profitability? Efficiency could not have been impressive within the local banking community either,[3] as there were no incentives to enhance efficiency in a system that was founded on lending to the government and reaping the benefits of high interest rates. The high profit margins, or net interest margins (NIM),[4] should have lured potential entrants with an edge in cost effectiveness into

TABLE 1
BANK PROFITS IN SELECTED OECD COUNTRIES

Pre-Tax Profits Scaled by Average Assets	1994–96
Turkey*	3.00
Austria	0.89
Germany	0.96
UK	1.43
Czech Republic	1.79
Hungary	0.84
Korea	1.69
Mexico	2.58
Poland	3.70

Note: * Average for 1997–98, after the correction for the impact of inflation.

Source: IMF Country Staff Report, *Turkey* (IMF, Feb. 2000), p.42.

the lucrative market. That clearly points to foreign competitors who could easily enjoy returns to scale. However, the presence of foreign banks in the sector remained extremely low compared to similar emerging markets for the 1994–99 period, as Table 1 illustrates. Signs of change have recently appeared now that the regulatory framework has been overhauled.

The paradoxical nature of the situation pertaining to the lax regulation period partially disappears when one realizes that the presence of foreign banks had exceeded their visibility. In other words, the share of assets held by those banks had been substantially lower than their share in government securities transactions. High visibility did not seem to be a prerequisite for making money in Turkish financial markets; neither did economies of scale matter in an environment characterized by high net interest margins. Highest pre-tax profits were actually accruing to small-sized banks while larger ones were also enjoying the high margins but suffering persistent net losses from activities outside the fixed income market, most notably the infamous connected lending being one of the chief reasons for loss generation.[5]

From the regulatory perspective, the low profile of foreigners can be partially attributed to the lack of prudent regulatory framework. The highly volatile and unstable economic environment operated as a perfect deterrent for potential foreign entrants, especially as political influence reigned supreme. Supervision was not only lax but also arbitrary, creating a potentially non-competitive environment open to favoritism. Nevertheless, foreign presence—although understated by foreign banking visibility—remained very low in comparison to other emerging markets due to the deficiencies mentioned above. Table 2 demonstrates the evolution of

TABLE 2

TOTAL ASSETS AND FOREIGN CONTROL IN THE BANKING SECTOR IN
SELECTED EMERGING MARKETS

	Total Assets ($ billion)		Foreign Control	
	1994	1999	1994	1999
Argentina	73.2	157.0	17.9	48.6
Brazil	487.0	723.3	8.4	16.8
Czech Republic	46.6	63.4	5.8	49.3
Columbia	28.3	45.3	6.2	17.8
Korea	638.0	642.4	0.8	4.3
Hungary	26.8	32.6	19.8	56.6
Malaysia	149.7	220.6	6.8	11.5
Mexico	210.2	204.5	1.0	18.8
Peru	12.3	26.3	6.7	33.4
Poland	39.4	91.1	2.1	52.8
Chile	41.4	112.3	16.3	53.6
Thailand	192.8	198.8	0.5	5.6
Turkey	52.0	156.2	2.7	1.7
Venezuela	16.3	24.7	0.3	41.9

Notes: Ownership data reflect changes up to December 1999 while balance sheet data are from Fitch IBCA's BankScope Database. Foreign control corresponds to the ratio of assets of banks where foreigners own more than 50 percent of total equity to total bank assets.

Source: IMF, *International Capital Markets: Developments, Prospects, and Key Policy Issues* (IMF, Sept. 2000).

foreign presence in the banking sector in major emerging market economies between 1994 and 1999.[6]

Credit extension to favored groups with no economic rationale or risk management—in the form of connected lending to group companies, most of which were troubled—exacerbated the status of the sector. The problem lingers, albeit much more transparent than it used to be, as I will discuss later on.

On top of all these regulatory deficiencies, a 100 percent guarantee deposit insurance scheme that was enacted during the 1994 crisis served as an extreme case of "moral hazard" and distorted the system in favor of the poorly managed, inefficient, and aggressive banks at the expense of the properly managed ones. Reckless behavior by small and aggressive banks in collecting deposits, in a way similar to that of the state banks who had a free hand in creating the so called "duty losses," weakened the status of the overall sector as the full guarantee worked as a risk cover for the small sharks, while the risk was being taken care of by the state. The guarantee has been lowered fairly recently, but quietly: sudden withdrawal from any bank based on rumors could have devastating effects. Trust in the banking sector is not fully established despite numerous takeovers by the Savings and Deposit Insurance Fund, the umbrella institution that handles the management of insolvent banks in the system with the ultimate aim of selling if possible, and, if not, liquidation. The BRSA has done a commendable job with the regulation, monitoring, and cleansing of the system, but the fragility of the system is believed to continue to exist, while fairly recent and vivid memories of bankers in trouble are a little blurred but still present. The sight of the once "untouchables" of society going to jail and uneasiness about future prospective inmates agitated a growing number of banking sector members and surprised the public at large. It was a huge blow to the credibility of a sector for which credibility means everything; restoration of confidence is an ongoing process.

The problems in the sector had been evolving over time in an environment of high inflation, lax and arbitrary regulation and monitoring, and acute political interference through the state banks. Nevertheless, the situation was mostly an open secret in the sense that the public was largely unaware of the colossal mess in the sector and the magnitude of the duty-losses problem created in the state banks. When the Banking Audit and Supervisory Board started the cleaning process in 2000, the Turkish public had a fairly abrupt introduction to the open secret in Turkish banking: corruption in the banking industry was rampant. People whose trustworthiness as credit customers would be questionable at best owned banks and blatantly abused them. The liquidity crisis in December 2000 brought the disclosure of the second open secret: the banking industry reform was the most vital of all steps to be taken during the disinflation program, and the systemic risk created by the poorly managed and aggressive sub-sector group of small banks in conjunction with the state banks was severely threatening the entire economic structure.

BANKS' OPERATING ENVIRONMENTS AND THE ROAD TO
DESTRUCTION, DECEMBER 1999–FEBRUARY 2001

The Operating Environment

Plagued by an increasing public sector borrowing requirement, chronic inflation, and boom and bust growth cycles that ultimately culminated in fairly low average annual growth rates, Turkey embarked on a disinflation program at the end of 1999. The program targeted single digit inflation levels at the end of three years by pegging the exchange rate to a US$-euro basket on a pre-announced crawling peg depreciation path and limiting money growth; these strategies were supported by an ambitious reform package involving privatization, public sector expenditure reform, and

TABLE 3

MAIN FISCAL INDICATORS (% OF GNP), INTEREST RATE (%)

	1995	1996	1997	1998	1999	2000	2001
Public Sector Borrowing Requirement (PSBR)	5.0	8.6	7.7	9.4	15.6	12.5	15.5
Duty Losses of State Banks	2.2	4.2	5.2	7.5	13.3	12.0	0.0
PSBR + Duty Losses of State Banks	7.2	12.8	12.9	16.9	28.9	24.5	15.5
Primary Surplus	2.1	1.3	0.0	2.1	-1.9	3.8	6.5
Consolidated Budget Deficit	3.7	8.5	7.6	7.1	11.6	10.2	17.4
Consolidated Budget Interest Payments	7.4	10.0	7.7	11.5	13.7	16.3	22.2
Domestic	6.1	8.9	6.7	10.5	12.6	15.0	20.3
Foreign	1.3	1.1	1.0	1.0	1.1	1.3	1.9
Public Debt*	37.6	40.3	40.5	41.3	51.8	53.4	97.8
Domestic	14.6	18.5	20.2	21.7	29.3	29.0	66.3
Foreign	23.0	21.8	20.3	19.6	22.5	24.4	31.5
Short-term Public Debt	8.0	10.2	8.1	10.9	4.1	2.1	10.8
Treasury Auction Borrowing Rate, Average	124.2	132.2	107.4	115.5	104.6	38.2	99.6
Average Maturity of Borrowing in Auctions (days)	188.0	186.6	393.5	235.1	502.3	426.8	146.3

Note: * Debt stock figures are for the end of the year. Foreign debt is converted to domestic currency by making use of the average annual exchange rate. Foreign debt stock for 2001 is for the third quarter.

Source: Treasury and the Central Bank, as reported in Fatih Özatay and Güven Sak, "The 2000–2001 Financial Crises in Turkey," Paper presented at the Brookings Trade Forum 2002 Currency Crises, Washington DC, May 2, 2002.

financial sector restructuring.[7] Table 3 displays the progress of deteriorating public sector balances, steadily swelling debt stock, and increased reliance on domestic borrowing for financing purposes, all of which—in the final analysis—set the stage for the demise of the banking sector.

As is clearly indicated by Table 3, the borrowing need of the Treasury was increasing quite drastically and was being covered through domestic borrowing—a situation that led to a surge in the domestic component of public debt, for which the local banking system was the main holder. Banking on the government seemed to be lucrative business until the risks carried throughout the process led to the catastrophic outcome in February 2001, when the price for delayed reforms and complacency—even after a serious warning in the form of the first liquidity crisis of November 2000—was finally paid.

Before illuminating the risks banks had exposed themselves to prior to the collapse in February 2001, a brief sketch of the monetary framework under which the banks had been operating should be given at the expense of using some economic jargon. The monetary and exchange rate policy section of the December 9, 1999, dated Letter of Intent prepared by the Turkish authorities and sent to the IMF had two crucial articles—31 and 33—that very clearly defined the new environment in which the Turkish banking sector would be operating:

31. Our monetary and exchange rate policies will be guided by two considerations. First, disinflation and a rapid decline in interest rates require that monetary and exchange rate developments become more predictable, so as to reduce the uncertainty on the value of financial investment for both residents and nonresidents. This requires a shift to a more forward-looking commitment on exchange rate policy. The strengthening of fiscal policy under the program, our level of international reserves, coupled with the financial support from the international community, make the introduction of such a commitment feasible. Second, there is a need to avoid being locked into a monetary and exchange rate framework that while appropriate for disinflation may lead to unnecessary rigidities in the long run, a problem that has affected many emerging markets in recent years. Hence, there is a need for a transparent and pre-announced exit strategy from this exchange rate regime.

33. Within this context, other than for short-term fluctuations, all base money will be created through the balance of payments and domestic interest rates will be fully market determined. Capital inflows will not be sterilized, allowing a rapid decline in interest rates and avoiding an excessively large interest rate differential, which would perpetuate the inflows. In the same vein, capital outflows will not be sterilized, so as to lead to a prompt increase in money market interest rates, which will help ensure that the floor on net international reserves (Annex E) is observed should pressures on the exchange rate arise. The interbank interest rates posted by the central bank will be adjusted daily in line with the movements of the overnight money market rates.[8]

As Article 31 indicates, the aim was to achieve disinflation and low real interest rates that would bolster growth and create an environment that was conducive to external and internal investment surges. A strictly controlled exchange rate regime was chosen in order to break down the inertial component of the inflationary process. Exchange rate uncertainty was to be eliminated from the system and from the minds of economic agents for the duration of the program, and disinflation was expected to benefit from this favorably. Note the prerequisites for the implementation of such a framework: the strengthening of fiscal policy (serving to assure the agents of the sustainability of improved public sector balances), the strong level of international reserves (necessary for intervention in the foreign exchange market to control the exchange rate), and support from the international community. More important, though, was elimination of exchange rate uncertainty for the upcoming periods. Another important issue was the possibility of unnecessary rigidities being built into financial markets because of perceptions of an excessively overvalued TL (Turkish lira) in the face of controlled exchange rates, in which case the system and the Central Bank would be pushed and tested frequently. The latter issue could have lead to a collapse of the program. In order to avoid this, a clearly defined exit strategy was announced and would have been in effect as of July 1, 2000. Finally, the fixed exchange rate supposedly eliminated the exchange rate risk for all those planning to borrow in foreign currency until that time (July 2001), and for the banks that had been sailing on a highly managed exchange rate regime and funding their TL positions through foreign borrowing.

Article 33 contained crucial implications for possible dangers awaiting the banks during implementation of the program. The disinflation and stabilization program, anchored around a crawling peg exchange rate, forced the Central Bank to put strict limits on its net domestic assets (NDA), which, in other words, limited the credit it could extend and thus create money growth. Growth in reserve money (the monetary aggregate that the Central Bank can fully control) could only come through an increase in the Bank's net foreign assets, or, more simply put, through foreign currency inflows. Note that the article emphasized that interest rates would be fully market determined and that this was not constructed by choice but was inevitable in the face of controlled exchange rates. Capital inflows and outflows would not be sterilized by the Central Bank, potentially leading to very volatile interest rates even within one trading day. Not sterilizing such flows would lead to sharp movements in interest rates, but would—at the same time—make sure that they did not become perpetual flows as the interest rate differential that induces such flows disappeared due to a lack of sterilization. In brief, the Central Bank was saying that with tight monetary rules embedded in the program and a strictly controlled exchange rate, there was basically no influence it was capable of exerting on the interest rates.[9]

The Road to Destruction

While base money—in the absence of foreign currency inflows— remained more or less flat throughout the year 2000, by the end of the year consumer inflation was 39 percent and real money supply had thus shrunk substantially. Foreign currency inflows would have provided much-needed relief in this case. After the initial euphoria in the first quarter of 2000, when the government's aggressive anti-inflation stance led to capital inflows and reduced interest rates, foreign capital became quite timid in the second half of 2000 due to the particularly discouraging signals being given by the government on the fiscal front and regarding the reform package. Moreover, the growing economy and the boom in imports led to a substantial widening of the current account deficit, and—although a bit misunderstood—the external deficit began to be perceived as a potential problem as well. Hence, a growing economy, rising price level, and—in nominal terms—a largely intact money supply initiated an upward trend in interest rates. This laid the groundwork for the vicious circle that would lead to the step-by-step demise of the system.

In the initial phases of the program some banks resorted to heavy commercial lending activity as the reduction in T-bill rates reduced the attractiveness of short-term (repo) funding and made a potential jump in short-term repo rates a much scarier scenario. On the other hand, other banks bet on a steady decline in funding costs and chose to invest in long-term government securities in an even more aggressive manner. The former group of banks had a reduction in their maturity mismatch,[10] while the latter further extended it—making them even more vulnerable to sudden interest hikes. As the rising interest rates and the deteriorating sentiment led to shrinking interest margins and lower profitability for the banking sector, some banks resorted to lending that had to be riskier by definition, while others further extended their maturity mismatch; both responses which were efforts to make up for falling profit margins. Maturity mismatch thus served as a time bomb waiting to explode when untoward developments on the macroeconomic front provided the opportunity. The group that shied away from government securities and chose to lend did reduce the maturity mismatch and thus the interest rate risk somewhat, but at the same time exposed itself to credit risk. Difficulty in short-term funding also led to the introduction of other instruments, such as "structures"—which will be discussed below. In short, the deteriorating environment culminated in increasing risks for some banks in particular, but, inevitably, in higher systemic risk as well.

Foreign exchange risk has been highly prevalent in the banking sector in the aftermath of the capital account liberalization in 1989. This is because the highly managed exchange rate system induced financial market agents to borrow in foreign currency in the absence of any anticipation of serious real loss in the value of the TL *vis-à-vis* other currencies. Hence, taking short foreign exchange positions to finance local securities portfolios has been rampant practice in the Turkish banking sector for more than a decade.[11] The extremely high returns on TL-denominated assets justified taking risks, especially under a highly controlled exchange rate regime. A sudden jump in short foreign exchange positions in 2000 reflected the fact that banks came to realize the importance of—and the profit opportunities in—carrying short positions in foreign exchange. However, the fact that it was a dangerous game to play became evident only after the initial liquidity crisis in November 2000. Table 4 demonstrates the steadily shrinking FX assets/FX liabilities ratio of the sector, which indicates the shorting of FX positions, and also the similarly shrinking liquid FX assets/FX liabilities ratio, which demonstrates a further increased vulnerability in the case of currency attacks.

While one reason for the appetite for increased short FX positions was the inability of local banks to borrow long-term from the locals, another was the firm commitment of the Central Bank to a pre-announced

TABLE 4

RATIOS, COMMERCIAL BANKING SECTOR (%)[a]

	1995	1996	1997	1998	1999	2000.3	2000.6	2000.9	2000	2001
Non-performing Loans / Total Loans										
	2.8	2.2	2.4	7.2	10.7	9.8	9.7	9.3	11.6	18.6
FX Assets / FX Liabilities[b]										
	90.6	93.6	89.6	84.9	79.4	74.3	73.0	71.6	75.9	81.0
Liquid FX Assets / FX Liabilities										
	44.8	44.6	41.0	39.5	40.0	36.6	35.2	34.4	35.9	38.3
Liquid Assets / Total Sources[c]										
	46.7	44.0	41.1	39.9	42.6	42.4	41.0	38.3	37.9	51.4
Assets / Liabilities (with 3 months or shorter maturities)										
	n.a.	n.a.	45.8	45.7	46.3	40.8	41.8	43.9	39.9	43.9
Share of Deposits with 6 months or greater Maturity in Total Deposits										
	26.1	26.6	24.7	22.9	28.2	19.8	18.7	19.3	15.1	11.6
Repos / (Liabilities + Repos)[d]										
	5.1	8.1	12.8	10.4	9.6	12.0	11.4	10.9	11.3	6.1

Notes: [a] End of period figures.
            [b] 'FX' denotes "foreign currency denominated."
            [c] Total resources = deposits + non-deposit funds.
            [d] Repos have been recorded off-the-balance sheet since 2002.

Source: Central Bank and the Bank Association of Turkey, as reported in Fatih Özatay and Güven Sak, "The 2000–2001 Financial Crises in Turkey," Paper presented at the Brookings Trade Forum 2002 Currency Crises, Washington DC, May 2, 2002.

exchange rate path—according to which all enthusiastic FX borrowers positioned themselves. When TL funding of their government securities portfolios became more and more difficult for those banks that relied heavily on overnight borrowing from other banks, they resorted to "structured loans" whereby government securities were used as collateral against FX borrowing. These instruments entailed certain stop-loss levels of interest rates that, when hit, the collateral holder automatically started to sell the collateral portfolio. They were indeed quite instrumental during the November 2000 crisis when financing difficulties experienced by Demirbank—the major market maker in the government securities market—led to an abrupt sale of the collateral portfolios and a surge in the demand for foreign exchange. Thus, the banking sector was carrying a full load of risks within the first year of the program, and the fragility was just waiting for a few triggering effects to lead to a full-blown crisis.

State banks had been notorious for distorting the deposit market by offering well above the market deposit rates while taking full advantage of complete deposit safety provided by the state. Such banks, then, had abused their privileges by serving as channels of subsidized lending and by covering the financing need of governments by extending loans to state institutions which ultimately became non-performing but were treated as receivables from the government in the books—hence the notion of "duty losses." Furthermore, the banning of short-term advances from the Central Bank to the Treasury by a legislation passed in 1997 enhanced the state banks' role in financing government activities. The Treasury was in charge of monitoring and supervising these banks, and—as mentioned in the regulatory framework section above—that inevitably created a conflict of interest, which, left unchecked, culminated in the severe accumulation of duty losses. These could only be taken care of after the collapse of the exchange rate-based stabilization program, and they very much contributed to the second crisis in February 2001.[12]

The nature of the problem with state banks was different than that of private banks. While the latter group had exposed itself heavily to exchange rate risk, state banks were largely exposed to interest rate risk. State banks also seemed to carry a much lower government securities portfolio than the private sector. Table 5 clearly shows the lower and steadily decreasing share of interest-earning assets of the state banks. However, the figure portrayed is misleading because the share of accumulated duty losses when added to the share of interest earning assets yields a total figure that exceeds that of the private sector banks' share of interest earning assets.

TABLE 5

STRUCTURAL CHARACTERISTICS OF PRIVATE AND STATE BANKS[a]

		1997	1998	1999	2000 /I	2000 /II	2000 /III	2000 /IV	2001 /I	2001 /II
Loan / GDI[b]	Private	113.72	119.28	82.52	93.26	102.49	111.39	130.70	139.00	144.97
	State	86.24	87.86	66.27	n/a.	n/a.	n/a.	59.22	n/a.	n/a.
Repos /	Private	123.36	83.27	106.61	95.23	93.73	105.41	53.48	23.62	25.37
Lira Deposits	State	22.49	19.07	13.64	30.29	28.67	29.50	27.27	55.36	41.52
FX / Lira	Private	212.20	201.63	274.65	285.07	279.99	299.90	209.24	205.37	237.54
Deposits	State	46.37	35.61	26.49	31.66	32.42	33.13	29.37	37.12	37.12
Share of	Private	14.01	13.97	15.91	16.28	16.51	17.10	19.84	20.02	19.55
FX Loans	State	3.07	3.18	2.30	2.13	2.78	2.85	2.54	3.36	2.78
Share of	Private	67.80	63.66	63.22	60.79	61.88	60.92	58.05	53.95	52.73
Interest										
Earning Assets	State	36.63	35.34	28.85	n/a	n/a.	n/a.	31.88.	n/a.	n/a.
Share of	State	27.07	27.59	32.01	n/a.	n/a.	n/a.	30.68.	n/a.	n/a.
Accumulated										
Duty Losses										
Share of	Private	9.13	9.87	11.29	12.16	12.83	13.85	12.39	11.25	9.65
Net Worth	State	5.38	3.85	3.80	3.78	3.50	3.20	2.69	3.78	3.50

Notes: [a] End of period figures.
[b] GDI stands for "government debt instruments."

Source: Central Bank and the Bank Association of Turkey, as reported in Fatih Özatay and Güven Sak, "The 2000–2001 Financial Crises in Turkey," Paper presented at the Brookings Trade Forum 2002 Currency Crises, Washington DC, May 2, 2002.

In summation, the banking sector—which has dominated the financial sector in Turkey—became extremely vulnerable to exchange rate and interest rate risks that inflicted serious, indeed fatal, damages on the sector, hence inflicting damage on the economy throughout the last decade and a half. Vulnerability sharply increased due to reckless positioning on the FX and TL funding fronts accompanied by very poor risk management.

While the quantitative performance criteria defined in the stand-by arrangement were fairly met during 2000, structural benchmarks were being missed and structural reform packages—particularly those pertaining to the banking sector and fiscal management and transparency—were not being put into effect. The coalition government was quite timid in displaying strong ownership of the program, and markets discounted the prospective achievements of the government heavily, on account of this perception of lack of ownership. Fiscal signaling was very weak: despite the absence of significant problems regarding the year 2000 budget realizations, budget performance in the remaining years of the program remained a mystery. Privatization became a hotly debated issue even within the coalition government, and extra-budgetary funds—which constituted another black hole in public sector finances—had mostly remained intact, despite the fact that the stand-by arrangement imposed the elimination of these funds as a structural benchmark.

The board of the BRSA had to be named by the end of March 2000 so that it could become fully operative by late August—another structural benchmark in the stand-by arrangement, but this was only achieved at the very end of August. In September 2000, the BRSA, presumably making up for the lost time, started very aggressively by launching a series of raids on the ex-owners of failed banks taken under the umbrella of the Savings Deposit and Insurance Fund (SDIF). The ex-owners were charged with "organized crime," a strategy that was probably devised to recoup the losses from them as it would have been extremely difficult to accomplish that through commercial law. These raids nevertheless increased jitters immensely within the sector and among the public at large as well, and bets were flying as to who would be the next to go under. The sector suffered a huge credibility loss, and reparation of losses in the sector became the hottest topic of debate—with estimates being in tens of billions of dollars; the very high variance of these estimates revealed the lack of transparency and accurate knowledge about the sector.

Furthermore, the deteriorating sentiment led to an increase in liquidity pressure and exposed the weaknesses of those banks that had positioned aggressively in the fixed income market and relied heavily on overnight borrowing in the hope of steadily decreasing interest rates. As the market became more reluctant to lend to such agents, the liquidity problem inevitably resulted in the November liquidity crisis, which began on November 20 with the funding problems of Demirbank and lasted until December 6. Initially, the Central Bank did not supply the needed liquidity so as not to breach the NDA limits, and the troubled market maker bank, Demirbank, was forced to start selling chunks of its huge government securities portfolio. This led to increased interest rates in the secondary markets, and the previously mentioned stop-loss levels of interest rates were hit,[13] generating further sell-offs in the fixed income market. Foreign currency demand surged as well due to the collateral problem, and the increase in interest rates continued. When the Central Bank decided to breach the NDA limits and supply the liquidity to the market, it was converted to FX and left the system—leaving the Central Bank with drained reserves and a market with still-increasing interest rates. With no solution in sight for Demirbank, the Central Bank declared on the last day of November that it would respect the NDA limit as funding the liquidity-drained market was only serving to further deplete the Central Bank reserves. The ensuing surge in the interest rates severely hurt the overnight borrowers, including the state banks, and the Central Bank ultimately had to fund Demirbank before it was taken over by the SDIF and the IMF announced its opening of a new credit line to Turkey.

As a result of this credit line, beefed-up reserves tranquilized the markets for a while, but the snowball had begun to roll. Interest rates remained high, FX demand was not subsiding, and concerns over the sustainability of the system were raised more vociferously than ever. Most importantly, the state banks had now replaced Demirbank as the major source of disturbance, a situation indicated by the surge in the repos/deposits ratio (indicating reliance on short-term TL funding of the securities portfolio) for state banks during the last quarter of 2000 and clearly demonstrated in Table 5. The reluctance of the political administration to deal with the state bank problem left the monetary authority and the counter party in the stand-by arrangement—namely the IMF—in a very awkward position. Thus, on February 23, the fixed exchange rate regime was abandoned and replaced with a float. The decision came after overnight rates had skyrocketed to above 4,000 percent on February 21, figures which followed the breech of 2,000 percent levels recorded on February 20 in the aftermath of the argument between the president and the prime minister during the National Security Council meeting on February 19. That was the final call to leave for all foreigners who had—for one reason or another—stayed put in the Turkish markets as well as Turkish banks that displayed a huge demand for FX, hence the decision to pull the plug and terminate the exchange rate-based stabilization program.

BANKS IN THE AFTERMATH OF THE COLLAPSE AND FUTURE PROSPECTS

Post-Crisis Outlook

Private banks that suffered huge losses with the abandonment of the fixed exchange rate regime and the move to the float—because of their open FX positions and high secondary market interest rates—barely survived 2001. Their FX risk exposure was eliminated in July 2001 with a debt swap that replaced their TL-denominated government securities with FX-denominated ones, virtually closing their short positions in FX and transferring the FX risk to the issuer—the Treasury. They experienced the annihilation of their capital bases due to the losses they incurred.

Consequently, the banking sector is undergoing a major restructuring process, which is formally labeled the "Bank Capital Strengthening Program." This program required that a triple audit process be implemented by the end of 2001 in order to gain a reliable picture of the actual soundness of the system, allowing for an increase in private banks' capital through public support if necessary. Those banks which would satisfy certain conditions would be allowed to receive one-time support in the form of SDIF's participation in Tier 1 or Tier 2 capital, if deemed necessary.[14]

The results of the auditing process indicated no need for such injections, mostly thanks to the re-evaluation of fixed assets and, therefore, Tier 2 capital. The non-performing loan (NPL) ratio of the sector was found to be more than three times the figure in the pre-audit phase, namely a 25 percent post-audit ratio versus a mere seven percent pre-audit figure. The transparency in the sector is thus immensely higher, and although one can question the standards of capital adequacy in the audits, the credibility of the audits—given the standards and measures applied—is beyond doubt.

Regarding the state banks that relied heavily on overnight funding and contributed immensely to the collapse of the stabilization package in 2001, a decisive move was made to overhaul the system and eliminate inherent structural weaknesses. The management of the banks has been transferred to the Common Board of Directors, which assumes responsibility to restructure and ultimately prepare the state banks for privatization. Financial restructuring of the state banks concentrated on liquidation of duty losses, elimination of short term liabilities, strengthening of the capital base, determination of deposit rates in line with the market rates, and efficient management of the loan portfolio.[15]

The Treasury supplied TL23 quadrillion (approximately $19 billion) in 2001 to securitize the state banks' receivables from the government. Regulations (around 100 Council of Ministers' Decrees and/or Laws) that allowed subsidized lending through state banks—thus creating duty losses—were annulled to prevent the generation of new duty losses. Financial restructuring of state-owned banks was completed by the end of 2001 and significant steps were taken regarding operational restructuring. One of the major outcomes of this restructuring was the merger of state-owned Emlakbank and Ziraat Bank in July 2001. Major employment reductions and branch closures have taken place: 788 branches were closed and 26,000 employees were laid off between April 2001 and July 2002. Inefficiencies and budgetary drains imposed by the state banks are finally over, but privatization does not seem to be possible in the foreseeable future, and the relative share of the state banks in the sector cannot be drastically reduced too quickly. The difficulty in reducing the relative share of the state banks' balance sheet stems from the need to actively use these institutions in internal debt rollovers.

PROSPECTS

Notwithstanding increased transparency, consolidation (indicating the survival of the fittest—note the number of banks in Table 6), and overall soundness, the banking sector continues to display some crucial weaknesses. The NPL problem has become more acute, at first merely due to recognition of the fact itself through increased transparency, but it has also got worse due to the severe contraction in the economy and the ensuing reduction in the repayment capacity of the borrowers. That problem is far from over, and there is no quick fix to the problem.

Economic recovery will undoubtedly ameliorate the asset quality problem of the banking sector to some extent, but to assert that the problem will be solved automatically via economic growth is a bit far-fetched. If the contribution of the export sector to growth is dominant and domestic consumption-oriented sectors register a lackluster performance, the asset quality problem may even get worse—as in the case of Mexico between 1994 and 1998. Provided that real interest rates remain high for some time to come, despite stability and growth, foreign exchange earning sectors will resort to alternative sources of finance, exit the local credit system, and

TABLE 6

NUMBER OF BANKS

	1997	1998	1999	2000	2001	As of Nov. 11, 2002
Commercial Banks	59	60	62	61	46	41
State	5	4	4	4	3	3
Private	35	36	31	28	22	21
Foreign	18	18	19	18	15	15
SDIF	1	2	8	11	6	2
Development and Investment Banks	13	15	19	18	15	14
State	3	3	3	3	3	3
Private	7	9	13	12	9	8
Foreign	3	3	3	3	3	3
Total	72	75	81	79	61	55

Source: Banking Regulatory and Supervisory Agency (BRSA), Unpublished PowerPoint presentation, "Bankacılık Sektörü Gelişmeleri, Kasım 2002" [Banking Sector Developments, November 2002].

TABLE 7

THE TURKISH BANKING SECTOR IN FIGURES ($ MILLION)

	I[a]					II[b]	
	1997	1998	1999	2000	2001	Dec. 2001	July 2002
Total Assets	94,645	117,767	133,535	154,955	119,974	116,661	117,814
Loans	40,349	41,997	36,891	47,404	29,090	23,899	24,638
NPL	1,014	3,248	4,309	5,895	6,123	9,595	7,969
Securities Portfolio	13,333	17,699	26,653	27,485	41,725	41,059	46,737
Total Deposits	55,552	69,630	80,316	87,680	76,686	75,938	76,202

Notes: [a] The year-end figures before the triple audit process, no inflationary accounting applied. [b] Inflationary accounting applied figures after the triple audit process.

Source: Banking Regulatory and Supervisory Agency (BRSA), Unpublished PowerPoint presentation, "Bankacilik Sektoru Gelismeleri, Kasim 2002' [Banking Sector Developments, November 2002].

leave the banking system with a pool of debtors that possess a lower payment capability. This will ultimately lead to a worsening of the NPL problem. Such a state of affairs would once again necessitate some form of state intervention, and there are limits to creative solutions on that front, as we have learned during the two recent programs.

A more significant problem lingers in the form of the seemingly irreducible borrowing need of the Treasury. As Table 7 demonstrates, the ratio of the securities portfolio to both the deposit base and the assets has been increasing. Such a state of affairs indicates that the banking sector will continue to be the main lender to the government, and that it will take time for banks to begin "proper banking"—whereby they assume the essential role of financial intermediary. Banks do have a profitability problem, and it would be unrealistic to expect a voluntary asset switch by banks from government securities to loans. The only way the sector could extend a higher volume of loans in the absence of such a switch would be either if the real rate of return on government securities was drastically lowered or if the sector was able to experience a boom on the liability side of its balance sheet, mainly in terms of an influx of deposits into the system. Such an influx—in the absence of an increasing borrowing need of the Treasury—would facilitate higher credit extension and underlie the financing of sustainable growth. Otherwise, with growth not forthcoming, the NPL problem is bound to worsen. The drastic real rate reduction—inspired by the vivid memories of 2000—should not be anticipated due to the adverse nature of the current exchange rate regime, which will always entail a not-so-negligible risk premium due to exchange rate uncertainty.

Therefore, a permanent solution to the banking sector problem ultimately boils down to the reduced borrowing need of the Treasury, and thus to increased fiscal discipline and improved public sector balances. Strong and prudent regulation and monitoring are in effect, which is a quantum leap forward for the sector, but these are necessary, not sufficient, conditions for the ultimate health and prosperity of the sector.

NOTES

1. Profitability is a hotly debated issue in the Turkish banking sector, and there are those who claim that profitability is high at the surface but, when corrected for inflation, it comes down drastically. That it comes down is true, but it is still very high indeed by international standards. For a more detailed exposition of the issue, see Osman Cevdet Akcay, Refik Erzan, and Reha Yolalan, "An Overview of the Turkish Banking Sector," *Boğaziçi Journal: Review of Social, Economic and Administrative Studies*, Vol.15, No.1 (2001), pp.13–23.
2. For profitability measures for selected Organization for Economic Cooperation and Development (OECD) countries during the mid-1990s, see Table 1.
3. For a detailed analysis of efficiency in the banking sector in the pre-crisis period, see Muhammet Mercan and Reha Yolalan, "The Effects of Financial Liberalization and New Bank Entry on Market Structure and Competition in Turkey," unpublished manuscript, 2000.
4. NIM = net interest income/total assets.
5. Connected lending corresponds to lending done to group companies, i.e., to companies that belong to the group that is also the main shareholder of the bank.
6. Despite the recent entry of HSBC through its acquisition of Demirbank and that of Uni Credito in the form of a 50/50 partnership with Koç Financial Services, Turkey still lags substantially behind the other emerging markets.
7. On the nature of the International Monetary Fund (IMF) "Stand by Arrangement," see The Undersecretariat of Treasury, Prime Ministry, The Turkish Republic, stand-by Arrangement— Letter of Intent, Turkey, Dec. 1999, available from the Turkish Treasury's website, <http://www.treasury.org.tr>.
8. For a detailed and critical investigation of this issue, see IMF, Country Staff Report, *Turkey* (IMF, Feb. 2000); IMF, *International Capital Markets: Prospects and Key Policy Issues* (IMF, Sept. 2000).
9. The float regime that has been in effect since the collapse of the first program has exactly the opposite set up: the exchange rate freely floats while the Central Bank controls the interest rate.
10. Maturity mismatch means taking long-term positions in TL-denominated assets while funding them through short-term TL liabilities such as deposits and repos. As long as the T-bill rates remain above the short-term funding rates the holder enjoys a positive return on the asset but remains vulnerable to hikes in funding costs until maturity.
11. Short positioning in foreign currency basically involves borrowing in foreign exchange, converting to local currency, investing in local currency-denominated assets, selling at or before maturity, converting back to foreign currency, paying back the loan, and hopefully enjoying a high return in local and foreign currency terms. A dirty or highly managed float system renders the practice fairly lucrative due to the absence of severe depreciation or devaluation.
12. For a detailed analysis and elaboration of the recent crises, see Fatih Özatay and Güven Sak, "The 2000–2001 Financial Crisis in Turkey," Paper presented at the Brookings Trade Forum 2002: Currency Crises, Washington DC, May 2002.
13. Stop-loss levels are predetermined levels for the market value of bonds (thus for interest rates as well), such that, when hit, an automated sell-off process is initiated.
14. Tier 1 capital is basically paid-up capital and legal reserves. Tier 2 capital is supplementary

capital in the form of fixed asset revaluation funds, provisions for revaluation of fixed assets of subsidiaries and affiliates, and subordinated debts. Turkish banks benefited greatly from the revaluation of fixed assets, and capital adequacy requirement was mostly fulfilled through Tier 2 capital. The system is still short of Tier 1 capital, and the questionability of standards of capital adequacy mentioned in the main text was implicative of this deficiency and the leniency of the regulatory authority in this regard.

15. For a comprehensive investigation of the Turkish Banking Sector, see Akcay, Erzan, and Yolalan (2001), pp.13–23.

9

Conclusion:
The Broader Ramifications of
Turkey's Financial Crises

ZİYA ÖNİŞ

The financial crises beginning in 2000 constituted, without a doubt, the biggest economic setback that Turkey has experienced in the post-1945 era. These crises resulted in a profound loss of output and employment, as well as a striking increase in poverty. The recent crises differ from the earlier 1994 crisis in the sense that their effects have been more widespread. All segments of Turkish society—rich and poor, skilled and unskilled—experienced the deep impact of the crises. Yet, the poor and the unprotected felt the pinch more than others. The various contributions in the present volume clearly highlight that the recent crises experienced by Turkey reflect both the impact of a more challenging external environment facing the country in the 1990s as well as the presence of deep-seated problems or imbalances in the domestic economic and political arenas.

Turkey is certainly not unique in experiencing acute financial crises during this period. Indeed, a number of important "emerging market" economies—including Argentina (2001), Brazil (1999), Russia (1998), South Korea, Thailand, Indonesia (1997), and Mexico (1994)—have experienced major crises with costly economic, social, and political consequences during this same period. Moreover, many of these other crises sprang from the same international roots that have helped bring about the Turkish crises. There is no doubt that an excessive push towards rapid capital account liberalization represents the weakest element in the neo-liberal policy agenda, or the so-called "Washington consensus." Clearly, a number of countries have been exposed in a rather premature fashion to the forces of financial globalization without attaining sufficient macroeconomic stability and before developing the appropriate regulatory institutions in the first place. Countries with nascent democratic regimes like Turkey and Argentina found themselves unable to cope effectively with the difficult environment of financial globalization. Consequently, they face a major challenge in terms of breaking out of the "low growth-high inequality equilibrium" in which they appear to be trapped.

The International Monetary Fund (IMF) has been a central actor in addressing Turkey's economic problems, as has been the case in other emerging markets during the 1990s. The contributions to the present volume attempt to provide a balanced interpretation of the role of the IMF. Clearly, key reforms promoted by the IMF in such areas of fiscal adjustment and banking sector regulation constitute positive developments that are likely to result in superior economic performance. At the same time, the role of the IMF itself has become the subject of critical appraisal. One of the recurring themes in this volume concerns the risks associated with exchange rate-based stabilization programs promoted by the IMF, not only in Turkey but also in other national contexts. Such policies designed to complement fiscal adjustment and achieve a drastic reduction in inflation over a short period of time have, in fact, proved to be counter-productive and have contributed to the emergence of financial crises.

The IMF is also open to criticism on the grounds that the organization pushed countries too rapidly in the direction of financial and capital account liberalization while underestimating the problem of establishing appropriate regulatory institutions during the process. Admittedly, though, the decision to open up fully Turkey's capital account in August 1989 was a domestic rather than an IMF-induced decision. Turkey was also unique in experiencing financial crises at a time when an IMF program was actually being implemented. This, in and of itself, might be interpreted as a sign that the program failed to provide sufficient insurance considering the major risks of failure involved. Given the fragile environment—that is, the presence of highly volatile and reversible capital flows and the massive economic and social costs of speculative attacks resulting in massive outflows of capital—that countries like Turkey find themselves in, various commentators in the present volume clearly favor at least temporary capital controls as a necessary part of an overall stabilization package. They are also well aware of the difficulties involved, as the IMF is not very sympathetic towards such arrangements.

There is a general agreement that the establishment of an effective regulatory state is likely to exercise a favorable influence over Turkey's development performance in the years ahead. The IMF has also been actively involved—both in Turkey and elsewhere—in the construction of effective regulatory institutions. The Bank Regulation and Supervision Agency (BRSA) has constituted a key component of such efforts. To be effective, however, such institutions need to enjoy a considerable degree of autonomy from day-to-day political pressures. At the same time, such institutions need to be politically accountable and enjoy a high degree of legitimacy. Clearly, if such institutions are perceived as mere creations of an external agency such as the IMF, they are unlikely to enjoy broad political support and their effectiveness will therefore be undermined. Arguably, the IMF has hitherto paid more attention to the autonomy issue than the legitimacy issue.

At present, it is doubtful whether or not key regulatory agencies in Turkey such as BRSA and the Competition Board enjoy either the degree of autonomy or the legitimacy that seems to characterize the operation of their developed country counterparts. It is also unclear whether such institutions possess the kind of personnel that have the expertise and commitment needed to make an effective contribution. Hence, simply achieving a high degree of autonomy from the political authorities is not enough, especially if such autonomy is misused in appointing the wrong kind of people to such institutions: actions of this sort will undermine the legitimacy of these institutions over time. Clearly, the appropriate mix of autonomy and legitimacy needed for such key regulatory institutions to be effective is a major challenge. At the same time, some of the contributors criticize the narrow focus of the IMF on the regulatory role of the state. They argue that the state should also be concerned with longer term developmental and income distributional issues.

The Turkish experience clearly demonstrates that partial reforms fail to generate the desired economic outcomes. There is no doubt that the coalition government that came into office in 1999 took significant steps in the direction of fiscal adjustment following the signing of the agreement with the IMF in December 1999. Although the coalition government projected a unified front during its early months—an image that seemed to contrast sharply with the earlier coalition governments of the 1990s—it soon became apparent that the government lacked the necessary coherence and commitment to the reform process. Key parts of the reform agenda such as bank regulation, privatization, and the reform of the system of agricultural subsidies faced considerable resistance, primarily—if not exclusively—from the major coalition partner, *Milliyetçi Hareket Partisi* (MHP—Nationalist Action Party). This, in turn, undermined the credibility of the program in the minds of private investors and increased the vulnerability of the Turkish economy to speculative attacks during 2000 and beyond. Hence, the domestic political arena is central to an adequate understanding of the crises that the Turkish economy has recently experienced.

The presence of informal networks has traditionally been a key element that has enabled Turkey to emerge from economic crises without massive social and political dislocation. A cursory examination of the post-crisis environment in 2001 seems to provide support to this proposition.

Compared to the massive wave of protests that Argentina experienced in the aftermath of its crisis, the social and political protests that Turkey experienced appeared to be quite marginal. Yet, several contributions to the present volume suggest that Turkey's social capital has been experiencing a steady process of erosion in recent years. Hence, there is no automatic reason to be confident that Turkey will overcome a future possible crisis as easily as in the past, given that the informal mechanisms of protection are being progressively weakened. Indeed, the contribution by Adaman and Çarkoğlu points towards an interesting link between crises, the decline of trust on the part of general public, and the process of pervasive corruption, with the authors drawing attention to the existence of a vicious cycle between trust and economic crisis. Loss of trust causes more corruption, which contributes to the onset of the economic crisis; economic crisis, in turn, leads to more corruption and further decline in trust and social capital, and so the process continues.

From a comparative perspective, the latest crises that Turkey has experienced have raised issues relating to income distribution and poverty, bringing them to the center stage of policy discussion. The Washington consensus, with its single-minded emphasis on efficiency and growth, has effectively relegated issues relating to income distribution to the background. Arguably, the neo-liberal consensus remained unchallenged in the Turkish context until after the February 2001 crisis. Certainly, the IMF as the key actor involved in the Turkish setting was hardly concerned with the income-distributional ramifications of its programs, although, admittedly, the World Bank has given some attention to this issue. One could in fact argue that Turkey's delayed encounter with the "post-Washington consensus," which places more emphasis on the social and income-redistributional aspects of neo-liberal restructuring, effectively occurred after the February crisis. Indeed, the "social liberal synthesis" put forward by Kemal Derviş, a former World Bank official and the architect of the economic program in the post-crisis era until the elections of November 2002, signaled the arrival of the post-Washington consensus in the Turkish setting. The contribution by Şenses underlines the point that growth is essential for the Turkish economy, and also makes the point that a single-minded concern with growth and efficiency will not be enough to achieve the desired trickle-down objective: complementary policies are required to deal with problems of poverty and income distribution directly.

One of the striking features of the recent economic crises concerns their dramatic impact on Turkey's politics. One major implication of the crises has been the unexpected acceleration in the process of reform, both in the economic and political arenas. The Helsinki summit of the European

Union (EU) in December 1999—where Turkey was offered the prospect of full EU membership—represented a major turning point. This prospect contributed to the emergence of a vocal "pro-EU coalition" in Turkey, which was willing to undertake the kind of reforms necessary to facilitate the country's progress towards the EU. Increasingly, EU membership has become a common motive creating a common bond between diverse elements of Turkish society. The potential material benefits of EU membership have become all the more attractive in the midst of an acute economic crisis. Consequently, Turkey has experienced a series of groundbreaking reforms designed to improve its democratic credentials during the course of 2002—reforms that would have been unimaginable only a few years ago. The impact of the economic crises, however, should be considered in line with the EU's impending Copenhagen summit of December 2002. The Turkish policymakers were well aware of the fact that the country's status as a potential EU member would be subjected to a critical review at the Copenhagen summit. Hence, they naturally felt the pressure to accelerate the momentum of the reform process.[1]

As part of this reform process, Turkey faces two interlocking external anchors in the form of IMF and EU disciplines. The international financial community has increasingly conceived of the EU-related reforms as a means of consolidating the economic reform process in Turkey. The fact that Turkey faces a double external anchor—rather than a single anchor in the form of IMF conditionality alone—is, on the whole, a favorable development for the future course of both the Turkish economy and Turkish democracy. Clearly, this is a feature that renders the Turkish case somewhat unique compared to other emerging market cases, such as Argentina.

The political earthquake that Turkey endured following the November 2002 elections also reflected the deep impact of the economic crises. Members of the coalition government were clearly penalized by the electorate for their poor economic performance. A number of other key political parties represented in parliament, which constituted key opposition groups of the coalition government, were also wiped off of the political scene. Consequently, a number of political leaders who had been influential in Turkish politics for a long time were forced to exit Turkish politics, a striking development that would have been hard to predict a few months ago. From a longer term perspective, what was even more striking was the very resilience of Turkish democracy in the midst of deep economic dislocation. This, in turn, illustrated the growing maturity of Turkish democracy itself as well as the impact of the EU as a powerful external anchor.

The November 2002 elections were also important in putting an end to the era of the political fragmentation of successive coalition governments with its costly economic consequences, a pattern present in Turkey since 1991. Successive coalition governments in Turkey had a poor track record in terms of their ability and willingness to undertake economic stabilization and structural reforms. The crises that emerged in 2000 and 2001 reflected the accumulation of disequilibria which successive coalition governments had been unable to prevent. *Adalet ve Kalkınma Partisi* (AKP—Justice and Development Party), a new party with Islamist roots but currently with center-right credentials, managed to obtain a clear majority in parliament. The fact that for the first time in many years Turkey enjoys a strong government constitutes a positive development. The party appears to be strongly committed towards advancing the course of economic reforms in cooperation with the IMF as well as achieving full membership in the EU, both constituting favorable signals. Falling interest rates in the early stages of the new government—which, if continued, is likely to exercise a positive impact on the country's debt burden—is a clear reflection of rising investor confidence. Hence, in spite of the dramatic impact of the November 2002 elections, we are likely to witness a considerable continuity rather than a major rupture in the direction of economic policy as well as in the nature of reforms on the democratization front. Moreover, in the presence of powerful external anchors a reversal of the basic policy stance appears rather unlikely.

In retrospect, one of the major reasons underlying the AKP's electoral success is the deeper commitment displayed by the party, relative to its competitors, in terms of dealing with the plight of the segments of the poor in Turkish society as well as small businesses deeply hurt by the economic crises. Consequently, the AKP's appeal to the poor and to disadvantaged groups in society proved to be far stronger than the "social-liberal synthesis" advanced by its principal rival, *Cumhuriyetçi Halk Partisi* (CHP—Republican People's Party).

The strong emphasis of AKP on the social dimension of neo-liberal restructuring, which has been so instrumental in its success, presents a major challenge for the future. To what extent will the party be able to stay within the boundaries of fiscal discipline imposed by the IMF and, at the same time, satisfy its broad electoral base? From the very beginning of the new government one can detect strong pressures from below towards relaxing IMF disciplines in such key areas as agricultural subsidies or tight regulations over commercial bank lending. However, the fact that the government has a strong mandate means that it can withstand such pressures for a considerable period. Furthermore, if the government is able to deal effectively with the problem of endemic corruption and increase tax discipline, it will be in a position to generate additional resources—part of which could be directed towards the much-needed social expenditures and anti-poverty programs.

Resumption of economic growth is clearly a central priority and there are signs that the Turkish economy is on the path to a recovery by early 2003, although it is too early to state at this stage that Turkey has fully recovered from the crisis. One can certainly not rule out the possibility that potentially adverse developments such as lack of coherence of government policy at home or the impending war on Iraq may seriously jeopardize the recovery process in the Turkish economy. Steady growth is essential to social and political stability in Turkey. As key contributions in the present volume imply, sustained growth significantly helps to reduce the country's heavy debt burden as well as the serious unemployment problem, which constituted a striking outcome of the recent economic crises. Nevertheless, it must be a durable kind of growth based on competitiveness, as opposed to a temporary growth based on a relaxation of fiscal discipline. Hence, the domestic political environment will continue to be central to the future course of the Turkish economy. In addition, in a globalized world where external actors are increasingly part and parcel of domestic politics, the United States, the European Union, and the IMF will continue to exercise a major influence over Turkey's economic and political trajectory in the years ahead.

NOTE

1. Indeed, the Copenhagen summit proved to be another turning point in the trajectory of Turkey-EU relations. Turkey was offered a conditional date of Dec. 2004 for opening accession negotiations for EU membership, depending on the country's ability to satisfy the Copenhagen criteria fully in the interim period. Whether this constitutes a case of total success from Turkey's point of view, however, is open to interpretation. Arguably, an earlier conditional date such as Dec. 2003 would have accelerated the momentum of the reform implementation process further and would have also contributed to the resolution of the Cyprus dispute over a shorter interval.

Abstracts

Domestic Politics versus Global Dynamics: Towards a Political Economy of the 2000 and 2001 Financial Crises in Turkey *by Ziya Öniş*

Populist cycles and recurrent macroeconomic crises have remained endemic features of the Turkish economy in the postwar period, in spite of the achievement of significant structural change. Populist cycles have become shorter and economic crises have become more frequent following Turkey's unrestricted exposure to the forces of financial globalization in the post-1989 era, with significant negative ramifications for economic performance. The objective of this contribution is to probe into the origins and the consequences of the 2000 and 2001 crises in Turkey from a broad political economy perspective, paying attention to the nature of domestic politics as well as the impact of global or systemic influences.

The Lost Gamble: The 2000 and 2001 Turkish Financial Crises in Comparative Perspective *by Hakan Tunç*

This study argues that at the core of the Turkish financial crises of November 2000 and February 2001 lay a financial panic characterized by a sudden shift in the expectations of foreign investors. This panic was accompanied by a vulnerable financial system, itself the result of a mismatch between the net short-term foreign currency liabilities of banks and the Central Bank's reserves. The conclusion of this study challenges common *ex post facto* explanations that regard the Turkish crises as accidents waiting to happen. In order to put the Turkish financial crises into perspective, this essay compares them with that of the Mexican peso crisis in 1994, the 1997 crisis in Thailand, and the currency collapse in Brazil in 1999. It also compares the circumstances under which the Turkish stabilization program was introduced with those that shaped the undertaking of similar programs in Brazil (1994) and Russia (1995).

On the Structural Weaknesses of the post-1999 Turkish Disinflation Program *by Ahmet Ertuğrul and Erinç Yeldan*

In December 1999, Turkey initiated an extensive disinflation program backed and supervised by the International Monetary Fund (IMF). In November 2000, however, Turkey experienced a severe financial crisis, which deepened and has continued to date. This contribution highlights the structural weaknesses of the exchange rate-backed disinflation program as manifested in its liquidity creation mechanism in a small and fragile financial system such as Turkey. This contribution also documents the fragility indicators of the Turkish banking system and demonstrates that the disinflation program led to an increased vulnerability of the banking system throughout 2000–1. Given the structural characteristics of the Turkish banking system, we argue that the orthodox policy of fully connecting the monetary expansion and liquidity requirements of the domestic economy exclusively to the speculative short-term capital flows was clearly a design flaw, overlooked by the IMF.

Domestic Needs for Foreign Finance and Exchange Rate Regime Choice in Developing Countries, with Special Reference to the Turkish Experience *by C. Emre Alper and Kamil Yılmaz*

Based on the analysis of exchange rate (ER) regimes, external debt accumulation, and recent economic crises, we argue that the choice of controlled ER arrangements in the post-capital account liberalization era provided ample incentives for rapid external debt accumulation in the emerging market economies. This claim is based on the annual data for 57 countries for the period 1975–2000 and on a cross-section time-series regression analysis of the debt accumulation. The lower the flexibility of the ER regime, the faster the external debt accumulation will be. Finally, this contribution discusses the ER regime and the macroeconomic policy framework suitable for sustainable long-run economic growth in Turkey.

Economic Crisis as an Instigator of Distributional Conflict: The Turkish Case in 2001 *by Fikret Şenses*

This contribution assesses the socio-economic impact of the recent crisis in Turkey, which started in the financial sector but soon made its presence felt in many other spheres. It argues that the impact of the crisis should be examined in the context of the neo-liberal policies that have been in force since 1980 and the momentum of powerful structural factors, most of which were carried over from an even earlier period. After a brief discussion of the main conceptual and statistical difficulties confronted in assessing and isolating the impact of the crisis, the study investigates the effect of the crisis in spheres such as production, employment, unemployment, wages, poverty, and income distribution, and draws attention to its negative impact. In order to provide a more complete view of its overall impact, the study also considers the response of the government, international organizations, and households to the crisis.

Social Capital and Corruption during Times of Crisis: A Look at Turkish Firms during the Economic Crisis of 2001 *by Fikret Adaman and Ali Çarkoğlu*

This contribution investigates whether lack of trust among business people towards the business community, as well as towards the general public, is conducive to more corruption in Turkey. Based on a survey study conducted in 2001, we establish a link between trust and corruption. Accepting the claim that corruption plays a role in the emergence and persistence of economic—and political—crises, we suggest that the latest crises that hit Turkey should also be approached from a trust-based perspective.

Towards a Sustainable Debt Burden: Challenges Facing Turkey at the Turn of the New Millennium *by O. Cevdet Akcay and C. Emre Alper*

Since the early 1990s, Turkey has been experiencing a major increase in its public debt. This contribution seeks to investigate the underlying causes of this deteriorating performance from a political-economic perspective. Our analysis, covering the 1990–2000 period, demonstrates that the current debt position of Turkey is unsustainable and that further fiscal austerity is needed. In establishing a link between budget deficits and inflation, one must adopt a very precise definition of the "budget deficit." Indeed, there appears to be a weak connection between the narrow definition of the consolidated budget deficit and inflation. Conversely, a strong connection has been established between the broad concept of the "public sector borrowing requirement" (PSBR) and inflation. In addition, the broad definition should be extended to include duty losses registered by public banks. The policy implications of our analysis are presented in the final section of the contribution.

The Turkish Banking Sector Two Years after the Crisis: A Snapshot of the Sector and Current Risks *by O. Cevdet Akcay*

The infamous 2001 crisis stemmed mostly from the fragility of the banking sector, which was not dealt with promptly. This contribution aims to paint a picture of the banking sector before and after the 2001 crisis and, more importantly, to emphasize the current risks the system still faces some two years later. There do not seem to be any "quick fixes" and a resolute stance on the part of the government regarding fiscal balances and reduced borrowing needs seem to be the only way out. Signs of progress in that direction will lead to increased confidence and improved market sentiment, which will also make it easier for banks to bolster proper banking and financial intermediation.

Notes on Contributors

Fikret Adaman is currently a professor at the Department of Economics in Boğaziçi University, Istanbul. He received his Ph.D. from Manchester University in 1993.

O. Cevdet Akcay received his M.Phil and Ph.D. degrees in Economics from City University of New York, Graduate School and University Center, New York. He served as an associate professor of economics at Boğaziçi University, Istanbul, until September 2001, and is currently the chief economist at Koçbank and Koç Yatirim, Istanbul. He is also an adjunct professor of economics at Koç University.

C. Emre Alper received his MA and Ph.D. degrees in Economics from Georgetown University, Washington DC. He is currently on sabbatical and is a visiting associate professor of Economics at the University of British Columbia, Vancouver. His permanent position is at the Economics Department, Boğaziçi University, Istanbul.

Ali Çarkoğlu is currently an associate professor at the Faculty of Arts and Sciences in Sabancı University, Istanbul. He received his Ph.D. from the State University of New York—Binghamton in 1993. He co-authored *The Political Economy of Cooperation in the Middle East* with Mine Eder and Kemal Kirişci (1998).

Ahmet Ertuğrul holds a Ph.D. from Ankara University. He is currently assistant professor of Economics at Bilkent University. Prior to this, he served as the president of Eximbank and Halk Bank.

Ziya Öniş is professor of International Political Economy at Koç University. He is the author of *State and Market: The Political Economy of Turkey in Comparative Perspective* (1998). His current research interests include the role of civil society organizations in the democratization process, Turkey-EU relations as well as the political economy of financial globalization and emerging market crises.

Fikret Şenses is a professor at the Department of Economics, Middle East Technical University, Ankara. His publications include *Recent Industrialization Experience of Turkey in a Global Context* (1994).

Hakan Tunç is a lecturer in the International Relations Program at the University of Pennsylvania. He has recently completed a study of privatization in 18 Asian and Latin American countries.

Erinç Yeldan received his Ph.D. from the University of Minnesota in 1988. He is currently professor and chair of the Department of Economics, Bilkent University. He also serves as an executive director of the International Development Economics Associates (IDEAs).

Kamil Yılmaz received his MA and Ph.D. degrees in Economics from the University of Maryland at College Park. He is currently assistant professor of Economics at Koç University, Istanbul and is also working on several research projects, including machinery investment and export competitiveness, trade liberalization and productivity growth in Turkey, and the political economy of stabilization.

Index

For Product Safety Concerns and Information please contact our EU
representative GPSR@taylorandfrancis.com Taylor & Francis Verlag GmbH,
Kaufingerstraße 24, 80331 München, Germany

Printed and bound by CPI Group (UK) Ltd, Croydon, CR0 4YY
08/06/2025
01897001-0016

.